ALIEN PHYSICS

The Physical Operation Performed Upon The Cosmos

By

Ronald F. Avery
www.AlienPhysics.com

1stBooks — rev. 09/03/02

TABLE OF CONTENTS

PREFACE

The seed for the concepts presented in this book was formed over 23 years covering a period of time while I worked in Architectural offices and encountered many professionals and settings in which the Gospel was a point of contention and misunderstanding.

Most of the concepts began to emerge in my attempt to first answer questions I had about salvation and how I could obtain it and then in response to argument concerning Jesus Christ and his power.

I had thought of the underlying concepts for years until an extended period of litigation hit me and my family forcing me to quit my professional and property development attempts. The periods between motions, trials and appeals left me with some time in which to develop these concepts into a more clear and concise theology that could be immediately recalled by anyone.

I asked my pastor, Bob Odom, to read my first manuscript and I attempted to have it published under the same title "Alien Physics" without success. I knew that the manuscript was not well done and that it needed more refinement and analysis. I asked Mr. Odom if he would work with me as a sounding board to develop a more precise and pointed work that would truly have new yet correct categories of concepts.

DEDICATION:

I would like to dedicate this work to my wife, Cynthia, who has stayed with me with devotion and love in conformity to the best biblical descriptions of womanhood. She has supported all my work including this book even when many of our friends and family thought it was a waste by a lazy reprobate. Obviously I dedicate this work to Christ Jesus to glorify him (as my pastor would say, "in new and fresh ways") in this present industrialized world. I think it's clear that now and then in history new things happen, even in the world of theology, as stated by Christ himself (Matthew 13:52):

> "Then said he unto them, Therefore every scribe which is instructed unto the kingdom of heaven is like unto a man that is an householder, which bringeth forth out of his treasure things new and old."

ACKNOWLEDGMENTS:

I want to thank my Pastor Bob Odom, an ordained Methodist minister, for taking the time to meet with me many hours on Sunday afternoons to discuss ideas for this book. I also want to thank Mr. Odom for meeting with me for almost two years on Tuesday mornings for an hour to discuss and review a number of other books on theology that we read. This eventually led to the conclusion that something very profound was missing from mainstream theology. This resulted in the publishing of this book. Those meetings caused excitement, exceeded only by the Biblical reinforcing discovered in the writing of this book. I look forward to what may be in the future for continued work together.

My Mother and Dad:

I would like to thank my mother, Joy for her unfailing support even if and when she does not agree with me on any issue. Even the world will support you if you side with it. It's a good mother that helps you when the world hates you. Hence the scripture (Exodus 20:12): "Honour thy father and thy mother: that thy days may be long upon the land which the Lord thy God giveth thee." My parents always maintained an environment of discussion in our home of the important issues of life even if it brought turmoil among us. I'm sorry my dad is not alive to read my best work but I think he would like it and will like it.

Editor/Memorial:

I also want to memorialize my editor, Mr. William, Richard (Dick) Tatum, a friend through thick and thin. Mr. Tatum died on June 13, 2002 without seeing this book finally published. But he faced death with calm patience and assurance of his destiny. Mr. Tatum had been a retired magazine and newspaper editor, who made a living with the printed word. Mr. Tatum was also a defender of republican ideas that were made part of the United States by the impact of Christ Jesus on the fundamental principles of civil government. He has been my teacher and mentor in the public arena. Mr. Tatum and I have had many a good time writing and working together on many issues. Mr. Tatum has been in the public eye for many years as a city treasurer, school board trustee and city newspaper editor. I am glad that he agreed to edit this book.

Lifegate Ministries:

I must mention my gratitude to Lifegate church. They had a great opportunity to kick me out of their congregation but chose to study the word of God as a means to make a decision as to my continued fellowship with them. In spite of those who left the congregation in protest of my opening and operating an Early American taphouse, the elders chose to allow my continuance with them. Most churches would have kicked me out in a heart beat. I am sure many of them have suffered for the word of God's sake over this issue. I pray that this book will bring much fruit to this worthy congregation that resists the temptations of success to maintain the integrity of the word of God. May we continue to rightly divide the word of God. I must also mention that one protestor became a good friend and another returned to this congregation. This return rates high in my eyes. It is my hope that we all be blessed in our propagation of the good news of what Christ Jesus has done to the cosmos.

Cover Photo Credit:

I have been in correspondence with Mr. Keith Mayes, an amateur astronomer in Scotland. I discovered this gentleman via his website at www.thekeyboard.org.uk. We started a lengthy and profound discussion over the Internet regarding our views of the cosmos, God, man, Christ and the concepts in this book. These e-mails are published on our websites. This internet debate is every bit as exciting and civilized as the 1948 BBC televised debate between Father F. C. Copleston and Bertrand Russel. One person e-mailed me and told me their life now had purpose as a result of reading this exchange.

When I was having trouble finding a background photo for my book cover, I remembered my Scotland friend who takes his own beautiful pictures of the heavens. He quickly e-mailed his photo of the Orion Nebula with his permission to use it. I invite you to visit Keith Mayes at his website and explore his vast knowledge and photography. Thank you Keith!

An Encourager:

I cannot forget Mr. Danny Hoffman, who read my first draft and never ceased to ask when this book would be published for he wanted the first signed copy. He also published far and wide the matter in my community. This man has the gift of encouragement among his brothers and sisters and is quick to tell all men why he is a happy man.

Further Mention:

I would also like to thank some people who traveled a long way to hear about my book before it was printed. I would like to thank them for their patience in its final printing. They listened to me present it in advance of its printing and that is most difficult. Therefore thank you David Jackson of Corpus Christi, Texas; Lauren and Joselyn Savage of Cuero, Texas. They read an early draft and encouraged me to print.

AUTHORITY

"By what authority do you do these things?" This is a question that modern and ancient society asks of all that do anything. We are obsessed with credentials and easily led astray by them. I have seen abuses of credentials in every profession including medicine, law, architecture, planning and theology. This question is asked many times only to intimidate. It is based on the assumption that the prudent always listen only to the "professional" or "licensed" or business success. Therefore, knowing that you will likely have the same question we offer the following biblical responses to the question of authority to create, organize and write theology.

❑ Prudence:

Jesus expressed a most interesting insight into the prudence of society in Luke 10:21:

> "I thank thee, O Father, Lord of heaven and earth, that thou hast hid these things from the wise and prudent, and hast revealed them unto babes: even so, Father; for so it seemed good in thy sight."

Therefore, my first qualification and authority to write theology is that I am a "babe" in Christ.

❑ Revelation is only authority:

Jesus answers the question of theological authority for all time and for all men in the very next phrase in Luke 10:22:

> "All things are delivered to me of my Father: and no man knoweth who the Son is, but the Father; and who the Father is, but the Son, and he to whom the son will reveal Him."

Authority then comes not from years and years of seminary scholarship, which can be undermined by years of incorrect or careless or corrupted teachers, but from a revelation from Jesus. We therefore declare that we have seen the Father and that we have access to the mind of Christ to develop and organize a modern theology that will not only survive modern society but reap a great and lasting harvest from it.

❑ "Work out your own salvation:"

The foregoing authority of revelation does not mean every Christian will be good at theology. But scripture does support the very real potential that major new theological work, can be produced by those that are truly attracted to it, even without training in seminaries.

In fact, we advocate that all be engaged in analysis of the Bible and what others, including ourselves, have to say about its principles and harmony. St. Paul admonished the Philippians to develop their own theology in Phil. 2:12:

> "Wherefore, my beloved, as ye have always obeyed, not as in my presence only, but now much more in my absence, work out your own salvation with fear and trembling."

Therefore, this book is an explanation of salvation for one ordinary man unschooled in any seminary but who invested much time, energy and research into understanding how Christ could save him and then, upon salvation, explaining that miracle to others (in and out of the Church). This endeavor produced fear and trembling many times but also has produced the fruit of more perseverance and confidence in the defense of the Good News from attack from any source. Many times this quest produced overwhelming chills and awe of the power and unity we have with God through Christ Jesus.

This effort has also led to a conclusion that it is not Christians or Christianity that can fail but one's undeveloped Christian theology that fails. It is unfortunate that whole denominations and whole cultures can have a Christian theology that is in some important way occulted.

INTRODUCTION

This work was started with the proposition that the Bible is true as revealed by our own passage from death into life by the operations performed and recorded for us in it. In the analysis of this operation we are led to the proposition that the Bible is not only true but that in some ways it is raw material, not theology in itself. In other words, theology is the work of anyone who tries to analyze the reality of their own transformation and communicate its availability to those around them and to condense its reality into memorable, related and harmonic concepts.

This endeavor could also be perceived as a response to the command of the risen Savior to, "Go ye therefore, and teach all nations, baptizing them in the name of the Father, and of the Son, and of the Holy Ghost: Teaching them to observe all things whatsoever I have commanded you: and, lo, I am with you alway, even unto the end of the world." What is our role in society as missionaries? We should consider ourselves missionaries wherever we are that Christ is not known. This is especially true in our own culture!

It is our prayer that this work will prepare you to better follow Peter's admonition to (1 Peter 3:15-16):

"sanctify the Lord God in your hearts: and be ready always to give an answer to every man that asketh you a reason of the hope that is in you with meekness and fear:

"Having a good conscience; that, whereas they speak evil of you, as of evildoers, they may be ashamed that falsely accuse your good conversation in Christ."

Apparent false presuppositions are revealed in the responses and expressions used by Christians and theologians as a result of a retreat from the scientific world. However, the truth of the Bible when fully analyzed and understood is dominant over science and gives a frame work to judge truth both within the church and outside the church in the world around us.

Our purpose herein is to provide a central theology that explains the Good News and power of Christ to modern society in its own terms and provide a system to resolve struggles within the modern evangelical church. Upon the question asked by others with insufficient theological Biblical understanding (Matt 22:29) Jesus replied:

"Ye do err, not knowing the scripture, nor the power of God."

They lacked two types of knowledge: knowledge of Scripture and knowledge of the power of God. The second type they could not have prior to Christ and that resulted in their inability to relate to and believe the truth of the scriptures.

To explain the power of Christ to deliver all mankind into the Kingdom of Heaven while they live on Earth unlocks all the scriptures and makes way for propagation of the Really Good News.

PART 1 - SOCIOLOGICAL EQUILIBRIUM:

CHAPTER 1 - FALSE EQUILIBRIUM - Social Decay

Our common perception of events and ideas are analyzed in terms of an implicit understanding of reality or the "real world." When various systems of knowledge interact or overlap subjects or events in question we resolve this in our minds with the present form of agreed equilibrium between the systems of knowledge.

Depending on the systems involved there may not be a conflict. And if both or several systems are all true there will not be a conflict. However, in regards to certain subjects and events, two or more systems of knowledge that are partially incorrect can operate in one's mind and must demand a resolution or equilibrium between them.

To complicate the situation, some systems of knowledge can actually adapt to the other system or compensate for the other system by rejecting its own truth or explaining matters in some other distorted manner.

What are the two biggest forces or systems of knowledge in America and in fact in the world today? Is it not Science and Christianity? We mention Christianity only, as opposed to other forms of "religion," because many forms do not argue with science nor have a means to do so.

It is the concern and care for the real world and the truth about it that makes science and Christianity the two most significant systems of knowledge involved in an equilibrium about the "real world." Truth that is applicable to both fields is of the utmost importance to the survival of mankind and to the ultimate destiny of each individual person.

It should be obvious that a social equilibrium is not necessarily based upon truth. In fact, it is contended herein that the present false equilibrium between science and Christianity has produced the epidemic social ills of our time.

Unfortunately, we have observed that being a Christian is no guarantee against adopting a false equilibrium between Christianity and science in an attempt to explain the world around us or ultimate destiny.

The following two statements are used to establish some evidence for discussion. The first statement made by Greg Russell in his essay reviewing the Ethics of Hans J. Morganthau:

> "A secular society doubtful about individual immortality in another world, and increasingly cognizant of the impending doom in the one

through which it tries to perpetuate itself here and now, buries itself in despair."[1]

Consider the following questions concerning Mr. Russell's statement regarding Hans J. Morganthau's world view:

1. Do you agree with his statement?
2. Does his statement make good sense to you?
3. Is there something wrong with that statement that in some way reveals the reason for the condition he refers to.

The second statement was made by Owen Gingerich, a Harvard astrophysicist and evangelical protestant, taken from a TIME Magazine article entitled "What Does Science Tell Us About God:"

"I passionately believe in a universe with purpose, though I cannot prove it. Purpose, like origin, is a point where the wisdom of empirical science ends and the quest for religious faith begins."[2]

Consider the following questions concerning Gingerich's quote:

1. Do you agree with that statement?
2. Do you perceive a problem with that statement?

Consider the answers to the following questions concerning both statements:

1. Do you believe it is possible that these men have illustrated problems in society by expressing them in terms of the false equilibrium that produced the problem to start with?
2. In other words could these statements inadvertently identify a problem while at the same time define it in terms of the underlying falsehood that initially produced the problem?
3. Have these two statements actually unknowingly described in some way the real false equilibrium between science and Christianity?

We will attempt to answer those questions in this book. The following statement questioning the reasonableness of atheism by a non Christian also points to the false sociological equilibrium:

"With respect for metaphysics comes respect for an idea central to many religions: The unknowable. Agnosticism—reserving judgement about divine purpose—remains as defensible as ever, but atheism— the confident denial of divine purpose—becomes trickier. If you

---

[1] Greg Russell, "Science, Technology, and Death in the Nuclear Age: Hans J. Morgenthau on Nuclear Ethics," in Ethics and International Affairs, vol. 5, 1991 (New York, NY: Carnigie Council on Ethics and International Affairs, 1987): 131

[2] Richard N. Ostling, "Galileo and Other Faithful Scientists," *TIME* 140, no. 26 (Dec. 28, 1992): 42-43.

admit that we can't peer behind the curtain, how can you be sure there's nothing there?"[3]

This foregoing statement will be shown to be in conformance to the false sociological equilibrium. Atheism is not supportable but not for the reason suggested therein. Thanks to Christ Jesus we not only peer behind the curtain, but we step behind and then we possess that which is behind the curtain.

It is asserted herein that men arrive at an equilibrium between science and Christianity with little conscious thought but reach conclusions based merely upon old arguments they have heard for years.

The amount of truth represented in the Equilibrium will determine the strength of the social environment and civilization. Few Christians would argue that the conditions of society producing poor education, the emergence of random recreational murder and "gang violence" are not the result of failure to teach moral and Christian principles. However, few would think that there exist a false equilibrium or a false assumption in modern Christian thinking that makes Christianity hard to spread or have power.

Where is the present equilibrium spelled out? The equilibrium will always, as is now, be mankind's view of the cosmos or the accepted cosmology. Christians must consider the cosmos as much as Carl Sagan and in order for Christians to communicate with their fellow men in America they will find that term of much use and power in describing God's plan for all men. Therefore, if there is a false equilibrium between science and Christianity it must be corrected in the area of Cosmology as described by both systems. That is why we gain little by discussing ethics and morality when it is mankind's view of the cosmos that has produced his morality and ethics to start with.

The concept of a false equilibrium presents science and Christianity as systems of knowledge that have accommodated each other in some way that is false to both systems. This concept is appropriate in order to correct both science and Christianity. In fact, it is just as important to correct Christian ideas as it is for Christianity to have an impact on society as a whole. But until the correction is made, the importance of a Christian impact on society is itself a question in evangelical circles. Modern evangelicals are questioning the need to reform society. This would not be a question in a correct understanding of theology.

The equilibrium concept also impacts science in an equally important way. In a false Equilibrium both systems of knowledge have been distorted where the real truth is hidden from both systems of knowledge. The implications of this upon society and its cosmology are explosive.

Therefore, it is reasonable to question why the socially beneficial institutions in the "best educated" country in the world are breaking down? The family, the legal structure, the public school and the "religious" quality of life are not standing up to pressures of modern demands. This is happening while there is so much "good will" between science and religion! Many scientist are, in fact, Christians yet the

---

[3] Robert Wright, "Science God And Man," *TIME* 140, no. 26 (Dec. 28, 1992): 44.

underlying perceptions of faith and empirical knowledge cannot be answered by them. Why is that?

Could there be some completely false assumption made by Christians that has prevented a clear perception of the cosmos and truth for both science and Christianity? What is wrong in the relationship between science and Christianity that in some way prevents all institutions from functioning properly as designed and intended by man?

It must be understood that sociological equilibrium is always in the process of finding equilibrium or rest, but not in finding the truth to both the forces involved; namely Christianity and science. If equilibrium is found without truth... society fails. It is imperative that we find truth before rest.

CHAPTER 2 - OCCULTED MAINSTREAM CHRISTIANITY

The first condition of our present day false Equilibrium is the occulting of certain Christian revelations or doctrines contained in the New Testament. The "occult" applies to modern mainstream Christianity today as much as to any other group or organization in society.

A proper understanding of the term *occult* is necessary to our discussion of contemporary society under a false equilibrium. Funk & Wagnall's dictionary defines *occult* in the following ways:

❑ **to cover from view or conceal**, especially by intervention; as, one heavenly body occults another.

❑ *Occult* can also be used as an adjective meaning concealed from knowledge or understanding; hidden.

❑ *Occultation* means the act of occulting, or the state of being occulted; especially, concealment of one body by another interposed in the line of vision, as of a star or planet by the moon, or of a satellite by a planet. It also can mean disappearance from view or notice.

❑ The term *occulter* used as a noun means the agent or device which covers something from view.

Notice that the term *occult* is not evil in itself as we hear it often used. This term is accurate for our use in discussing the compromises and distortions of knowledge in both Christianity and science. Obviously, there can be degrees of occultation that applies to Christian theology and denominations. And it appears that Christianity itself is in, and has always been in, a march towards more freedom in expressing and establishing the truths of the Gospel into society or the world system. From Roman persecution through the Reformation to the settlement of North America and the United States Constitution, the progression and understanding of Christian revelation grows and needs freedom to express itself. This freedom of progression was recognized by the Founding Fathers of America and its movement is guaranteed in the First Amendment to the Bill of Rights. This freedom reserved in America protects all expression of Christianity and other religions but does not determine the truth of such expression.

The preoccupation of many Christians about the Devil or "Satan worship" and animal sacrifice, while merely memorizing Christian slogans and formulas and caring little to discern the deep truths of the Gospel, is amazing. The wholesale acceptance by our entire society of much error in modern Christian theology and contemporary science, while being totally consumed with the sensational aberrant behavior of a handful of sick and demented people, is astonishing.

The only explanation for this condition is that people are most afraid of a few nuts when they do not understand the foundation of their own lives. Therefore, "Christians" with little understanding of their own foundation are both weak and fearful of a few bizarre events and totally ignorant of the real pervasive, and continual threat to their peace and security at work in the mainstream of society. However, this is becoming more clear to more Christians everyday.

What is almost amusing among Christians today is their protection of denominational colors won in the battle for truth or balance years ago while most all denominations swallow the false precepts of the science / religion debate without argument.

I remember a young associate pastor told me once that he felt that the more the "spirit" was lost in a congregation the more "pomp" was observed in the church meetings. This is really perceptive of him. Yet he also told me on another occasion that one of his hobbies was reading everything he could about Albert Einstein, especially his religious works concerning his view of God. Undoubtedly, Einstein was big in the Methodist Seminaries and pulpits of Houston, Texas. This Methodist pastor, as perceptive as he was, failed to perceive the complete atheism of Einstein.

This is not to say Christians cannot and should not derive pleasure from reading works of science and Christianity from non-Christians and atheist etc., but in this case a complete failure by a "Christian Pastor" to recognize the quality of an atheist is alarming. This pastor was mislead merely by the use of religious terms and inner questions, prompting and yearnings as proof of a belief in God. What is in operation in our society that occults the perception of a pastor of the essential and simple quality of one who believes in God? It is none other than the false equilibrium between science and Christianity that goes unchallenged in main stream society and accepted as true by both thought systems.

The Christian Reconstruction movement presently led by Gary North and Gary Demar of Tyler, Texas, ably point out the weakness and partial falsehood of the popular Evangelical Premillennialist position of escape and retreat from the world. The Reconstructionist expose the practical and effectual unity of liberal theology and the secular humanism with the Evangelical retreat from working to reform society. This Evangelical Premillennial view asserts that this world is ruled by Satan and Christians cannot change it nor save it. This conclusion leads to pessimism regarding salt and light in society and chains the holder to "personal" or "spiritual" experience.

The Reconstructionist point out that this is a relatively new concept and one not held by the early church nor was all the evangelical and cultural advances of western civilization made with this futile view of the gospel in the world. However, the Reconstructions rest on the law or essentially the Old Testament as the answer. They maintain that knowledge of the law and obedience to it is both personal and cultural and leads to freedom for both (cultural and personal freedom). They use the analogy of the fish bowl. The Premillennialist position is to save the fish only while the older and more accurate Postmillennialist position is the salvation of culture or society via civil and political reform where all fish can live till all are saved individually.

I tend to agree with the Reconstructionist in their assessment of the modern Evangelical retreat from the real world about them to personal experience. But the Reconstructionists did not offer one explanation for this retreat from the world nor any new revelation of the Gospel or theology to encourage their return to the world. I also reject the notion that a return to old testament law will be effective for those who could not be saved by it to start with as well discussed by Paul in the New Testament.

John MacArthur's recent book *Reckless Faith* also illustrates precisely and in good detail this same retreat from the world and turning to rote ceremony and structure of mere traditional religion and mindless experience. MacArthur exposes the abandonment of reformation principles by modern Evangelicals in the document entitled *"Evangelicals and Catholics Together."* MacArthur argued well the notion that sound doctrine established by the blood of Protestant martyrs is abandoned by modern Evangelicals for some perception of security in numbers to fight for "family values."

ABC televised the News Special entitled *"In the Name Of God"* which supposedly investigated the several "evangelical" movements in the United States. One was the "laughing revival." Much of the "documentary" covered several very large urban churches with "paid musicians and worship leaders." The emphasis of all the movements was mindless expression of "spirit" in the form of tongues, jumping up and down, laughing, falling on the floor in convulsions etc. ABC summed up the Special by saying they could not discern the validity of such things. However, the commentator did not establish his perception or his own persuasion. To most people that is an adequate answer but not for me and a few others. I have no doubt that ABC would not hesitate to degrade any Christian movement and saw this as an opportunity to do so again.

It is clear that the similarity between all these recent discussions and news specials is the abandonment of mental faculties by modern Christians. Both John MacArthur and the Reconstructionist complain of the abandonment of the mental faculties and sound doctrine on the part of modern Evangelicals and fear that a serious set back is ahead for this movement and all Christianity as a result.

The Reconstructionist have hit the Evangelicals hard in their view of the future and their abandonment of social responsibility and pessimism concerning the redemption of God's Kingdom. MacArthur totally destroyed the Biblical and reasonable basis of the *"Evangelicals and Catholics Together"* document and the many bizarre forms of reckless faith being pursued mindlessly.

MacArthur explained the reason for this movement as a desperate move to fight the evil of abortion and homosexuality. The Reconstructionist gave no explanation for the retreat of Evangelicals but explained in detail the practical results of their new theological positions and retreat into "personal experience."

Neither the Reconstructionist nor MacArthur gave the Evangelicals any solid ground to stand on but merely destroyed the little bubble they are stranded on at sea. This is not to say that they did not scream in their ear to return to sound doctrine in the word of God. But the screaming of this directive when the Bible has always been in their hand seems a little cruel and short sited.

The real reason for the abandonment of the mind and sound doctrine is that Christians in the work day world five days a week cannot win a mental and truthful argument with a modern scientist without retreating into the "other world," or the "personal" world or the "spiritual" world. But all forms of this argument or defense is a retreat and escape rather than a frontal challenge of scientific concepts based upon the real physical truth contained in the Holy Scriptures.

The Reconstructionist nor MacArthur helped these Evangelicals equip their congregations with this type of pseudo science whipping theology. Sound doctrine in the past was developed, not all at once, but in sequential response to challenge from within and without the Body of Christ. The Reconstructionist and MacArthur show the errors clearly within the Body but do not offer one ray of hope for Evangelicals to resist the incredible every day humiliation and retreat from the scientific world. In other words, no new doctrine has been developed since the reformation to resist new challenges upon the Body from the secular scientific world. Screaming century old intrabody doctrines in the ears of modern Christians being beaten into submission every day is useless if not cruel.

Christianity cannot resist doctrinal corruption if it cannot resist and challenge outer intellectual attack without retreat into a fictitious realm. Not only must Christianity resist attack it must challenge and win offensive assault on the world of mythological science in order to give Christians courage to go to work and be strong and confident in their minds and its power. No Christian will abandon this kind of mind for the practice of mindless experience. They abandon their minds now because no modern theologian has put anything in them that will do what needs to be done with the Gospel - namely to Challenge and subdue all Rome and the known world. This is precisely what Paul did. He developed theology for the world he encountered.

The only way back to sound doctrine for the Body is to soundly and intellectually defeat the modern world of science. Equip the modern Christian with the tools and armor for battle and victory without retreat into the "other" world.

The truths contained in the Bible can do that very thing but few are engaged in developing such a system of theology but rather use the Word to find "personal peace" outside the "scientifically" described world. But this is precisely the primary and first doctrinal error which produces all the others. The Gospel is for this real world of science. The revelation of Christ is the supreme reality in the entire eternal cosmos of space and it is more than sufficient to subdue and contain all other knowledge.

Evangelicals take their "beliefs" to work all week where they are humiliated intellectually and mentally beaten into submission with modern science. Then on Sunday they no longer want to hear about Reformation Doctrine or "sound doctrine." They want to feel alive, yet the pastor presents old doctrines of old challenges left in the dust centuries ago. These doctrines are not wrong but merely irrelevant for their current external challenges from the modern world of science. Modern Christians don't care about the Trinity when they are viewed as idiots for

9

believing in God at all. Modern Christians cannot establish, by their lacking theology, what or who God is. In most cases the pulpit presentation of the Trinity will be mystical or something to be accepted as a "matter of faith" rather than a logical and simple mental explanation.

After the "Theologian" presents the "Doctrines" of the Middle Ages phrased and framed in that context, the "believer" returns to the scientific work world for another week of humiliation and defeat.

Finally the "believer" can take it no more. He looks for something that will give him a lift "believing" now that the "intellectual doctrine" is not adequate or even necessary, or worse, maybe non-existent. He now looks to the "spirit" or "personal experience" as the real defense to modern science in the every day world. He is right back to the first theological error producing our false equilibrium.

We must eventually look to the failure of the modern "doctrinally sound" intellectual theologian to provide a defense for the modern Christian in the modern scientific work place. Theology has been neglected and new doctrine has been left undeveloped. The pursuit of sound new doctrine has not been encouraged, accelerated or elevated in defense of modern attack from outside. This neglect by modern theologians has forced Evangelicals to retreat to anything they can. Seminaries in the last three decades have been busy undermining scriptural authority and sound theology while ignoring the pursuit of new and necessary theology to equip the modern Christian. These seminaries were more concerned with producing a modern preacher that blends with modern society rather than one that can explain Christ and the Gospel in scientific and pseudoscientific terms.

Mainstream doctrine propounded today is mostly sound but was developed from the attacks of old. New doctrine in harmony with old doctrine and the scripture is needed for new attacks on the modern Christian Church.

Most all doctrine expounded today is to defend the Church from within the Body because it is very evident that many Christians feel that the external world cannot be successfully resisted or defeated without a retreat to the "other world" or "personal world" or the "spiritual world." The existential, mindless, spiritual harbor is all that is safe for the modern Christian to anchor the storm. In fact there is much argument going on in the Body today but little assault on science from theologians, as was once common place.

This is detrimental to the modern Christian church and all the Saints or redeemed should be hard at work looking to develop new explanations and organizations of the truths of scripture. This effort should result in the construction of a mental, real intellectual port that can weather any storm and send mighty battle ships into the roughest of seas to bring God's will and salvation to all men.

Therefore, there are two questions we need to ask and answer to defend Christianity in the new Millennium:

1. Is there some empirical truth of Christianity that has been blocked from view by a gigantic falsehood about the real cosmos developed by modern science and accepted by the Church and by society in general?
2. What happens to the occulting agent when it covers up truth? Has Science itself been altered or polluted in the process of occulting Christianity?

Our task must seek a critical quantity or shared field or element between Science and Christianity to be resolved correctly. This shared field can be found and corrected giving both modern Christianity and modern science truth, accuracy and purpose.

PART 1- SOCIOLOGICAL EQUILIBRIUM

CHAPTER 3 - RELIGIOSITY OF SCIENCE

The interest of scientists in explaining "religion" is support for the hypothesis that a critical element or field shared by both Christianity and science exists in an occulted form. Scientists have become interested in explaining "religion" and the purpose and origin of the world. Scientists presume that they approach these subjects from principles of observation and discovery. But today we will see that they end up with propositions that are not supportable in the truth revealed by Christ Jesus nor by the nature of the observable environment about them.

A scientific principal comes to mind when we think of the hiding or occultation of truth by another field of study. It is similarly stated in Newton's third law of motion: to every action there is an equal and opposed reaction. Therefore forces exist not singly, but always in pairs. This principle, modified to apply to our analysis of a shared field of truth between Christianity and science, would sound as the following: One field of study cannot hide the truth of another field without itself becoming critically flawed or polluted in some way.

Therefore, the suggestion is that if some actual truth of Christianity has been occulted by science, that science itself has been altered and polluted in its use, purpose and understanding of the cosmos. In other words, the natural result of the occultation of Christian truth has been the pollution or "religiosity" of science.

It is interesting that the term "religiosity" was used in the writings of Albert Einstein. He tried to use the term in a "positive" way to describe what he had experienced in his quest for the truth in the world around him. Or better yet, Einstein used the term "religiousity" to describe that force that drove him to seek truth about the world through science. The term "religiosity" is used herein in a "negative" sense to describe what happens to objective observation when the truth of Christianity is occulted by science. Therefore the "religiosity" of science is the same as the pollution of science from the point of view proposed herein. Funk and Wagnall's defines "religiosity" as religiousness or pious sentimentality.

Funk & Wagnall's dictionary defines religion in the following ways:

❑ A belief binding the spiritual nature of man to a supernatural being, as involving a feeling of dependence and responsibility, together with the feelings and practices which naturally flow from such a belief.

❑ Any system of faith and worship.

❑ An essential part or practical test of the spiritual life; as, pure religion is to visit the fatherless, etc. (this is one of the only three times the word religion is used in the Bible - James 1:27)

❑ Conscientious devotion in practice; scrupulous care; as to make a religion of his work.

❑   The rites or cult of a religion.

The very little use of the word "religion" in the Bible (four times) suggests that the authors were not as concerned with making a religion as with describing the acts and directions of God.

Religiosity as used herein, and most accurately so, is the creation of a religion from secular non-religious objects of worship. Scientists have made their "quest for truth" their "faith" and an object of religiosity. Early Christians were challenged by science from the beginning but not nearly to the degree that it is now. Paul rightly understood that the power of Christ to redeem the whole world forever was consistent with true science but that false understandings of and uses of science were a threat to the spread of the good news. Saint Paul admonished Timothy to avoid useless babblings and false theories passed off as true science (1 Timothy 6:20-21):

> "O Timothy, keep that which is committed to thy trust, avoiding profane and vain babblings, and **oppositions of science falsely so called**:

> "Which some professing have erred concerning the faith. Grace be with thee. Amen."

(Emphasis added)

It is obvious from Paul's admonition that he regarded true science as correct and to be a valuable pursuit. But not everyone expounding theories of "so called" science, even in those days, were to be taken seriously. It is also apparent that Paul could discern the difference between real science and science that was "falsely so called." How would Paul be able to avoid and resist such theories without some profound knowledge of truth about the world revealed to him by Christ Jesus? It is that confident knowledge of truth to test science that we seek to establish herein. The power of Christ to physically operate upon the cosmos is that which establishes the truth about the cosmos and mankind's relationship to it. This is knowledge that can check science. This knowledge is supported by the most convincing evidence of experience, unlike those of "so called" theoretical physics in science today.

It is evident from Paul's letter to Timothy that this science "falsely so called" was professed by those who erred from the truth of Christ. Therefore, not only was there talk concerning false science but that talk was causing error concerning the faith. This error might have caused doubt about the power of Christ and Christians. This error concerning the faith therefore could have caused the preclusion of salvation within the church and the incorrect perception of Christ and his rejection outside the Church.

Therefore, the purpose of this presentation is to search for this truth that Paul knew about reality that has been occulted in modern times by science "falsely so called." If this truth is found and revived in the modern church it must restore the power within the church and the power of salvation that brings others into the church. This is the best and most accurate meaning of the term "revival." Revival must be more than a mere self-induced frenzy or emotion that rapidly comes and goes. Revival must bring to consciousness something that was once commonly recognized but now occulted.

Prior to a discussion of the religiosity of science, it is essential to recall the notion that Western Christianity lies at the foundation of the most advanced scientific pursuits. The late Francis Schaeffer has pointed out in his books that it is the Western belief in the creator, redeemer God, that revealed himself, his purpose and his desire to mankind that became the intellectual foundation for modern science. It was the belief of Western Christianity that this revealed relationship between God and man and the world around us could be explained in more detail by use of the human mind. The Biblically revealed purpose and relationship of all things gave man a framework to seek more detailed information about the world around us that would also fit within the general order of all things as revealed in the Bible. That is to say, an intelligent creator with purpose and desire and destiny has created a world containing forces that can be explained and discovered. Schaeffer went on to contrast this Western view and the accompanying scientific advances with the Eastern view and its sluggish scientific advancements resulting from a lack of hope in understanding what lies behind the order of things, if there exists order at all. The East was stuck in a naturalist view of the world without a spatial explanation of the relationship of all things, which the revelation of Christ Jesus provides.

It is the Western view of the world and God, which resulted in the development of the scientific method that produced the scientific advances, that the world is most proud of. Schaeffer demonstrated that less scientifically advanced cultures did not view the world as designed nor discoverable because no discernible being or force was at work over it. Religious and social development in general was dependent on attainment of naturalistic wisdom or "ways of the world." Some of these natural religions produced very good perceptions and some close to the nature of God but never based upon an actual revelation of the supreme act of God himself—His redemption of the cosmos and all therein. Therefore the hope of discovery of scientific principles at work in the world did not attract Eastern men to invest themselves in such apparently futile efforts, in the absence of this knowledge of Christ Jesus and his operational power.

To understand how science has become polluted we must know what unpolluted science is. What is meant by pure, true or unpolluted science? Pure science is the use of the scientific method to determine the principles at work in the environment around us in order to explain a phenomena and to accomplish some type of beneficial use without regard for ultimate meaning in the cosmos. Today scientists are as much concerned with the origin of man, his destiny, and his purpose or ultimate meaning as they are the immediate beneficial adaptation to his environment. That is to say, with the occultation of the Christian explanation for the ultimate meaning, purpose, and destiny of mankind, scientists have turned their attention to such ultimate questions and answers completely outside the revelation of the truths contained in the Holy Bible. This quest has produced some very interesting information yet many times the implications of the new findings are completely distorted by scientists outside the revelation of the truth of Christ and his physical operation over the cosmos. The resulting "scientific" propositions for mankind are so distorted that they violate other obvious scientific laws of the world around us. This distortion of scientific findings to create hope for man outside the revelation of Christ, God, Man and space is "so called science." In other words it is important always to separate the actual findings of science from the propositions set forth by the scientists supposedly based upon such findings.

This attempt by modern scientists has produced some very interesting information but in the absence of the spatial principles of the New Testament the result is completely absurd propositions for mankind's future. This movement in the scientific community was termed "modern modern science" by Schaeffer. This movement has abandoned the foundation of modern science, supported by the revealed Biblical relationships, to build a religion of its own. This movement is called the *religiosity of science* in this book. When "modern science" is used in this book it will mean the same kind as Schaeffer referred to as "modern modern science" for convenience only.

Before offering an explanation of how the pollution or religiosity of modern modern science developed, it must be said that this tendency has been around almost since the dawn of mankind. Pythagoras, 582-507 B.C., was the earliest and most notable of the ancient philosophers / mathematicians and religious mystics to develop a religion around science. Pythagoras developed the idea that because things in the world could be reduced and explained in numerical relationships that numbers were the essential and fundamental basis of life and therefore became the central focus of his religion. Pythagoras founded the Pythagorean Brotherhood, a school in Croton in southern Italy, with two classes of students. The students (mathematikoi), who alone received the full scientific and religious instruction and the auditors (akousmatikoi), or lay followers who merely pledged to observe the Pythagoran way of life.

It may be absurd and impossible to have a completely pure science void of all concern for ultimate questions about man. But this does not mean that science must become a complete religion as it became to Albert Einstein and to many other scientists since. It does appear that the revelation of ultimate answers about man and his world totally explained by Christianity liberated the Western mind for focused quest of more detailed forces at work in the world for mankind's benefit devoid of religious overtones in the scientific method or resulting assertions. In other words, when Christianity was the underlying belief of the scientist, science was at its most pure and its logic the most clear and its propositions for man the most realistic.

Certainly the truth revealed by science must fit in the Christian revelation of Christ Jesus. But, it is the revelation of the spatial principles of Christ Jesus that determine the truth of the propositions made by scientists and which theories are scientific truth and which are "science so called."

However, It is more absurd to expect to attain a religion devoid of science. Who in their right mind would want to "believe" in a "religion" that is totally unsupportable by "science?" Unfortunately, this is what some "Christians" mean by "faith." But it is essential for an honest man and a sincere and powerful man to "believe" in something that is real. What Christ did was to reveal a greater understanding of science based upon real spatial relationships rather than to request that we follow him without knowledge or question or intellectual satisfaction based in reality. And herein lies the difference between "faith" and "grace" which we discuss later. However, modern Christianity has virtually accepted this non-dimensional, indiscernible, nonintellectual "spirituality" where "truth" is found only by the abandonment of the mind. This is also the position of many "scientists" that accept the religious realm where the potential for religious meaning lurks behind an "impenetrable curtain."

This may be stated another way. The mind that makes use of the scientific principles of observation and discovery is the same mind that discerns the truth of the spatial principles of Jesus Christ. There are other qualities of man at work besides the mind as will be discussed later. However, because man comes to his **knowledge of God** by the application of other faculties rather than the sole use of his mind does not mean that once unified with God that his mind is still ineffective as a sufficient tool to explain the truth. Nor does it mean that the truth itself is not solely intellectually explainable. The climbing of a mountain may be used as an illustration. Because one may need their feet and hands to climb a mountain, does not mean they need their feet and hands to tell someone the complete and essential truth about the top of the mountain. Nor does it mean that the mind is dependent on other human capabilities to communicate the whole truth of a matter. Also, because many Christians experience Christ with tears and powerful emotions does not mean that the mind is not essential nor that the mind is not required to complete salvation nor to explain the power of Christ to others. Nor does it mean the powerful revelation of the mind cannot produce tears. Yet, the mind, upon revelation of the power and unity with Christ and his Father, produces chills and physical strength as well.

Having tried to establish the necessity of a Christianity that is intellectually explainable to a scientific mind and a science that is not a religion itself for both Christianity and science to be correct, let us examine how we arrived at this strange place in history. There are numerous reasons for the rise of religiosity in science over the last five hundred years. The first reason was to defend certain scientists after finding facts that appeared to be in conflict with the church's understanding of the world. Copernicus and Galelio did not use "religiosity" as a defense of their work but they were later explained by more modern scientist (Einstein and Sagan) with "religiosity." Unfortunately, the church has accepted at times (as is the case presently) certain scientific explanations for the world around us that became virtually canonized into doctrine. The greatest of these being Ptolemy's geocentric theory (127 AD) that the Earth was the center of the universe and the Sun and stars moved around it. When these canonized scientific mistakes were challenged by Copernicus in 1543 AD and other better and more advanced findings the church assumed that its Scripture was under attack. However, nothing in Scripture ever appeared to support Ptolemy's theory. It is imperative that the church stick to its own scriptural explanation of the cosmos and its relationships. Now if you think this was a simple error and easy to avoid please continue herein to observe a much more serious error in the perception of the cosmos. The geocentric error pales in comparison to the error that is swallowed by both Christian and modern science presently.

The resulting embarrassment over the defense of insupportable and canonized and mistaken "scientific" theory led to the virtual rejection of all science by the church in general. This is the contemporary stand of many Christians today. Other more recent arguments include the debate over evolution and the ape trials. Creation and Evolution are in hot debate at the present. But this argument is a well defined agreement between scientists and Christianity in the false sociological equilibrium. It is very unfortunate that the church becomes embroiled in the trees rather than maintaining its cosmic truth from over the forest. The rejection of *all* science as valid for an explanation of the cosmos by Christians and the **unwillingness** of theologians to argue the holistic revelation of the Bible with scientists has led to the oversight of the spatial realities. The spatial realities are the relationships revealed in Scripture, which explain the power of Christ Jesus to translate the cosmos from death into life. This oversight has crippled the spread of the Gospel in more intellectual circles and crippled those in the church that see the importance of reality as a foundation for their belief and missionary zeal. This phenomenon accounts for the focus of common Christians on the "heart" and the abandonment of their minds resulting in almost complete subjection to a world of emotions and mere feelings.

Our place in the cosmos and the cosmos itself can be further explained and more accurately described in American culture by the use of the totality of Scriptural revelation rather than mere isolation and defense of a few Biblical passages in the book of Genesis. This holistic approach also applies to the origin and essence of man versus the simple "scientific" theory of biological evolution of man from apes.

Secondly, the concept of evolution further justified and accelerated the religiosity of science. No longer was religion itself seen as a revelation of some truth (much like, if not completely identical to scientific findings) but religion was evolved by man as his needs changed in order to adapt to his new situations. This notion is taught in public schools through out America today and has been rightly termed situational ethics and secular humanism. The idea that man evolved religion gave rise to "functionalism" in the study of religion. Functionalism studied only certain aspects of religion, namely, its structure or its organization and its effect on society. Functionalism was a tool of sociology and anthropology to organize the study of religions. Some have accepted this organizational tool of sociology as correct Christian theology.

Now scientists could clearly see their own quest for truth as a "religion." This conclusion is a logical development when the term "religion" is seen as a functional unit in society that "evolved" in response to mankind's needs. The scientific quest itself became a religious experience and a ritual for scientists. Einstein claimed this to be a religious experience sometimes very lonely and trying, yet representing the highest degree of religious devotion. Einstein claimed that his search for scientific truth and principles was driven by the highest sense of religion or "religiosity."

Finally religiosity continues to escalate as the result of the vacuum created by the occultation of Christian doctrine. With the church and science in agreement over their respective realms of study, as is the case now, the world around us continues to parish. What are the agreed realms? The church studies the "other world" that cannot be known by any means except through "faith" or the abandonment of the mind and a forced or surrendered mind to the power of the emotions and possibilities. Meanwhile, scientists get to claim priesthood over the known observable measurable world around us. What scientist wouldn't agree to this arrangement? This is completely contradictory to the message of the Gospel and to the laws of God. The first and greatest commandment is to Love the Lord thy God with all thy Heart, Soul, Mind and Strength. Christians cannot abandon the Mind nor shrink from scientific challenge. It is the job of the modern Christian to explain the Gospel to an advanced scientific community in their own language of science.

Einstein established the religion of science in his essay entitled *Science and Religion*. However he focused only on the creed of science rather than the whole functionalistic study of science as a religion. It is interesting that modern modern scientists have been eager to establish science as a religious endeavor, yet they are very reluctant to use their functionalist approach to determine the effects on society from their own new "religion." This is for good reason. Our industrialized societies are in deep trouble in this new false sociological equilibrium. It would not take them long to determine that the teaching of evolutionary, situational ethics in public schools across America has produced desolation unknown in American history. Ignorance and barbarism are so great in many schools that armed police enforce order in halls and classrooms. It is quickly discernible that the effects of their new religion on society are ineffective and destructive.

Modern modern scientists suggest that true religion should be changed to go with the times because they see their own religion of science evolve and change. They conclude that all other religions should do the same. And some "theologians" are buying this logic. Dr. Norman Beck, professor of theology at Texas Lutheran University, is advocating the complete rewriting of the Bible to leave out all "derogatory" information about Jews. He has written two books on the need to do this as well as a Bible that has put this matter in the footnote areas. See website www.AlienPhysics.com for a newspaper debate between us.

Most questions related to modern modern scientific research relate to concepts that come from the ignorance of Biblical spatial reality. Religiosity of science takes place as a direct result of a loss of the concept of man and his place and future in the cosmos provided by Christianity. This loss is perceived by all men and felt by modern modern scientists who ask questions like:

- ❏ "Are we alone in the universe?"

- ❏ "Is there life in outer space?"

- ❏ "Can we go to the stars and visit other galaxies?"

- ❏ "What do creatures in outer space look like?"

- ❏ "Are these creatures superior to us?"

Early Christians did not ask all these questions, not because they were not smart or less advanced, but because they knew the real cosmos and what it was in relation to human beings. They did not perceive the cosmos as well as modern modern particle scientists in relation to light characteristics but rather held a complete and accurate view of what the cosmos is and their relationship to it.

One might ask: "If society receives scientific advantage and useful implements from the scientific quest for who is out there, who cares if it is founded on error?" We forget that some of the most advanced institutions have come from man's revelation of Christ Jesus and what he has done to the cosmos. The United States Constitution is one. The advances in liberty for the common man in Europe and America have been achieved through this revelation. The quest for ultimate truth through science, in rejection of Biblical based revelation, has tyranny as a foundation. For without knowledge of Christ we do not know what man is and what his place is in the cosmos. Science has flourished in the environment of freedom in America. But, tyranny and oppression can endanger true science, economy and liberty for the whole world if science "falsely so called" goes unchecked based on error concerning mankind. Men will prefer liberty to Teflon frying pans, cell phones, Internet, smart bombs, satellite surveillance, and credit card implants. Christianity can and must challenge modern science in the definition of mankind and what our relationship is to the entire cosmos.

PART I - SOCIOLOGICAL EQUILIBRIUM:

CHAPTER 4 - DE-OCCULTING CHRISTIANITY:

After making the point that modern mainstream Christianity exists in a state of occultation in contemporary "scientific" America, it is our task herein to remove that which occults it and let its light shine upon all.

There is a real and true equilibrium between science and Christianity where both coexist and where the doctrines, laws, principles and reality of both are true. This, of course, is not the condition today. This condition has existed more fully in history but probably never in complete harmony.

We have allowed science to define Christianity and limit the parameters and definitions of terms to encompass only, that which is outside human observation and detection. Christians, for the most part, will not venture out of common biblical terminology to describe any Christian phenomena nor "trespass" upon the real world of science to describe their experience of Christ's power.

For example, in Sunday school a teacher asked the class what we thought it meant to be "sealed" in the Holy Spirit in relation to Ephesians 4:30 and John 3:33. They read as follows:

"And grieve not the holy Spirit of God, whereby ye are sealed unto the day of redemption."

"He that hath received his testimony hath set to his seal that God is true."

Several of the class said it related to the royal practice of sealing their important documents and decrees with a symbol of royalty. Others said the seal was a symbol of earnest of something to come. Finally, someone said that he thought the term "seal" implied in this context the containing of something within, or the act of placing a lid, top or seal on a jar. The teacher injected further that it might mean the completion of something. It appeared that the teacher missed the point of what the man had said, which related to a spatial physical condition of being contained in a sealed vessel, and went back to a legal interpretation.

This discussion reinforces the notion that the good news of Jesus Christ, as a result of what he has performed, is covered up or occulted. This good news is limited by the fear of Christians to perceive or describe the acts of Christ in any way that does not use biblical legal terminology. Christians avoid any terminology that infringes upon the world of science. This fear is produced in Christians and Christianity by the world of science. A Christian cannot use the word space or cosmos to define the biblical term Holy Spirit. Christians tend to think that they can use no words in common use to describe their Christian experience and that if they did use such terms they could be challenged by the scientific mind. In one sense this fear is good, in another sense this is detrimental to the propagation of the true Jesus Christ and how he exercises power over the world.

First, we will see later that the word space is ultimately an inanimate word used by scientist to define The One Eternal God of the Living. In fact, the word "space" was carefully chosen by philosophers and scientists to avoid this very character of the real world around us. In this regard Christians should not use the lifeless, characterless, and powerless term "space" to pray to our Father. We should fear the use of non-biblical terms in this manner! However, it is imperative to use the word "space" to communicate to non-Christians the one real essence of the reality that both God and men share together. An example would be to express the Kingdom of Heaven as the "final frontier." Likewise: "Heaven—the final frontier!" The dual world cosmology has produced a culture where heaven and the observable cosmos are in two different dimensions. This error is worse than believing in multiple Gods for Christians and worse then believing that the Earth is the center of the solar system for scientists.

In order for our society to maintain a safe equilibrium and for the truth of the gospel to be propagated once again, Christians must not be afraid to describe their Christian experience in terms that the modern scientific American mind can understand. A meaningful modern description of one's salvation may require use of terms not in the Bible or part of "church jargon." A revival may also require a fearless use of terms that scientists use or make up to avoid God.

For example, it has now become acceptable in Christian circles to use the word "universe." But don't try the word "cosmos" yet! The problem with these words, however, is that they do not hold the same definition for both Christians and scientists and cause confusion in both circles. When a Christian says the universe is infinite a scientist will argue with him. But Christians are very dubious of the word "cosmos" merely because Carl Sagan used it in his showbiz astronomy presentation entitled "The Cosmos." Scientists use the word "universe" to describe the outer limits of the exploded matter from the Big Bang, which astronomers say is between 18 and 20 Billion light years across.

The word *universe* however does not include the unlimited space, which contains the smaller area of exploded matter. The term *cosmos* is a much larger definition which still generally implies spatial infinity and all therein. If a Christian says that the cosmos is infinite or that space is infinite a scientist is less likely to argue that point. Agreement is made and the next level of revelation can be explored and discussed and possibly agreed upon.

A black, female, evangelist friend of mine refused to read a pre-edited copy of this book because she said it contained explanations of Scripture that did not use Scriptural terminology. She returned the book after scanning it and finding the use of words like cosmos, space, and impletion, etc. She said she did not read anything that was not Scriptural in nature. This is like being an evangelist to Russia and refusing to learn Russian. How are you going to tell them anything? America has become a culture that is far different than it once was. It has a technological, scientific language that has no definitions of words used in the Bible. If you are going to be relevant to this new American culture you will learn their language and what their terms mean and how to describe the real power of Christ to operate on the real world in terms they hold dear and understand.

My evangelist friend is not unusual. In American church circles today, suspicion is immediate if words are used that are not quotes from the Bible. The church seems not to care which version of the Bible you quote but it better have the words that are in some translation. I prefer the King James but be prepared for trouble if you describe some event in your Christian life with terms that a scientist can understand.

This process of analysis of Salvation or Alien Physics has also shown that many Christians do not know the full significance of what Christ has done and what their inheritance is. While writing this chapter my daughters and I met one of their teachers. We began to talk about Memorial day and the sacrifice of our forefathers and such:

I said that even though I had a great, great, great Grandfather that died as a patriot in the battle of King's Mountain that my main roots were in Christ. He agreed and said wouldn't that be great if all knew that. I said, "yes and why would anyone fight over the east bank or the Golan Heights." He continued to agree and I added, "If everyone knew that they possessed the Galaxies and would go there at will, they would be less concerned with local property." I said this knowing that the right of private property is also a God ordained principle. He looked shocked and bewildered and stated, "if we only knew how to go to the galaxies?" I said, "I know how to go to the Galaxies." He replied, "You do!" I said, "Yes, the same way Christ Jesus travels to them in the twinkling of an eye." This made him very uncomfortable and he immediately made light of it and went for the door.

I later asked my girls if they noticed the shock on him and they agreed that he was indeed amazed. Yet this should be common knowledge to students of the Holy Bible of which this man is well acquainted. My boldness in stating this truth in an every day scientific language is what shocked him and he probably thought I was a little tired or crazy. But where does the Bible say that Christ went in his ascension? Did the Bible say; 'into another dimension' or; 'up into the sky above them'? If you go up into the sky above long enough do you end up in another dimension or in deep space?

All this we have discussed can be summed up by saying that modern Christianity has succumbed, acquiesced, and deferred to scientists in the use of terms and their definitions resulting in fear to describe their own experience in words that a modern American can understand. This has paralyzed Christians and Christian theology as discussed earlier resulting in the retreat of the modern church to the "heart," or the "spirit" and the "other world."

Many Christians, including some real scholars, seem to be unconcerned by contradictions they make in discussing the Scriptures and the misuse or interchangeable definitions they use for Biblical terms and the spatial reality they describe. Many preachers and laymen interchangeably use phrases that might mean different things and progressions in the life of a Christian. It is not uncommon to hear the following terms and phrases to mean and describe different experiences or just one experience in the life of one believer: "When I first met Jesus; When I got saved; When I received the Holy Spirit; When I got baptized by the Spirit; When I was baptized; When I was born again; When I accepted Jesus as savior; When I let Jesus into my heart, etc...etc." These can have the same meaning or different ones and the modern Christian could care less. Why is that? Many preachers and laymen use the words "faith" and "grace" interchangeably. These terms cannot have the same definition without destroying the essential difference between the Old and New Testaments.

The confusion caused by the interchanging and misuse of these terms and phrases is common in modern Christianity. This is so because the modern Christian Church does not have a theology that defines these different terms and experiences in a comprehensive interrelated way. Modern Christianity lacks a consistent real world model as a foundation that explains Christ's power to transform people. The natural consequence of this lack of sound theological framework based in reality is a legalistic, memorized, labor intensive, mystical, naive, vulnerable, contradictory and impotent witness. Joy and peace in this present predicament is not found except with those of their own kind struggling to maintain their personal life-styles rather than spreading the good news of what Jesus has done in the world.

A defense and comparative contrast of Christianity and other world views is well drawn in David Knoble's book entitled *Understanding The Times*. But we cannot explain our experience of salvation by telling everyone what we are not and by avoiding all terms that they may understand. Why is it that we think we should learn a foreign language to be missionaries in a foreign land but we should not use any language common to those of our own culture but must withdraw and use only biblical terms in common use centuries ago? This is not to advocate another translation of the Bible to current language. This is about shaping the meaning contained in the King James version into theology that can be propagated in modern America.

A most remarkable example of the problem of explaining theological ideas without an interrelated consistent definition of terms based upon Christ's power to transform the cosmos is contained in a book called *Joy Unspeakable*, which is a collection of sermons and writings by Martyn Lloyd-Jones. Jones goes into great detail about how one should not come up with his own ideas and have experiences that are not consistent with the word of God. Then he immediately begins to commit that very error. His whole work is the attempt to establish an experience he calls "Baptism of the Holy Spirit" as something independent of salvation and regeneration. He attempts to make it clear that "Baptism of the Holy Spirit" is the act of Christ himself acting independently of the general operation of the Holy Spirit of God. In other words, he develops the concept of a Holy Quaternion; God the Father, God the Son, God the Holy Ghost, and God the Holy Spirit of Jesus. How can this be? How can one so carefully explain the error of making desired behavior into theology inconsistent with the Bible and go directly to doing so? In our modern world of public education, we could call this type of doctrine "outcome based" theology.

The Introduction to *Joy Unspeakable* explains the motive of Jones:

"So the conviction as to what Scripture taught, and the concern that he had about the increasing aridity in the lives of many Christians around him, caused him to change both his views and his emphasis. He became increasingly burdened to pray for revival—indeed the desire for a revival was to dominate the rest of his ministry."[4]

The way he was to help this prayer come to being was to theologically make the "Baptism of the Holy Spirit" a "thing" that happened after regeneration:

"He believed passionately in the baptism with the Holy Spirit as a distinct, post-conversion experience."(13)

Notice the carefulness of Jones to alert all men to the dangers of placing their experiences ahead of the Scriptures to arrive at their theology:

"Perhaps the greatest danger of all for Christian people is the danger of understanding the Scriptures in the light of their own experiences. We should not interpret Scripture in the light of our experiences, but we should examine our experiences in the light of the teaching of the Scripture."(16)

After this great admonition he goes right into doing that very thing that he warned us against.

"That, then, is our first great principal. All I am trying to establish is this—That you can be regenerate without being baptized with the Holy Spirit. The Scriptures that I have adduced to you show quite clearly that to say, as so many have said, and are still saying, that every man at regeneration is of necessity baptized with the Holy Spirit, is simply to fly in the face of this plain, explicit teaching of the Holy Scriptures."(32)

Jones fully understood the problem but not the answer of how to avoid the problem. The answer is not to merely check your experience with the word of God but to fully analyze and define all biblical terms consistently in harmony with the actual process by which Jesus transforms a dead world into the Everlasting Kingdom of God. In contrast to Jones' approach, the principles that will be developed later in this extent book are interrelated and checked against the necessary physical and spatial operations required for the translation of men from death into life. Anything concept that violates, encumbers, impedes or unnecessarily complicates the essential relationships and processes exercised by Christ to redeem the cosmos, is error.

---

[4] Martyn Lloyd-Jones, *Joy Unspeakable - Power & Renewal in the Holy Spirit*, ed. Christopher Catherwood (Wheaton, Illinois: Harold Shaw Publishers, 1984),13.

Jones built his defense of "the Baptism of the Holy Spirit" as a distinct operation of Jesus rather than God the Father by failing to define every term that he used such as regeneration, rebirth, salvation, sanctification, redemption, Christian, faith, and grace etc. We shall see later in this book that some of these terms which theologians painstakingly make separate cannot be made distinctive without violating the physical operation of Christ upon the cosmos. Likewise, we shall also see that some of the terminology used by modern theologians interchangeably cannot be so used without violating the same physical operation of Christ upon the cosmos. This is to say that modern theology contains no recognition of physical reality of how Christ saved the world. And without this knowledge theology cannot be unraveled (with or without the Holy Scriptures).

Jones' book was read in a home study group setting and most everyone enthusiastically accepted the theology that Jones was developing. The following logic that Jones used to support his theology will prove the need for a real world model of Christ's power to save all flesh for all time.

Jones opens his argument with a reference to John 1:26,33 where John the Baptist testifies of Christ as the one who will baptize with the Holy Ghost as opposed to the baptism of John by water. Jones then makes a dilution of Scripture at John 1:16, which is characteristic of the impotence of theology under the false sociological equilibrium:

"And of his fulness have all we received, and grace for grace."

Jones says that as a result only of our baptism of the Holy Spirit, which is beyond mere regeneration, we receive "something" of the fullness, receiving it "increasingly" and our finding Christianity "increasingly true." All of this Jones says we experience with "large and great measure," when we are baptized with the Holy Spirit by the Lord Jesus Christ. Notice that his statements do not convey the totality of the fullness of God as stated in the Scripture but he has now made it something less that grows continually. Something that grows bigger and better is not something that is full at one time. John clearly says they received the FULLNESS not the ever-shrinking PARTIALNESS.

Jones then refers to Luke 3:1-17 saying that the doctrine of Christ is enhanced by the baptism of the Holy Ghost. Jones says that those who have been baptized by the Holy Ghost have the same doctrine of Christ but in greater fullness. This cannot be. Doctrine cannot be in more fullness. Either you have a doctrine or you don't. Either you know a doctrine or you don't. One cannot hold the same doctrine as another but in more fullness. Another person cannot hold the doctrine of Christ, as the creator of the cosmos, in more fullness. Either you perceive that or you don't.

Jones tried to make the point that Christians were becoming more arid all the time because they were not baptized by the Holy Ghost. But this is not a problem of Christians without the Holy Spirit. It is a problem of Spirit filled Christians without a theology that explains their state of being to the modern scientific world they live in. It is bad theology that stifles the Spirit in its expression in the real world not a failure of the Holy Spirit itself. One can be filled with the Spirit and not know how to explain that to his fellow man.

Jones clearly states: "It is possible for us to be believers in the Lord Jesus Christ without having received the Baptism of the Holy Spirit."(21) This is logical but mere believers are not regenerated either. Jones continues: "Basically, therefore, you have to start by saying that no man can be a Christian at all without the Holy Spirit."(21) But Jones has not established his definition of when a man becomes a Christian; at belief, at baptism by water, or at rebirth or regeneration.

Now Jones defines the term Christian: "But then we can go further. It is the Holy Spirit who regenerates us, it is he who gives us new life. The Christian is a man who is born again. Yes he is a man who is 'born of the Spirit'."(22) Jones continues to refine his error: "I am asserting at the same time that you can be a believer, that you can have the Holy Spirit dwelling in you, and still not be baptized by the Holy Spirit."(22)

It is truly amazing that our home study class was unconcerned with the distinction that Jones is making here. Clearly Christians today do not have a way of discerning scriptural truth from scriptural error. Now Jones makes it clear that he is saying that there is two Holy Spirits:

> "But as you notice in the teaching in the first chapter of John's Gospel and which we see so clearly in the preaching of John the Baptist, the baptism of the Holy Spirit is something that is done by the Lord Jesus Christ not by the Holy Spirit."(23)

Not only does Jones make a distinction between the general operation of the Holy Spirit and the Holy Spirit of Christ but unknowingly makes a distinction between the general operation of Jesus Christ and the Baptism of the Holy Spirit by Jesus. To support this Jones says, "If you think that the Old Testament saints were not children of God you are denying the whole of Scripture. They were. But they had not been baptized with the Holy Spirit."(24)

The general operation of Christ is his death resurrection and ascension. This is a physical operation performed on the cosmos and all therein by the body of Christ Jesus. The operation of the Holy Spirit by Jesus is that which operated in himself and in us today. The Old Testament saints were sometimes filled with the Holy Spirit and this is the same as was in Christ and in those who believe in Christ today. What the Old Testament saints lacked was the general operation of the body of Christ, which brought grace into reality... the death of death and eternal life. It wasn't the lack of the Baptism of the Holy Ghost, it was the lack of the person Jesus Christ and his physical operation upon the cosmos opening the door to the Kingdom of Heaven.

Like most other theologians of our day Jones applies the term "regenerate" without cause when other Scriptural terms appear, supposing regeneration to be synonymous with belief and water baptism etc. Jones applies the term "regenerate" to those Christ is addressing or speaking of in John 15:3 and all of John 17. But the term "regenerate" is not to be found there nor implied there. The Scriptures referred to mentions their belief and knowledge but not their regeneration. In fact in chapter 17 of John, Jesus prays that they be with him in the future after his resurrection and prior to their expiration on earth. So they cannot be regenerate but merely believers in Christ and filled with the Holy Spirit. But they cannot be regenerate because Christ himself had not performed the act of regeneration upon the cosmos in his death, resurrection and ascension.

The error that Jones makes is implying that belief by those coming to Christ is the same as being regenerate. He makes no distinction between mere ascent or belief in some truth to the teachings of Christ and the full participation in the operation of Christ upon the cosmos resulting in their death, resurrection and ascension. Why does Jones make so little distinction between belief and regeneration and the general action of the Spirit yet make so much distinction between the Holy Spirit, the Holy Spirit of Christ and the Baptism of the Holy Spirit by Christ?

The account of Acts 8 is used to prove Jones' faulty theology of the "Baptism of the Holy Spirit." Jones again indiscriminately ascribes and implies the term "regenerate" to the Samaritans who had just heard about the account of Christ from Philip. It is reported there that they were in one accord. They were hearing and seeing the miracles Philip did. They were baptized in water in the name of Jesus after believing Philip. Jones quotes verse 14 of Acts:

> "the apostles which were at Jerusalem heard that Samaria had received the word of God, they sent unto them Peter & John: who when they were come down, prayed for them, that they might receive the Holy Ghost (for as yet he was fallen upon none of them: only they were baptized in the name of the Lord Jesus.) Then laid they their hands upon them, and they received the Holy Ghost."

But still this does not support the idea that a man can be regenerated through the operation of Christ without the full baptism of the Holy Spirit required to place oneself into this operation and perceive its impact on the whole cosmos. It is the Holy Spirit that nails you to the cross with Jesus and places you in the grave and raises you from it and causes you to ascend with Christ into the heavenly places. These people in Samaria were mere believers not regenerate new creatures. I dare say, also, that even after they had received the laying on of hands and the Baptism of the Holy Spirit they were not necessarily regenerate. Just because regeneration is not synonymous with Baptism of the Holy Spirit does not mean that regeneration does not include Baptism by the Holy Spirit as a necessity.

In a further attempt to support his faulty theology, Jones recites the conversion of Paul on the road to Damascus as proof. Paul only *believed* on Jesus after the vision. Where does the Scripture imply that Paul was regenerate immediately before or after Ananius was sent to fill Paul with the Holy Ghost. He then makes the reasonable point that you can be baptized with water either before or after Baptism of the Holy Spirit. But what does that have to do with regeneration? It is clear that Jones has a very loose definition of regeneration. It is a term used very little in the New Testament and one that indicates that it is the actual work of the body of Christ on the cross. One must fully participate in this event to completion in the heavenly places or they are not regenerate in Christ as a new creature in a new creation by the operation of Christ. One cannot experience this outside the fullness of the Holy

Ghost. In other words one must be completely immersed in the Holy Spirit of God and Christ to be able to experience this. This is missing in the theology of Jones.

Jones reiterates his position, "But what is established beyond doubt is that one can be a believer without being baptized by the Holy Spirit."(31) Yet did not he say earlier that one cannot believe without the Holy Spirit? He can only say this if there are two or more Holy Spirits. This is simply not the case. There is only one Holy Spirit. It can be established that one could be Baptized with the Holy Spirit and not be born again or regenerated or saved. But it does not work conversely to that because to be born-again, regenerated or saved, one must have been baptized in the Holy Spirit. Because it is the work of the Holy Spirit that permits your body to participate in the death, resurrection and ascension of Christ Jesus and have the resultant state of being a new creature.

Finally Jones leaps from the term "believe" to the term "regenerate" for the last time and we see clearly the resulting error. In an attempt to make his argument sound, without success, Jones quotes Ephesians 1:13-14:

> "In whom ye also trusted, after that ye heard the word of truth, the gospel of your salvation: in whom also after that ye believed, ye were sealed with that holy Spirit of promise,

> "Which is the earnest of our inheritance until the redemption of the purchased possession, unto the praise of his glory."(32)

It is clear that Jones does not distinguish between belief and regeneration nor does he have a clear understanding of the power of Christ to save the cosmos which allows him to err. Jones wraps up his error with this statement:

> "That, then, is our first great principle. All I am trying to establish is this—That you can be regenerate without being baptized with the Holy Spirit. The Scriptures that I have adduced to you show quite clearly that to say, as so many have said, and are still saying, that every man at regeneration is of necessity baptized with the Holy Spirit, is simply to fly in the face of this plain, explicit teaching of the Holy Scriptures."(32)

Why is this so important? Who cares if there are two or more Holy Spirits, anyway, if they are both from God and Christ and result in our salvation? This question is the result of our false sociological equilibrium. It is absolutely critical to the propagation of the good news of what Christ Jesus has done in and to the cosmos.

Not once did Martyn Lloyd-Jones mention the power of Christ to save all mankind. When he quoted comprehensive power delivering Scripture, he diluted them to partial power interpretations. Jones reads of receiving the fullness of Christ in John 1:16 and he says we can have "something of the fullness." Jones is really talking about getting people or "Christians" whipped up in a state of something, rather than having them understand the awesome power of Christ and the excitement of telling their fellow man about how Christ has done this miracle.

Rather, Jones is content to have Christians full of the Spirit instead of being full of effectual power coming from the revelation of the power of Christ.

In fact Jones missed the importance of Ephesians 1 entirely. Verse 13 and 14 were only a prelude to the rest of the chapter. These verses really relate to our being sealed with the Spirit as an earnest until the redemption of the purchases possession. The redemption has already occurred. The promise is fulfilled when one has come into the revelation of the knowledge of what Christ Jesus has actually done as described in the rest of the chapter. Therefore, let's see what the seal of the Holy Spirit holds in earnest for us, rather than getting hung up on being "Baptized with the Holy Spirit." Let's get what the Holy Spirit wants us to have (Ephesians 1:17-20):

> "That the God of our Lord Jesus Christ, the Father of glory, may give unto you the spirit of wisdom and revelation in the knowledge of him:

> "The eyes of your understanding being enlightened; that ye may know what is the hope of his calling, and what the riches of the glory of his inheritance in the saints,

> "And what is the exceeding greatness of his power to usward who believe, according to the working of his mighty power,

> "Which he wrought in Christ, when he raised him from the dead, and set him at his own right hand in the heavenly places,"

And at Ephesians 2:4-6:

> "But God, who is rich in mercy, for his great love wherewith he loved us,

> "Even when we were dead in sins, hath quickened us together with Christ, (by grace ye are saved;)

> "And hath raised us up together, and made us sit together in heavenly places in Christ Jesus:"

Now, how many of us are aware that we are sitting in the heavenly places with Christ Jesus? Is the aridness of Christians because they, who are believers, reborn, and regenerated, have not been baptized by the Holy Spirit? Or does this aridness come from the occultation of the power of Christ over the cosmos? In all this commotion over the number of Spirits and who's operating them we have lost the harmony that explains the power of Christ to save the world and all that is in it for all time. With the loss of this power we have lost the evangelical thrust and desire.

The church has lost an explanation of the good news. We are lost in our own Bibles. We are in retreat from the world of science. We live as the "brave" prophet in the bottom of the well. We need to deoccult Christianity and take the power of Christ Jesus to the streets of modern science. And demonstrate the operation of Christ over the cosmos and show the spatial relationships of the triune God the Father, God the Son and God the Holy Ghost and how all three have power over the cosmos. Therefore, be filled with the Holy Spirit and also pursue perfection in grace until you receive it and sit in the heavenly places with Christ Jesus. What you believe and know about how Christ operated over the cosmos effects not only your theological structure but how you perceive everything in society and how you express the truth. The baptism of the Holy Spirit is a vehicle to a place, not an end in itself.

The aridity of the modern church is not due to a lack of the Holy Spirit. Rather, it is due to the occultation of Christian doctrine conforming to science "falsely so called." Faulty incomplete doctrine has crippled evangelism in the modern world.

A woman told me once that she was a Methodist and that she had never heard of being filled with the spirit or being born again. Then one day she decided to go to a charismatic Pentecostal church. She was afraid to go in until she said to herself that she would just forget about her mind and go in and let it happen.

This simple statement by this woman reveals two very important consequences of the same problem with modern Christianity. The statement reveals the occultation and ineffectiveness of modern Christianity in our American culture. First it tells us that she was never exposed to the spatial principles required for salvation in her Methodist background. Secondly, it tells us that she had to leave her mind outside the door to enjoy and participate in the Pentecostal experience. Both result in ignorance and impotence in the everyday reality of American culture.

The first component testifies to the lack of understanding of the spatial principles of impletion and envelopment in the Methodist Church necessary for salvation and its proclamation. These concepts impact the soul of mankind. The second component testifies to the present necessity of mind abandonment to survive in some church circles. We are not required, by any statement made by Christ or the prophets, to abandon the mind in order to love, serve or experience God. In fact, just the opposite is true we are commanded to love God with all of our mind. It is time that people be able to attend a church in America where they can take, exercise, and rely upon their whole heart, mind, soul and strength to obtain eternal life and power! Mindless "Christian" voodoo will not sustain us in the days to come very shortly.

This chapter proves that modern Christianity cannot discern the meaning of its own theological terms and exists in a state of occultation. The task in the remainder of this book is to provide a model based upon the real observable world around us to show the power of Christ Jesus to save all mankind for all time. When this model is known all theological terms can be known with precision. This model will also be able to challenge modern science "falsely so called."

PART II - ALIEN PHYSICS / COSMIC OPERATION

CHAPTER 5 - RESTORATION OF THE QUATERNION MAN:

In order for the church to cast off from the sand bar of the "other world" the definition of man must be restored to its full uniqueness described by Christ Jesus and referred to herein as the Quaternion Man. In order for a correct equilibrium of science and Christianity to occur, two things must take place. First, pseudo-scientists must understand that man is not merely a thinking rock. Second, pseudo-Christians must perceive that Jesus saves more than the heart. Mankind has four components described by Christ, the heart, the mind, the soul and strength. These are the faculties that mankind is commanded to use in Loving God in Mark 12:30:

> "And thou shalt love the Lord thy God with all thy heart, and with all thy soul, and with all thy mind, and with all thy strength: this is the first commandment."

Modern Christianity is hobbling along using only its Heart. The awesome power of the rational Mind, as a valid instrument to be applied in Christianity, has been captured as the property of modern science exclusively.

It must be stated for the physiologists among us, that all these terms such as the "heart," "soul," and "mind" are all dependent upon the brain. And certainly it could be argued that the scriptural reference to the mind refers to rational thought processes and not the brain as an organ. It could also be argued that certain thoughts processed in the brain act upon the heart, as an organ, and cause deep emotional feelings of sorrow and happiness resulting in tears. The sensation of the soul seems to effect the whole body in the sense of weightlessness and the unity with space. Strength seems to relate to our will to do things that we sense are our obligations and to resist things, which are wrong. This component can also stand alone from the other components of the "quaternion man." It could also be said that all these properties can overlap with others but each can operate alone.

The Heart

The first property of the quaternion man is the heart. All Christians know more about the "heart" than any other human component. Much of the good news of Christ Jesus appeals to the heart of man. Many of Christ's statements regarding mercy, forgiveness, and justice appeal to the heart of mankind. Many of Christ's parables appeal to the heart especially in the prodigal son (Luke 15:11-24), returning home after wasting all his father's gifts, to make himself a servant to avoid starvation and finding the love of his father and restoration of his place as a son:

> "And he said, A certain man had two sons:

"And the younger of them said to his father, Father, give me the portion of goods that falleth to me, And he divided unto them his living.

"And not many days after the younger son gathered all together, and took his journey into a far country, and there wasted his substance with riotous living.

"And when he had spent all there arose a mighty famine in that land; and he began to be in want.

"And he went and joined himself to a citizen of that country; and he sent him into his fields to feed swine.

"And he would fain have filled his belly with husks that the swine did eat; and no man gave unto him.

"And when he came to himself, he said, How many hired servants of my father's house have bread enough and to spare, and I perish with hunger!

"I will arise and go to my father, and will say unto him, Father, I have sinned against heaven, and before thee,

"And am no more worthy to be called thy son: make me as one of thy servants.

"And he arose, and came to his father. But when he was yet a great way off, his father saw him, and had compassion, and ran, and fell on his neck, and kissed him.

"And the son said unto him, Father, I have sinned against heaven, and in thy sight, and am no more worthy to be called thy son.

"But the father said to his servants, Bring forth the best robe, and put it on him; and put a ring on his hand, and shoes on his feet:

"And bring hither the fatted calf, and kill it; and let us eat, and be merry:

"For this my son was dead, and is alive again; he was lost, and is found. And they began to be merry:"

The parable of the one lost sheep of such value that the herder abandons his flock to find it and upon saving it rejoices more over it than the 99 left in the flock (Luke 15:4-7). Crying over these parables is to love God with all our hearts. We can feel the action, undeserved mercy and love of God in our hearts.

The Soul

The second property of the quaternion man is his soul. This is the spatial component of mankind, where the Two Complementary Image Capacities are acknowledged and gratified. These two capacities of man will be discussed in later chapters. These two capacities are completely unheard of by modern scientists. This capacity of man allows him to be at one with God and Christ Jesus and the Holy Spirit. This property revealed in the New Testament, and confirming the Old Testament, is the one property most related to the "image of God." The property of the soul takes time to develop and understand and it can operate independently of the heart or the mind. Yet, it can operate simultaneously with all other properties to cause chills to run up and down the spine in great adoration and praise to God. The soul is the spatial property of man that is most connected to God through Christ Jesus. One must understand this property and surrender to its operation in order to be "born again." This concept will be developed further in this book.

The soul is where the sensation of filling and containing space resides within ones own body. The first description of this phenomenon is given in the account of the baptism of Jesus (Matthew 3:16-17):

> "And Jesus, when he was baptized, went up straightway out of the water: and, lo, the heavens were opened unto him, and he saw the Spirit of God descending like a dove, and lighting upon him:

> "And lo a voice from heaven, saying, This is my beloved Son, in whom I am well pleased."

One cannot perceive that operation of baptism, or how Christ could raise the dead without some idea of a unity of space and what space has to do with life itself. Certainly, if one, i.e., Christ, could contain all space and fill all space and never break that unity, he would certainly have power to do miracles and ask the Spirit to enter again into the dead bodies of men and women.

The raising of Lazarus (John 11:39-44):

> "Jesus said, Take ye away the stone. Martha, the sister of him that was dead, saith unto him, Lord, by this time he stinketh: for he hath been dead four days.

> "Jesus saith unto her, Said I not unto thee, that, if thou wouldest believe, thou shouldest see the glory of God?

> "Then they took away the stone from the place where the dead was laid. And Jesus lifted up his eyes, and said, Father, I thank thee that thou hast heard me.

> "And I knew that thou hearest me always: but because of the people which stand by I said it, that they may believe that thou hast sent me.

> "And when he thus had spoken, he cried with a loud voice, Lazarus, come forth.

> "And he that was dead came forth, bound hand and foot with graveclothes: and his face was bound about with a napkin. Jesus saith unto them. Loose him, and let him go."

Notice that the foregoing scripture causes chills not tears. The account of the baptism of Jesus should cause the sensation of weightlessness. Both scriptures relate to a spatial component of mankind—the soul. Hear in this next account how Jesus had to work in the face of disbelief of his power (Matthew 9:23-26):

> "And when Jesus came into the ruler's house, and saw the minstrels and the people making a noise,

> "He said unto them, Give place: for the maid is not dead, but sleepeth. And they laughed him to scorn.

> "But when the people were put forth, he went in, and took her by the hand, and the maid arose.

> "And the fame hereof went abroad into all that land."

All accounts of healings and raisings of the dead involve this component of man—the soul and its ability to link up with the Father and the Son and the Holy Spirit. Christ tells us to possess our souls in patience (Luke 21:16-19):

> "And ye shall be betrayed both by parents, and brethren, and kinsfolks, and friends; and some of you shall they cause to be put to death.

> "And ye shall be hated of all men for my name's sake!

> "but there shall not an hair of your head perish.

> "In your patience possess ye your souls."

This certainly says we have a connection to an existence wherein we have physical character (e.g., hair) that cannot perish. We shall see how this works later. Notice also the word possess. The possession of your soul will be shown to be involved in the essential difference between faith and grace in a later chapter herein. Seeking and possession are the key elements of faith and grace respectively.

The Mind

The third property of the quaternion man is the mind. This is the most distrusted and misunderstood property of the modern Christian. Things that are difficult to understand are immediately placed into this category and dismissed as unnecessarily complicated, irrelevant, expedient or evil. It has been said many times by Christians to those who are trying to understand it, "it's simple!" Well some of it may be simple but it's not always simple to explain. In a great movie (I consider it to be the best ever made, called '*Jesus of Nazareth*') Jesus says to Judas, "Use your heart Judas, not your mind." Of course, this is not found in scripture but reflects the modern distrust of the mind regarding Christianity. In fact modern Christians believe that the betrayal of Christ was Judas' use of his mind rather than his heart. This is serious error in modern Christianity.

It has become acceptable theology to dismiss intellectual argument or to attempt to understand the power of salvation and to merely believe one is saved "because it says so," rather than to understand and possess one's soul with confidence, power and authority. The modern presentation of the Trinity or Triune nature of God is treated this way by preachers, theologians and laymen. They say the Trinity must be a thing to be accepted on "faith" rather than to comprehend and know the relationships and therefore possess fully their resulting power over the cosmos and every thing in it.

This willingness to give up thinking and rely on "faith" deprives man of the power of the good news. Those who do not know and cannot explain the relationship of the Triune God (God the Father, God the Son and God the Holy Ghost) can not explain their own salvation. As a further result they cannot explain this means to be saved to anyone else nor defend their own state of being when attacked by nonbelievers. The Heart cannot fill all the duties of Christianity towards God and Mankind. Christ, the "SON OF MAN," and Man must be seen as a Quaternion in order to demonstrate man's physical relationship to the cosmos. Therefore the admonition of Paul in Ephesians 1:17-18:

> "That the God of our Lord Jesus Christ, the Father of glory, may give unto you the spirit of wisdom and revelation in the **knowledge** of him"

> "The **eyes of your understanding being enlightened**; that ye may **know** what is the hope of his calling, and what the riches of the glory of his inheritance in the saints,"

> (emphasis added)

It is obvious that Paul knows and understands with his mind and prays that his followers do the same. We must stop saying that we don't know how or why Jesus loved us! We do know why and how. If we don't know, our salvation is questionable. If we do know we must state it fearlessly.

It is the mind and the soul that must explain the miraculous events and hard to believe statements regarding Jesus Christ. It really is not sufficient to merely say: "because the Bible tells me so." That's not loving God with all of your mind. When Jesus says; "before Abraham was I Am," something must be stirred in the mind of the reader (John 8:58). How can this be? The mind then begins its journey to answer that question. The mind is what is challenged when Paul says (Colossians 1:12-17):

> "Giving thanks unto the Father, which hath made us meet to be partakers of the inheritance of the saints in light:

> "Who hath delivered us from the power of darkness, and hath translated us into the kingdom of his dear Son:

> "In whom we have redemption through his blood, even the forgiveness of sins:

> "Who is the image of the invisible God, the firstborn of every creature:

"For by him were all things created, that are in heaven, and that are in earth, visible and invisible, whether they be thrones, or dominions, or principalities, or powers: All things were created by him, and for him:

"And he is before all things, and by him all things consist."

This is a most colossal statement to make about a man and it is true. And it is to be understood completely as it had to be understood in order to express it. Why would we not want to know exactly how this can be and what this means to us? But many Christians pay little attention to this statement and many other similar statements in the Bible. But, due to the fear of the scientific world around us, many preachers tend to gravitate to the mundane rules and traditions of Christian theology. How could Jesus respond as he did to the questions of the Jews in John 2:18-20?

"Then answered the Jews and said unto him, What sign shewest thou unto us, seeing that thou doest these things?

"Jesus answered and said unto them, Destroy this temple, and in three days I will raise it up.

"Then said the Jews, Forty and six years was this temple in building, and wilt thou rear it up in three days?"

We shall see later in this book how he could say this and not be lying, joking, teasing or deceiving these men as to his power. Many theologians today do not have a clue of the cosmic power behind that statement made by Jesus some 2,000 years ago. We shall see that it is not the heart but the mind and the soul that reveals the meaning of that scripture. We will explore and explain the truth and reality of that statement in later chapters.

Therefore, Christianity is not simple, nor is it merely a matter for the heart. It is not confusion, however either. The opposite of simple is complex not confusion. The transformation power of Christianity is built upon learned interrelated principles and relationships not confusion (I Corinthians 14:33):

"For God is not the author of confusion, but of peace, as in all churches of the saints."

Strength

Finally, we come to the last component of the quaternion man. "Strength" is seldom regarded in Christian circles or the clergy. We do not love God until we become aware of the fact that it takes strength to do it. How do we become aware of our need of strength? The world resists the knowledge, expression and presentation of Christian principles. It takes strength to be the light and salt in the world. It is like putting your hand to the plow (Luke 9:61-62):

"And another also said, Lord, I will follow thee; but let me first go bid them farewell, which are at home at my house.

"And Jesus said unto him, No man, having put his hand to the plough, and looking back, is fit for the kingdom of God."

There are times, however, when it seems as though Christians operate only upon their own strength. This is approved of God if they are in this condition as a result of pressing on towards the mark (Philippians 3:14) or by running the race (I Corinthians 9:24). Even Jesus felt this condition on the cross (Mark 15:34):

"And at the ninth hour Jesus cried with a loud voice, saying, Eloi, Eloi, lama sabachthani? which is, being interpreted, My God, My God, why hast thou forsaken me?"

But if men are hard of heart, empty of soul, and lazy of mind and merely attempt to do things in their own strength they will have no fruit at all. Loving God with the heart, soul, and mind takes strength and it will call and rely upon God's strength when it comes to a moment of helplessness (John 15:5):

"I am the vine, ye are the branches: He that abideth in me, and I in him, the same bringeth forth much fruit: for without me ye can do nothing."

Another very important idea behind the component of strength is how one goes about increasing it and building it. Jesus told the disciples where he got power or sustenance in John 4:31-34:

"In the mean while his disciples prayed him, saying, Master, eat.

"But he said unto them, **I have meat to eat that ye know not of**.

"Therefore said the disciples one to another, hath any man brought him ought to eat?

"Jesus saith unto them, **My meat is to do the will of him that sent me, and to finish his work**."

(Emphasis added)

Fulfilling the purpose of God for you is meat and food and strength. The more you express God and receive the affliction of the world's resistance the stronger your foundation and strength becomes.

Now this brings up another very elusive area of theology today under the false sociological equilibrium. This is the method of determining the "will of God." There have been many books written on this and few of real merit. One of the worst books on the subject makes a twisted, contradictory labyrinth of ideas to attempt to prove their own seven steps to know God's will:

"1. God is always at work around you;
2. God pursues a continuing love relationship with you;
3. God invites you to become involved with him in His work;
4. God speaks by the Holy Spirit through the Bible, prayer, circumstances, and the church to reveal himself, His purposes, and His ways;

5. God's invitation always leads to a crisis of belief that requires faith and action;
6. You must make major adjustments in your life to join God;
7. You come to know God by experience as you obey Him and He accomplishes His work through you."[5]

This can be unraveled by showing the written will of God for all men (II Peter 3:9):

> "The Lord is not slack concerning his promise, as some men count slackness; but is longsuffering to usward, **not willing that any should perish,** but that **all should come to repentance.**"

(Emphasis added)

Now that is the universal will of God for all men and secondary to that is that we be involved in the pursuit of God's will for all men. And the way to determine your actions is to do the following from Psalms 37:4:

> "Delight thyself also in the Lord; and he shall give thee the **desires of thine heart.**"

(Emphasis added)

If one is delighted in knowing the revealed mysteries of the Lord Jesus and spreading them around, then it follows the above premise that what your heart wants is in the will of God already. Therefore seek your delight in unlocking the treasures of Jesus and you can do as your heart wishes at one with the will of God.

But to attempt to find God's will somewhere in the circumstances of daily life, and in and around the church, is going to bring nothing but grief and despair and confusion. Certainly we cannot say that doing God's will must bring "crisis of belief" and "major adjustments." This sounds like those that are as straw blown by every wind of change. This is not the will of God for you! Finally, to do the work of God we must do the following (John 6:28-29):

> "Then said they unto him, What shall we do, that we might work the works of God?

> "Jesus answered and said unto them, This is the work of God, that ye **believe on him whom he hath sent.**"

(Emphasis added)

Therefore believe and be transformed by Christ Jesus and the desire of your heart will be the will of God for you. If you do this you will be in the will of God and be doing the work of God. It is only natural that you will want to share this profound and great knowledge with others in the continuation of that will of God.

---

[5] Henry T. Blackaby and Claude V. King, *Experiencing God - Knowing and Doing The Will of God* (Nashville, Tennessee: LifeWay Press, 1994), 19.

When you are translated by that knowledge you will be in God's Kingdom and you will want others to join you there. Any lesser activity will lead to stumbling in the ditch as the blind cannot lead the blind.

The revival of Christian truth is dependent upon the correction of the present sociological equilibrium by the de-occulting of Christian truth. Revival under the scientific age must be more than whipping people up into a temporal "spiritual" frenzy. Revival must be the revelation of empirical evidence of Salvation Mechanics acting on the cosmos.

The true evolution of men into new creatures equipped to dwell and travel in deep space forever is the answer to the hopes and dreams of modern America and to the nations. This event of course is dependent on the proclamation of New Testament spatial properties and dynamics of Jesus Christ our Lord and Savior. This will be shown clearly in the last section of this book.

It is so common today at church and in Christian social settings to hear the phrase; "Lord, open our hearts to your word today." The prayer should be expanded to include all the components of the Quaternion man required to love God: "Lord break our hearts, unite with our souls, reveal yourself to our minds and give us strength to perceive and express what you have done in Christ Jesus." And we should not be content with tears of repentance and forgiveness. We should press on to the expansion of our souls into space, to the chills of the mental perception of eternity, and the weightless power of all space within us in unity with God to experience the full sensation of the quaternion man sitting in the heavenly places.

PART II - ALIEN PHYSICS / COSMIC OPERATION:

CHAPTER 6 - THE DOMAIN TRIAD:

In order to reveal real Christian concepts and truth about the world and the nature of mankind and his ultimate potential, we cannot leave unchallenged a common and false notion held by secular society and many "Christians." This false notion is that the observable world around us is the domain of science and that we cannot know, in life, what is beyond the veil of death. This false notion is not one proposed by Biblical scripture. However, many "Christians" believe that we can only hope for salvation after death and that we become whole only after death. They also believe that the Kingdom of Heaven is obtained only after death. They also conclude that the observable world around us, including space and stars, is separate from the Kingdom of Heaven. This view is relatively new and incorrect. It will be shown herein that this view cannot be correct if Jesus is to have power at all to save anyone at any time.

Obviously, if "Christians" can make such an error, how much easier for secular society? Modern society is saturated with the distinction between the world of the living and the world of the dead or either the world of the living and the nonexistence of God. These views are all related to the concept of God and His domain. The secular man cannot accept the idea that God is in or operates in the observable world. Therefore, if God exists at all he must exist and operate in another world, the "spirit" world. Further they conclude; "if this other spirit world exists, it may be known and experienced only after death."

As you might see here both views held by the "Christian" and the secular society are essentially the same and results in a prevention of salvation and a stagnation of evangelism for Christianity and a profusion of ridiculous propositions for the hope of mankind presented by modern science.

The following is a Biblical description of the domain of God which establishes the power of God and Christ Jesus and which is consistent with science in the observable world about us. Since there are three components necessary to establish the domain of God we can call it the "domain triad." The domain triad can be remembered easily as; "I...Am, One, Living."

Eternal Existence

The first component is eternal existence as revealed in Exodus 3:13-15, John 8:57-59 and Revelation 1:8.

Exodus 3: 13-15:

> "And Moses said unto God, Behold, when I come unto the children of Israel, and shall say unto them, The God of your fathers hath sent me unto you; and they shall say to me, What is his name? what shall I say unto them?

"And God said unto Moses, I AM THAT I AM: and he said, Thus shalt thou say unto the children of Israel, I AM hath sent me unto you.

"And God said moreover unto Moses, Thus shalt thou say unto the children of Israel, The Lord God of your fathers, the God of Abraham, the God of Isaac, and the God of Jacob, hath sent me unto you: this is my name for ever, and this is my memorial unto all generations."

John 8: 57-59:

"Then said the Jews unto him, Thou art not yet fifty years old, and hast thou seen Abraham?

"Jesus said unto them, Verily, verily, I say unto you, Before Abraham was, I am.

"Then took they up stones to cast at him: but Jesus hid himself, and went out of the temple, going through the midst of them, and so passed by."

Revelation 1: 8:

"I am Alpha and Omega, the beginning and the ending, saith the Lord, which is and which was, and which is to come, the Almighty."

These scriptures present the concept of God as eternal existence. No other description is as basic. Jesus identifies himself with this type of "I AM" existence and is at one with it. This also illustrates the timeless and infinite nature of God and the start and finish of all other things within himself. Jesus voices the notion that he has existed always and is in a constant state of existence.

Undivided Oneness

The second component of God's domain is his "oneness." This is best illustrated in Mark 12: 28-29:

"And Jesus answered him, The first of all the commandments is, Hear, O Israel; The Lord our God is one Lord: And thou shalt love the Lord thy God with all thy heart, and with all thy soul, and with all thy mind, and with all thy strength: this is the first commandment."

This does not, as I once thought, relate to polytheism at all. Many believe this statement relates to monotheism, instead of polytheism, peculiar to Judaism as opposed to other religions with multiple gods. However, other scriptures relate to that concept much better then what Jesus says here. One of the Ten Commandments states the monotheism concept much better: "Thou shalt have no other gods before me."

All the persons present in the conversation with Jesus in John chapter 8 were well aware of monotheism. But "the Lord our God is one Lord" relates to HIS quality of existence, or his **undivided existence**. This quote reveals to us that God is not split into two or more worlds. We may be split in our understanding of reality in terms of life and death and other worlds but this is error about reality and God. Some would say that Christ and Deuteronomy 6:4 is a strong argument against the ages old doctrine of the Trinity (God the Father, God the Son and God the Holy Ghost). We shall see later how God can be undivided yet have three representations and be at one with them all. We shall see that it is eternal space that is common between all three, the Holy Spirit.

Historically, men have believed in more than one god, wherein each was responsible for some facet of life or death e.g., goddess of fertility, god of war, god of the sea etc..etc. Yet Jesus' reference to Deuteronomy 6:4: ("Hear O Israel: The Lord our God is one Lord:") is more about the domain of God then the multiplicity of gods. God is not split up nor does he split his realm of operation or interest. This statement reveals that God does not function in two different worlds. Jesus reinforces that with his own statement that he had the commandment of God: Life Everlasting (John 12:50). The statement, "The Lord our God is one Lord," indicates that if we view the world as split between the living and the dead or the observable world and the spirit world or some other world we are wrong about God and reality. So far we have an eternal God in one dimension. Christ makes this one dimension of God more clear by limiting where God lives and works in the next component of the Domain Triad.

World of the Living

The third component in the domain triad completes the revelation of where God is to be found. Mark 12: 24-27:

> "And Jesus answering said unto them, Do ye not therefore err, because ye know not the scriptures, neither the power of God?

> "For when they shall rise from the dead, they neither marry, nor are given in marriage; but are as the angels which are in heaven.

> "And as touching the dead, that they rise: have ye not read in the book of Moses, how in the bush God spake unto him, saying, I am the God of Abraham, and the God of Isaac, and the God of Jacob?

> "He is not the God of the dead, but the God of the living: ye therefore greatly err."

A spirit world outside the observable cosmos does not exist. Christ says it plainly; there is no other world of the dead or any other kind to discover upon death or any other kind of spiritual probing. The domain triad is important because today the Trinity of Personality, (Father, Son, and Holy Ghost) has been buried in the "other world" of the dead or unknowable spirit world by modern physics. Who cares about the relationship of the Son to the Father when most men do not perceive the existence or domain of God in the world? Who cares about the Holy Ghost and His relationship to both the Father and the Son, when the whole union is bound in a spirit world where they cannot impact the world in which we live. Many "Christians" who can experience the Holy Ghost have a tendency to limit His power by holding this same split world view of the real world of science and the spirit world of religion and the kingdom of heaven to come.

Modern cosmology defined by secular science has a split worldview that goes off into infinity where the two never meet. The domain triad not only puts God back into the cosmos but indicates that God is the cosmos and that the cosmos itself is the Kingdom of God. This view is not new but has been occulted by modern secular science and modern philosophy for over 100 years. However, the real coming doom that modern secularist attempt to avoid is the promise of Christ to return to this planet from outer space just as he ascended into outer space. Acts 1: 9-12:

> "And when he had spoken these things, while they beheld, he was taken up; and a cloud received him out of their sight.

> "And while they looked steadfastly toward heaven as he went up, behold, two men stood by them in white apparel;

> "Which also said, Ye men of Galilee, why stand ye gazing up into heaven? This same Jesus which is taken up from you into heaven, shall so come in like manner as ye have seen him go into heaven."

Now, we see that one day the secular world of the living and the dead will one day come to a collision. The two worlds will not stay separate even for those who resist the Lord. Notice the use of the word "heaven" for the space above them in which they saw Jesus ascend. This was not a place beyond the grave but the space above their heads where the clouds were. Now if Jesus ascends far enough into the sky above, does he go into another dimension or does he go into deep space? And when he returns, will he come from another dimension or from deep space? We shall also see that Christ came from deep space in the first place. What we have learned to call outer space is the Kingdom of Heaven. Now how Christ travels in deep space, and how he performed a physical operation upon the cosmos, we shall see in other chapters. Does this begin to tell you about how men translated by their revelation of Jesus Christ shall travel through out the galaxies?

Who do you know today who say, "I looked up to heaven to see the planes fly over head?" What weatherman says, "a picture was taken from heaven by a satellite?" They don't see the space above as heaven. Heaven to modern secular man is an impregnable fortress that is penetrated only upon death and in which all men are somehow equal. This is totally incorrect. The Kingdom of Heaven is the space we inhabit all around us and which is infinitely large and small. We shall see also how Jesus, the Son of Man, fills all space and contains all space and therefore has power over the smallest of particles and the largest of celestial bodies. This is how he can be a healer as well as a mover of galaxies.

We shall also see that the possession and habitation of this kingdom can only be acquired through the transformation power of Jesus upon all those who can perceive what Christ did in his death, resurrection and ascension. We shall see also that this transformation must occur to men while they inhabit this known observable world in which we live or they never ever will possess nor enter into the Kingdom of God.

Let us conclude what the domain of God is. It is at least a triad of the components of continual existence, undivided oneness and living in the sphere of living human beings rather than "dead" ones. The domain triad is expressed simply in the phrase, "I Am One Living." Therefore the Father, Son and Holy Ghost say in unity, **"I Am, One Lord, of the Living."**

PART II - ALIEN PHYSICS / COSMIC OPERATION

CHAPTER 7 - THE SINGULAR ESSENCE OF GOD

The essence of God has been debated for centuries and many attempts to describe God's uniqueness have been pursued for many years. And, many Christians have problems in understanding what the real difference is between God and Jesus. And many preachers avoid the description of the Trinity and its clear relationships. The reason again is that few theologians will trespass on the domain of modern science and its claim on the observable cosmos.

Everyone, I think, has heard the expression "God is love." Certainly this is true but this is just one attribute of God and not His singular essence. And it is demonstrable that God is also justice, and judgement and greatness and beauty and power etc. We need a singular essence of God that explains the power of Christ to save all flesh that believes in him. And certainly it could be said that we don't know the definition of love any more than the definition of God. Therefore it's just as easy to say Love is God. But this does not explain the power of Christ to save men and how that power operates. Without knowing the singular essence of God and His relationship to Jesus we can not know what Jesus meant in his prayer recorded in John 17:1-2:

> "Father, the hour is come; glorify thy Son, that thy Son also may glorify thee:

> "As thou hast given him power over all flesh, that he should give eternal life to as many as thou hast given him."

Christ defines his Father as a Spirit and this means that God is not material in his most basic essence. He therefore must be nonmaterial or spatial. Certainly, we don't want to say God is neither spatial nor material, for then we have God, as a nothing. "Nothing" is what many theologians come up with in their fear to define God. They mistakenly think that it is blasphemy to define God. Many Christians believe God is not definable and when one attempts to do so we automatically fail and we anger God. We must have some definition or we cannot believe in him as required to please Him. Finding God, as He wants us to, cannot be done without defining God, at least to the point of knowing His power to work upon the cosmos and us. Therefore, defining God is not disrespectful arrogance or blasphemy but required work to receive the reward He has for those that believe in Him.

Jesus, in speaking to the Samaritan woman at the well as recorded in John 4: 1-26, not only tells the woman that God is a Spirit but that she worshiped what she knows not. Therefore how can we not have a definition of God and worship Him well? For Christ says there also that we will worship Him in truth and in Spirit. One cannot worship contrary to popular Christian thought, in ignorance without definition even with the Spirit. Christ said the true worshipers would worship in Spirit and Truth.

John 4: 22-24:

> "Ye worship **ye know not what**: we know what we worship: for salvation is of the Jews,

> "But the hour cometh, and now is, when the true worshipers shall worship the Father in **spirit and in truth**: for **the Father seeketh such to worship him**.

> "God is a Spirit: and they that worship him **must worship him in spirit and in truth**."

(Emphasis added)

As we see in the above Scripture, Jesus is ending the idea that one can please God and worship Him and not know Him or what He is. If it ever was, it is no longer any good to attempt worshiping God in ignorance of Him. It is implied that the woman did little good to worship what she knew not. And how do we do any better today if we worship what we have no definition of either? We have been until now worshipping, as she did, what we know not. This teaching of Jesus should tell us that there is no reduction of awe, inspiration, or reverence in defining what God is and His true magnitude and essence. This should end our present day theology that insists that awe of God require ignorance of God. We will cover this more in later chapters as well, for this old faulty theology shows itself in other ways as well.

The correct definition of Spirit in this case is not something from another dimension but the total of that which is opposite of material. The Spirit in this context is space. And God in this case would be all of eternal space. But in this age of the false sociological equilibrium the definition of "spirit" has been reduced to a force from the "spirit world" or "other world" or from some "other dimension" outside the observable cosmos. This notion is great error, every bit as great as believing in false gods for Christians and every bit as great as believing in a dual world of the living and the dead by scientists. This false definition of spirit has allowed the following falsehood as well.

Another critical term being defined in error in this present false sociological equilibrium is the word "heaven" which is now meant to be some "impenetrable other world." Meanwhile, we refer to God and His Kingdom as mere empty lifeless yet never ending space. God and His Kingdom have been removed to the "other world" rather than where we live at present. Modern men seek God by attempting to penetrate the "other world" with their "spiritual minds." Satan has been loosed to again deceive the nations by removing God from the real world in which we live. Satan now resides in the real world of science. But God is eternal space and His Kingdom is that same eternal space that we presently live in and observe on a daily and constant basis. Satan lives and has his dominion in the false theology and science.

As we can see it is modern science that has claimed the domain of the observable cosmos. But this is error. The observable cosmos is God and the Kingdom of God as is clearly expressed by St. Paul in Acts 17: 28:

> "For in him we live, and move, and have our being: as certain also of your own poets have said, For we are also his offspring."

Philosophers have argued that God is existence itself but even this definition falls short of the singular essence of God that would explain the power of Christ to save all flesh. This quantity or entity that would explain such power must be eternal space. There is nothing bigger than eternal space. And if God were that, nothing can be bigger than that. If God's singular essence were that of looking like the daddy of Jesus, then space is a larger entity than God. God therefore, would not be the biggest. Most importantly eternal space is the one singular essence that makes it possible for God to share his essence with man in the form of His first born Son, Jesus Christ and His adopted sons in and through the Holy Spirit.

Further, nothing, nor anyone, including Jesus himself can actually become exclusively God. Yet Christ first and then all men can share God's singular essence by becoming one with all space and time.

John 14: 28:

> "Ye have heard how I said unto you, I go away, and come again unto you. If ye loved me, ye would rejoice, because I said, I go unto the Father: for my Father is greater than I."

Because Jesus Christ is at one with the Father does not mean that Christ could become exclusively God. Christ obviously regarded this Father as greater than himself even though they exist as one by sharing the same essence. The singular essence of God, defined as eternal space, does not disallow other attributes such as Love, Biggest, Justice, Judgement, Power, Creator, Designer, Sustainer, Healer etc.

Arriving at this singular essence of God, as eternal space reveals a very powerful concept. It means that we live in the source of life itself and that space, as we have come to call all above us and around us, is alive. **Space is Alive**. This means that astronomers and scientists stare into life itself every day and night looking for life on other planets not knowing that they are staring into the face of Life itself. This accounts for the statement of Jesus in John 5: 37 and John 6: 46:

> "And the Father himself, which hath sent me, hath borne witness of me. Ye have neither heard his voice at any time, **nor seen his shape**.

> "Not that any man hath seen the Father, save he which is of God, he hath seen the Father."

> (Emphasis added)

Now for the good news! Jesus proclaims that you too will see the Father or God in Matthew 11: 27:

"All things are delivered unto me of my Father; and no man knoweth the Son, but the Father; neither knoweth any man the Father, save the Son, and **he to whomsoever the Son will reveal him.**"

(Emphasis added)

Have you seen God? Well, according to this, all who know Jesus have or will see God. This means you will not only perceive of God in the sense of His many attributes such as Love as discussed above, or in the form and person of Jesus or the Holy Spirit but in his singular essence. That is to say we shall perceive him as the infinite space that we experience all around us every day...the Kingdom of God. The only shape of eternal space is the human form of Jesus Christ and now us.

This does not mean that we seek and find God in trees and rocks and created things. God is to be sought in prayer, in and through Christ as the mediator between God and man, knowing that God exists and that He is Real and that we live in His Kingdom now and forever upon revelation of what Jesus performed on all space.

Until now the "Spirit" has been interpreted under the false sociological equilibrium as some feeling of the "other world." Chapter one clearly presents evidence that our contemporary false sociological equilibrium holds that people somehow believe that there is a "spiritual" connection with the "other world" beyond the observable world and the touch of the rational and scientific mind of man. This is a violation of the Quaternion Man requiring his complete attention and use of his mind in Loving God. One cannot Love God by abandoning his mind as is required so often in modern evangelical churches.

If it were possible to have a world outside of eternal space e.g., a spirit world, which was impregnable to the human mind, then God would be teasing and tempting us to challenge us to use all our minds. More importantly, a relationship revealing the power of Christ to save men forever would not be perceivable, conceivable or discoverable.

Therefore, God's singular essence must be the eternal infinite observable space that we live in presently and the Kingdom we one day will travel through out. God's Kingdom is visible from here and permeable by the human mind in fulfillment of God's commandment contained in Christ's quaternion description of how man must love God.

Jesus told the Sadducees that they did not know the POWER OF GOD. They did not know the Scriptures precisely because they did not have the underlying secret of the POWER OF GOD that Jesus embodied and was about to exercise upon the entire cosmos. This brings up the important reason to have a model of the major relationships of all things spoken of in the Bible that is in harmony with each other and that results in effecting the power and promises of God. It is irrelevant to be able to quote the entire text of the Bible if you do not know how the pieces fit together to work out your own salvation and to confidently possess your own soul.

Let's review some Scriptures that at first glance appear to contradict our notion that God's singular essence is eternal space or heaven. It is hoped that it has been established earlier herein that this book will use the general concept of heaven as the same as eternal space and as God, except where specified otherwise.

Upon first reading it appears that God cannot be space or heaven according to Genesis. If God is space or Heaven, how could it be said that God created heaven in Genesis 1:1?

"In the beginning God created the heaven and the earth."

But this statement gets further defined in Genesis 1:7,8:

"And God made the firmament, and divided the waters which were under the firmament from the waters which were above the firmament; and it was so. And God called the firmament Heaven. And the evening and the morning were the second day."

Obviously then, God made the heaven by dividing the waters on earth from the waters in the sky. The first heaven separates the rain, clouds and water in the sky from the lakes and oceans on the earth. But is this all there is to heaven? The rabbinical teachings included a three-layered model of heaven that is a rational and useful observation of Scripture. The first layer was just described and the second layer is that space which contains the stars and celestial bodies. The third layer (or third heaven) is the space above all matter and contains everything. II Corinthians 12: 2-3; Paul says;

"I knew a man in Christ above fourteen years ago, (whether in the body, I cannot tell; or whether out of the body, I cannot tell; God knoweth;) such an one caught up to the **third heaven**."

(Emphasis added)

We will define the term *universe,* as all that is included in the *second heaven* of the Bible and the *cosmos* shall include all things within the *third heaven* or God (eternal space). Our definition of universe will be consistent with the modern scientific use as approximately 18 billion light years across.

Einstein's expression of the "infinite ocean of space" will be consistent with the Third Heaven except it can be shown that this expression can be expanded to include the attribute of a living, feeling, jealous and powerful creating and destroying God.

The Domain Triad and the Singular Essence of God establish the foundation for the Power of God through the Trinity of Personality to work in the real observable world to affect what scientists have hoped for but not understood...THE EVOLUTION OF MAN. These two theological categories (Domain Triad and Singular Essence) begin to explain the reality of the power of Christ to translate all flesh in the operation of the Trinity of Personality which is the Father, Son and Holy Ghost. Other theological categories in chapters to follow will more completely explain the power of Christ to transform people from one type of creature to another.

This is not to say that one must express these concepts prior to the transformation of an individual. American Christians understand the principles of spatial and physical transformation subconsciously but they live in culture where they can only express it in "spiritual" terms. But they learn to express their transformation in terms that both the church and scientists have agreed is a personal, non-provable "other-world" experience that lead to their transformation.

This has happened in the life of the author of this book. The theological categories in this book were derived after transformation to help explain to the present culture of America how Christ has such power. This was done to strengthen the testimony, witness, and confidence of those Christ has transformed and to increase membership in the Kingdom of God from the modern Western culture. The Scriptures reveal these relationships of space and personality during the process of salvation but it took years, after salvation, to be able to express these components to contemporary Western culture.

It should be evident now that when the Bible speaks of God creating the heaven and the earth, it is referring to the first and second layers of heaven and not to the third heaven or the Kingdom of Heaven in which God presents his most fundamental essence—**Eternal Space**. This idea can be illustrated by the following questions: On what platform can God stand upon in order to create eternal space? None! That which is and cannot be created or shaken is God. And if outer space is not infinite what lies at its perimeter, Jell-O? Is Jell-O infinite? Or is God Jell-O? If God's singular essence is not eternal space, is God only a smaller entity traveling within the ether, Jell-O or space? If God were merely a moral force floating around in space would he not be equal with Satan? Do you perceive what must be here? God is Eternal Space! He is not a thing moving in space. He is all the space. He is constant unchangeable space that cannot be shaken, reduced or expanded. What can lie outside the domain of eternal space? Only the "other world" which is a totally fictitious creation of Satan in an attempt to destroy the effectiveness of God and Christ in the modern real world. However, this is the place reserved for Satan and his converts, outer darkness where the worm never ceases and where wailing and gnashing of teeth is the only pastime. To be cast out of the Kingdom of God or presence of God is to be cast out of all space and time—the ultimate black hole! And many modern physicists are on their way there and many are already dead and awaiting their eternal home in hell at this moment.

The most prevalent characteristic of the present Western culture is the incorrect idea that there is a "spiritual world" and an "observable world" and the two worlds meet only in death. This idea kills the effectiveness of God and Christ in the real observable world for many that would otherwise give them consideration. This idea is used to discredit those who have been transformed already and to quietly bury them in the coffin of a "personal religion" that every man makes for himself. Our society therefore concludes that weak "religious" men like those deserve no serious attention in anything they do. Our culture looks for those who independently blaze the trail in the observable world void of God. Has there been a greater lie believed in the Western world? Was Ptolemy's geocentric theory a greater misunderstanding of the cosmos? Nothing in the geocentric view of the Earth at the center of the solar system removes God and His Son and their power from the observable cosmos. The incorrect idea of two worlds (spiritual and observable) that meet only in death can be called the **dual world cosmology**. When this erroneous cosmology of today is pointed out, it explains the meaning of part of John's revelation.

It is hard to avoid the implication of the Dual World Cosmology in John's Revelation that the dragon will be let lose for a short period after the dominion of Christ has been established in the world. This has always been a hard Scripture until now (Revelation 20: 7):

> "And when the thousand years are expired, Satan shall be loosed out of his prison, and shall **go out to deceive the nations** which are in the four quarters of the earth, Gog and Magog, to gather them together to battle: the number of whom is as the sand of the sea."

(Emphasis added)

It could be shown, somewhat convincingly, that Christ has ruled the world through his church and Christian societies in the West and that Satan had been rather effectively chained for a 1000 years. It could also be shown that for the last 75 years Satan has been let loose and has made a place to reside in this very concept of a dual world cosmology. It is interesting to note what "chaining" and "unchaining" Satan consists of in Revelation 20:1-3:

> "And I saw an angel come down from heaven, having the key of the bottomless pit and **a great chain** in his hand.

> "And he laid hold on the dragon, that old serpent, which is the Devil, and Satan, and bound him a thousand years,

> "And cast him into the bottomless pit, and shut him up, and set a seal upon him, **that he should deceive the nations no more**, till the thousand years should be fulfilled; and after that he must be loosed a little season."

(Emphasis added)

The chain in both Scripture references refers to **chaining Satan's power to deceive the nations**. When Satan is chained he can no longer deceive the nations. Likewise, when he is loosed from chains he is able to deceive the nations. This refers to the nations in our observable world and known in our real world history. It can be easily shown that Christianity has successfully liberated the nations of all kinds of falsehood since Saint Paul journeyed to Rome. It is the teachings of Christianity that prevented the growth and spread of false gods in Greece and Rome and also brought much of Africa and Latin America out of the clutches of voodoo and black magic. The Christian West was a light to the entire world for at least a thousand years culminating in the Christian self-governing republic of the United States of America. The age was not perfect but it did effectively chain Satan preventing him from deceiving the nations.

But in the last 75 to 100 years it is Satan again who is able to deceive the nations. What better way to deceive the nations than to describe the Kingdom of Heaven and God as an "infinite ocean of space?" What better way to deceive the nations than to link the first atomic bomb blast and its destruction of cities to the very one who proclaimed that we live in an "infinite ocean of space?" It is that great false hope of mankind in the Space Age and its resultant doctrine of the "spirit world" and "real world" existing together where Satan is once again loosed to deceive the nations on a worldwide scale. Forget the pathetic cults and forget the dumb Satan worshippers. Instead, beware of the false sociological equilibrium that permeates all of our churches, colleges and work day world that will lead us all to the One World Order where "scientists" will rule without the knowledge of what man is, as revealed by the "Son of Man!"

The above Scriptures in Revelation cannot relate to a period after Christ returns in bodily form for no one will stand who is not His and none of His will rebel. Further, if Satan can subdue Christ Himself upon His return, who can put Satan back into the pit? These Scriptures relate to this present time period when **Satan is presently deceiving the nations by locking Christ and the church out of the known observable cosmos.**

It is indeed time for a "revival" of actual Christian fact that has been occulted by "science falsely so called." It is time to perceive that the Singular Essence of God is the eternal space that we live in and observe all around us. It is time to perceive that God's real domain can be expressed in His own words as "I AM, ONE LORD, OF THE LIVING."

The infinite ocean of space is the One and Only Living God who has provided a way for all men to obtain eternal life and travel to distant galaxies forever. **Do not be deceived by Satan about an "impenetrable curtain"** that we will know only in our death! But follow Christ's words, **"He that believes in me shall never die."**

In the Revelation of St. John, Jesus tells us that Satan dwells in ideas. Jesus warns His churches to beware of the doctrines of Satan. Jesus further promises His churches rewards for their resistance of the ideas that are promoted by Satan.

Jesus also tells his churches how he will fight against them if they give in (Rev. 2: 13-16):

> "I know thy works, and where thou dwellest, even **where Satan's seat is**: and thou holdest fast my name, and hast not denied my faith, even in those days wherein Antipas was my faithful martyr, who was slain among you, **where Satan dwelleth.**

> "But I have a few things against thee, because thou hast there them that hold the **doctrine** of Balaam, who taught Balac to cast a stumblingblock before the children of Israel, to eat things sacrificed unto idols, and to commit fornication.

> "So hast thou also them that hold the **doctrine** of the Nicolaitans, which thing I hate.

> "Repent; or else I will come unto thee quickly, and will fight against them with the **sword of my mouth**."

(Emphasis added)

Notice that one of the rewards that Christ promises to His church is the power over the nations. It should be clear then that we fight with Satan to establish the truth in the world for the control of the nations. Satan to deceive the nations and Christians to educate the nations about the door to the stars of heaven (Rev. 2:26):

> "And he that overcometh, and keepeth my works unto the end, to him will I give **power over the nations**:"

(Emphasis added)

Christians have work to do because it is Satan who is out successfully deceiving the nations and Christians have retreated and been pushed out of the observable world into the other world that is impenetrable to the human mind. Christians need to get back in the world of man and God and expose Satan's dwelling place in his lies about the cosmos and its meaning to mankind.

PART II - ALIEN PHYSICS / COSMIC OPERATION

CHAPTER 8 - TRINITY OF PERSONALITY

The concept of the Trinity has been around about 1,840 years and less understood today than in its inception. Modern preachers are taught to explain the concept of the Trinity as a "mystery." God must be shown as monotheistic while at the same time having three independent identities. This apparently is hard for some to understand and has caused mainstream Christianity to merely say; "accept it as a mystery on faith." Some "Christian" denominations reject it altogether. Therefore there own salvation becomes a matter of faith not experience.

The Trinity (of personality) cannot remain a mystery! Nor can it be ignored or rejected if we are to explain God's power in Christ to save all flesh that believes on him. This relationship is required in order to explain Salvation Mechanics. If this remains a mystery then so is your salvation a mystery. People are not saved by and through mysteries. To quote a song lyric sung by Stevie Wonder: "If you believe in something you don't understand...then you suffer." That is a good common sense observation and it applies in Christianity as in anything else. Thus, one of the main theses of this book is that **Man cannot live in a state of being that he does not intellectually perceive**.

The doctrine of the Trinity of Personality (the Father, Son, and Holy Ghost) was first developed by Turtullian, the father of Latin theology, in 150 AD. This doctrine is so sound that it has survived though it is accepted by mainstream Christianity in a formal but "mysterious" way. It is, none the less, one of the most fundamental and primary Christian concepts.

The three personalities are mentioned by Christ Jesus in his command to go forth and teach all nations and Baptize them in the name of the Father, Son and Holy Ghost (Matt 28:19). However the three personalities are never mentioned in Scripture as a "Trinity."

The doctrine of the Trinity of Personality was developed to defend against the accusation by Jews and Greeks that Christianity was polytheistic. However, the Trinity of Personality was not the first doctrine developed to defend against this charge. The "Logos" was the first doctrine to defend the Christian belief in one God. Logos simply translated means "word." The word logos was used in those times to mean "reason, purpose, wisdom." This was a rather impersonal and academic doctrine that left the idea of salvation out of the picture. The doctrine of the logos adopted terms familiar to philosophers of the period but left out personality and the pathway to salvation. The logos explained the connection between the Father Creator and the Son but left the Holy Spirit or you and the rest of us out of the picture.

Socrates, Plato and Aristotle all lived before Christ was born and had all believed in a god who's essence was wisdom, reason and purpose but believed in many lesser gods in human form with human emotions e.g. Athena. The Greeks also held a concept of unity that was "perfect oneness" excluding any internal distinctions. We can see the logos coming out in Tertullian's Apology XXI:

> "God made this universe by his word, reason and power. Your philosophers also agree that the maker of the universe seems to be Logos—that is word and reason...(for example, Zeno and Cleanthes)...We also claim that the word, reason and virtue, by which we have said that God made all things, have SPIRIT as their substance...This Word, we have learnt, was produced from God, and was generated by being produced, and therefore is called the Son of God, and God, from unity of substance with God. For God too is SPIRIT."[6] (Emphasis added.)

However, the most interesting illustration is given immediately following the above to explain the substance:

> "When a ray is projected from the sun it is a portion of the whole sun; but the sun will be in the ray because it is a ray of the sun; the substance is not separated but extended. so from spirit comes spirit, and God from God, as light is kindled from light...This ray of God...gilded down into a virgin, in her womb was fashioned as flesh, is born as man mixed with God. The flesh was built up by the spirit, was nourished, grew up, spoke, taught, worked, and was Christ."(112)

This is a good illustration especially for that time in which Tertullian lived, but there is a better illustration for today. Why select light to explain spirit rather than space? If the substance they share is spirit why was that not described as space rather than light? Why even unto this day do we speak of the essence of God as "existence" or "love" or "power" or "light" or some other very elusive ideal rather than a direct interpretation of the word spirit (incoporeal — not consisting of matter — space)? Even though this "light ray" is a nice WARM illustration it is not as accurate, permanent or comprehensive as a spatial illustration in which all three personalities share fully the identical essence of Eternal Space. This is why David could say in Psalms 139: 11-12 that even darkness was light to God.

> "If I say, surely the darkness shall cover me; even the night shall be light about me.

> "Yea, the darkness hideth not from thee; but the night shineth as the day: the darkness and the light are both alike to thee."

This is why God is not energy or force, etc., in the cosmos but is the spatial cosmos itself. Certainly darkness is identical to lightness to the Holy Spirit or

---

[6] Everett Ferguson, "Tertullian," in *Eerdman's Handbook To The History Of Christianity*, ed. John H.Y. Briggs, Dr. Robert D. Linder, David F. Wright (Carmel, New York: Guideposts, 1977), 112.

Eternal Space. There is no better translation of spirit than space! Yet we avoid this translation with vigor. Why? The explanation for our reluctance to call spirit "space" is due to external pressure and fear of our modern world. Satan has convinced this age that the observable world of science is separate from the "spiritual world." But the spiritual world of old is the same as the spatial cosmos of today. Modern Christians are afraid to tread on the world of science and the observable world about us. Christians are content to hold authority over the "spiritual other world." But this place is non existent and renders the power of Christ unexplainable and opens the door to mindless Christian voodoo.

There was much confusion up until about 400 AD about the Trinity of Personality and many Jewish Christians and the Docetist of the day believed that Jesus was not God. The Monarchians as in "monarchy" (Greek "single principle") believed God existed in different but separate modes (Father, Son, Spirit) and were sometimes called Modalist.

Tertullian developed the Trinity of personality around the divine "economy" or plan for the world. His economy stressed the successive activities of the Father, son and Spirit. God (Father) created the world, then he (Son) saved the world and then God (Holy Ghost) works in the soul of man.

But it wasn't until Athanasius (296-373) who further defined the doctrine of the Trinity of Personality to correct the belief of Arius and his followers. The importance of the Trinity to salvation is magnified. Arians said that Christ was a created being, made by God before time and less than God. Athanasius argued that if Christ was less than God was, then he could not be our savior; only God could restore man to communion with himself. This is very good logic and rationale. If Christ's Space or Spirit did not extend to the ends of Eternal Space or God then there would be a time in which his domain and affect would be exceeded. In this regard the principle of "**all or nothing**" applies. How would one know where this perimeter was? He (Christ) that had all space and time (without measure—hyper) did not hesitate to perform a Cosmic Operation. But he that does not possess all space and time would not even think or attempt to operate upon the cosmos with his body. If Christ has not all space and therefore all time, how do we know when we have exceeded his influence? It is all or nothing. Christ transforms the cosmos or no one has ever been translated and no one ever will be translated.

Athanasius presented the importance of salvation mechanics provided by Christ as the key to understanding the Scriptures and developing doctrine and adopting creeds. This emphasis must remain the core of sound theology and endeavor. The test of every doctrine must be its ability to support and clarify the mechanics of Physical Salvation. If we do not make the path clear to Physical Salvation, what is the point of all the talk about Father, Son, Holy Spirit, creation, evolution or anything else? For precisely the same reason, the Trinity of Personality cannot remain a mystery. **Salvation Mechanics, or the means and power of Christ to save men must be shown clearly to men**.

Paul said in 1st Corinthians 14:33: "For God is not the author of confusion, but of peace, as in all churches of the saints." Therefore, let's try to really explain the Trinity of Personality to our own generation and culture. Paul is clear in chapter 2 of

1st Corinthians that we have the full revelation of the mysteries of God in Christ Jesus. We now possess the mind of Christ or God. **Why do we need to fall back into the mysteries** of the ancients instead of explaining clear spatial relationships that we now know?

It is clear from our review that the SPIRIT is the essential element of the Trinity. The Spirit is what unites all three personalities. There was less concern in 400 AD for the Holy Spirit in men and what men really became as a result of The Spirit is really the third personality and it is that which can enter men as well as Jesus, the first Son of God. The Singular Essence of God as anything other than Eternal Space seems to lead to confusion. Today the "Spirit," is perceived by many modern men as temporal moody feelings of remorse or brokenness, or one among many spirits, i.e. demons, angels, devils, etc...a good spirit or a bad spirit or sadness and joy. Or worse, moderns assume that the Spirit is in the other world! Check out the bookstore sometime, you will find Christian books in the "spiritual" section, beside the books on witchcraft.

But God is not a spirit but **THE SPIRIT**. If God is merely one Spirit among many He is not a great and powerful God. Yes, you can be the slave of the spirit of Satan. But the SPIRIT OF GOD has no equal and is greater than Satan and is the only power that can overcome Satan's grip on men. Therefore, Satan and demons are spirits, but they are temporal and do not share the domain of God fully, and their spirit is not synonymous with the SPIRIT OF GOD. The spirit of Satan is the spirit of the world systems at work i.e., the work of unregenerate groups of men under the fear of death. Take for instance, the United Nations plan for world disarmament. The plan is called "Freedom From War." Compare this title to the battle cry of Christian lawyer, Patrick Henry, "Give Me Liberty or Give Me Death." Who here fears death? And who here loves liberty for all men?

The prophets and apostles did not think of the Spirit or of Heaven as another dimension. They thought of Heaven as the space about and above them. We must return to this perception of reality. Therefore, in this age of pseudoscience, it would be good to always distinguish the SPIRIT OF GOD as the one and only Eternal Space Entity rather than just another spirit.

We have established the concept of the Spirit Of God as Eternal Space in the preceding chapter, now let us turn to the Scriptures again to see how the concept of the Trinity of Personality works:

The Virgin Birth of Christ (Luke 1:35):

> "And the angel answered and said unto her, The Holy Ghost (Eternal Space) shall come upon thee, and the power of the Highest shall overshadow thee; therefore also that holy thing which shall be born of thee shall be called the Son of God." (Parenthesis added.)

The baptism of Jesus by John the Baptist (Matthew 3: 16-17):

> "And Jesus, when he was baptized, went up straightway out of the water: and lo, the heavens (plural - all 3) were opened unto him, and he saw the Spirit of God (Eternal Space) descending like a dove, and lighting upon him:

"And lo a voice from heaven, saying, This is my beloved Son, in whom I am well pleased." (Parenthesis above added)

Those Scriptures show how the Spirit of God came into the world through Jesus. How does Christ Jesus transmit his essence (eternal space) to his followers (John 14:16-20):

"And I will pray the Father, and he shall give you another Comforter, that he may abide with you for ever;

"Even the Spirit of truth; whom the world cannot receive, because it seeth him not, neither knoweth him: but ye know him; for he dwelleth with you, and shall be in you.

"I will not leave you comfortless: I will come to you.

"Yet a little while, and the world seeth me no more; but ye see me: because I live, ye shall live also.

"At that day ye shall know that I am in my Father, and ye in me, and I in you."

What day is Jesus talking about? It is the day that we realize that God or Eternal Space is in Jesus and hence, in you and I, and everything else. We also know on that day that Jesus is in us. How do we know? By the recollection of His recorded word, and being transformed into new creatures by the death, resurrection and ascension of Christ. See John 14:26, 15:3 and 15:7.

Is the Comforter the Spirit? (John 14:26):

"But the Comforter, which is the Holy Ghost, whom the Father will send in my name, he shall teach you all things, and bring all things to your remembrance, whatsoever I have said unto you."

What do the two terms, spirit and ghost have in common? They both lack material qualities. But this does not mean they are otherworldly. The "Comforter" is a term used to describe the function of the Spirit in the Scripture above just as the "Spirit of truth" is used to describe another function of the Spirit of God or Eternal Space. The Holy Spirit or Ghost has these two functions of bringing comfort and knowledge of the truth concerning our observable cosmos.

Jesus never referred to God as mere space. This is because Jesus knew that Eternal Space was alive and that this entity was his Father. Jesus was at one with this entity and was loved by it and would not use a non-personal word like space to describe his Father. Neither should any Christian view this entity as an empty dead "ocean of space," as Einstein did. But we live in another time where society in general cannot see God as anything anywhere much less as a Father. The singular essence of God as eternal space is essential to describe the power of Christ to operate on all men forever and explain what has gone wrong in Christianity and the world around us.

Men up until recently have never thought of mechanically travelling out into the stars. They saw this as part of the Kingdom of God and knew that there was a way to go there. They never would dream of attempting to go to Heaven in a contraption. No one would dare think of talking of such a place in cold terms like space. The whole notion of space at that time was sacred. That epic magazine headline "God is dead" was proclaimed when the great "ocean of space" was proclaimed.

God died in the industrialized world when we began to think we could travel eternally in the stars by a man made contraption. This is still entertained by most. Our human bodies are the most complex star and galaxy visiting devices ever made. And, if anyone can perceive of the operation of Christ over the cosmos, they shall use their bodies forever to travel eternally in the stars of Heaven. But other men trying to break into Heaven with contraptions will not join the Saints.

It is clear now, that modern scientists are as bound by the great expanse of space as man have ever been. We can play around close to earth but we can't go to the stars mechanically without sacrificing every American and earth inhabitant in the process. The space program has become like the pyramid program of Egypt. Paul said it well in speaking of God's power to the Anthenians in Acts 17:22-28:

> "Then Paul stood in the midst of Mars' Hill, and said, Ye men of Athens, I perceive that in all things ye are too superstitious.

> "For as I passed by, and beheld your devotions, I found an alter with this inscription, TO THE UNKNOWN GOD. Whom therefore ye ignorantly worship, him declare I unto you.

> "God that made the world and all things therein, seeing that he is Lord of heaven and earth, dwelleth not in temples made with hands;

> "Neither is worshipped with men's hands, as though he needed any thing, seeing he giveth to all life, and breath, and all things;

> "And hath made of one blood all nations of men for to dwell on all the face of the earth, **and hath determined the times before appointed, and the bounds of their habitation;**

> "That they should seek the Lord, if haply they might feel after him, and find him, though he be not far from every one of us:

> "For in him we live, and move, and have our being; as certain also of your own poets have said, For we are also his offspring."

(Emphasis added)

This proclamation at Mars' Hill is still profound and should be made on the floor of the United States Congress and the United Nations. We still worship the unknown God in ignorance, as we shall see momentarily, and the bounds of our habitation are as fixed and sure as they have ever been. It is interesting to note also here that Paul saw that we live, and move and have our being in God, not in an other worldly sense that we pretend today, but in the present physical observable reality.

Why did God restrict mankind's bounds of habitation? So that mankind would seek the Lord! And why did God want us to seek him? So that we might haply FIND HIM! Finding God is not ignorantly worshipping him in MYSTERY!

It is clear from all modern science that scientists have failed to deliver hope of everlasting life to mankind or men individually either on earth or in space or anywhere else. Without Jesus (the Hyperspace Alien) and his evolutionary process of Salvation Mechanics via Spatial Physics, scientists will not only fail to travel in deep space, they will fail to exist anywhere.

It is instrumental and critically important for us at this time in history to have several ways of describing God. First through a domain and then in character and then through singular essence. This allows us to make the necessary Biblical connections required for salvation and at the same time explain many other concepts and actions of God in the Bible. Bible scholars believe that the Seven Spirits of God in Revelation 5:6 refer to the seven churches mentioned in the first three books of Revelation:

> "And I beheld, and, lo, in the midst of the throne and of the four beasts, and in the midst of the elders, stood a Lamb as it had been slain, having seven horns and seven eyes, which are the seven Spirits of God sent forth into all the earth."

But what do the seven Spirits of the Church say and what is the meaning of horns and eyes other than how God is heard or seen. Is it possible to locate and know God in a Trinity of Personalities and a Domain Triad and one Singular Essence? That totals seven ways that God is known or located in our observable world. We can know God as a Father, as a Son, by the Holy Ghost or Spirit. We can observe God by his Singular Essence of Eternal Space. We can also locate God as I Am, Undivided One, Of The Living. This totals seven ways that the power of Christ is made known in the world and certainly they have been revealed or sent forth into the world by God's word. Could these Spirits actually be the channels that God makes himself known to man and the way He perceives mankind? It is chilling to think that each candlestick of the Menorah represents one of these primary means of knowing God. Eternal space is the singular essence with each character of the Trinity on one side and each component of the domain triad on the other. Each has its own independent meaning but all are in unity with the essence of God.

Christ Jesus was the first man to demonstrate mankind's created capacity to implete, or fill, all of eternal space and to envelop, or contain all of eternal space. This concept will be shown shortly in this book. It is man's endowed and created capacity to contain Eternal Space. This is what Christ meant in Matthew 11:27:

> "All things are delivered unto me of my Father: and no man knoweth the Son, but the Father; neither knoweth any man the Father, save the Son, and he to whomsoever the Son will reveal him."

There is only one way that God could give Christ all things; that is through uniting with him spatially so that all things contained in eternal space become the property of Jesus Christ. If you want to see the very outer limits of eternal space look in the mirror. Jesus looked a lot like you. If you want to possess the Kingdom of Heaven and inherit the Earth then look to Jesus the Hyperspace Alien and humble yourself and learn of him and his power to translate you from death into eternal life. And this opens the door to eternal space habitation and travel.

Men can be transformed by the physical operation of Christ's death, resurrection and ascension as the second person of the Trinity without being able to explain how it happened to another person. But subconsciously the Holy Spirit or Eternal Space at one also with God the Father and God the Son work on the individual until they experience the operation for themselves. But to defend the Trinity in any way other than to say, as their pastor will, that they must perceive the Trinity as a mystery and accept it on faith can come only after years of analysis. In fact, my pastor said as I was writing this chapter, "we cannot worship that which we are familiar with." Now that may sound good at first to those that are praising God but this is a dangerous statement to the doctrine of the Trinity as well as power of salvation itself. And didn't we just here what Paul said about being too superstitious and worshipping God in ignorance?

The church has confused knowledge with magnitude or greatness or majesty. How can we worship God if we don't know Him? How do we know that He likes the ignorant and lazy of mind to say meaningless slogans to Him? For if we know Him not, our words must be uttered in ignorance and this would bore me. How much more would God be bored and annoyed by such praise and adoration? "We love you Lord yes we lov lov lov ya! You are beyond our comprehension but we lov ya anyway. Now let's eat lunch!" The Trinity is not a mystery nor should it remain a mystery by the insistence of some bunch of theologians somewhere teaching preachers how to present this concept or theological relationship to laymen. It is impossible to praise God if He is not known completely. You are complete in God and you have complete knowledge of God through the possession of the mind of Christ. Therefore the secret and mystery of the Trinity is made known to you as well. But the modern church does not acknowledge this fact. This again is evidence of the false sociological equilibrium between science and Christianity.

As evidence of the false sociological equilibrium and the maintenance of the Trinity as a mystery let's review the subject in Grudem's book, *Systematic Theology*. Grudem devotes about 40 pages in his book on systematic theology. You will be amazed at what he reduces it down to as a result of a lack of a spatial model explaining the Trinity.

> "This tri-personal form of being is far beyond our ability to comprehend. It is a kind of existence far different from anything we have experienced, and far different from anything else in the universe."[7]

---

[7] Wayne Grudem, *SYSTEMATIC THEOLOGY, An Introduction To Biblical Doctrine* (Grand Rapids, Michigan: Zondervan Publishing House, 1994), 255

Man must be able to experience this triune relationship or he cannot be transformed! So why does Grudem insist that we cannot comprehend this? It is none other than the false sociological equilibrium at work. Mr. Grudem then clearly states his opinion that "the Trinity is a mystery that we will never be able to understand fully."(231) Then he starts to tell us what we should know only partially.

"However, we can understand something of its truth by summarizing
the teaching of Scripture in three statements: God is three persons.
Each person is fully God. There is one God."(231)

He then makes the accurate point that simplistic solutions to the so-called "mystery" of the Trinity historically have not worked out well. Historically, movements have occurred that attempt to solve the "mystery" by denying one of the three components.

Then Grudem makes another accurate point in saying, "all analogies have shortcomings." He reviews some of the analogies drawn from nature to help explain the "mystery" of the Trinity. He then covers the analogy of the three-leaf clover but it fails because each leaf cannot be said to be the whole clover. He brings up the analogy of the tree with roots, trunk and branches as one tree. He recalls the analogy of the three forms of water as liquid, steam and ice and shows how this fails as it is not all three at one time.

Grudem also covers analogies from human experience such as the farmer who is also mayor and elder in church with three roles to perform. Also he recites the intellect, emotions and will of a person. But the farmer is just one man and the three parts of a person does not constitute one complete person. He draws the conclusion that no analogy adequately presents the Trinity.

Mr. Grudem then makes an interesting statement, "it is interesting that Scripture nowhere uses any analogies to teach the doctrine of the Trinity." Without thinking a whole lot, this appears to be true. However, Grudem is referring to an analogy, and an analogy is not required if there has been a record made of the direct action and direct relationship of the Trinity. Why give an analogy of the baptism account of Jesus when itself is a direct explanation of the Trinity?

In the Baptism account, God-the-Son is obedient to "fulfill all righteousness" and be baptized by John. God the Son fills all of heaven or God with his spirit and then the Spirit of God descends like a dove and lights upon God the Son. Then God the Father says "this is my beloved Son, in whom I am well pleased." We have a direct account of the Trinity joining together and consummating the power of Christ Jesus upon the earth to the ends of the cosmos.

Why do we need an analogy of something we have a direct account of? And why should not man-made analogies fail by comparison to the direct explanation of the actions of the Triune God. Here we have not only the different roles played by each person but the state of being of each person and also a description of how they all are one undivided God. Jesus is obedient servant and Son acting upon the will of His Father. The Son perceives the heavens opened to him and his soul fills all the heavens. Upon completion, the Holy Spirit of God descends upon the Son as a dove uniting the Soul or Spirit of Christ with the Spirit of God. The voice of God the Father verifies the event proclaiming Christ as His beloved Son.

We therefore have at least one direct account of all three personalities acting in different ways and we also perceive here that each one is fully God and that there is only one God. The Son fills all of space or heaven uniting with the singular essence of God. As a result of that event, all of space or God or the Kingdom of God descends upon The Son as a dove wherein the Son then contains all of space or the Kingdom of God or God Himself. Wherein the Son can then without hesitation proclaim, "the Father and I are one." And obviously, Christ says, later, that his disciples will be at one with the Son and the Father through the action of the Holy Spirit. We also know that eternal space is not divided up but continuous and shared by each distinct personality wherein each shares the essence and totality of God. And this also means that we who have been transformed also share the identical eternal space that the others share. What lack we?

The answer to the "mystery" of the Old Testament prophecies concerning God, the Messiah and the Holy Spirit of God are revealed in the New Testament in this very baptism account. The answer is in the spatial unity not in trees or rocks or clover or sponges or human experience, or sunbeams, etc. A spatial understanding of the relationship does not violate the requirements of the triune God but gives a complete understanding of how all three are fully God yet distinct entities all at one.

Now we will see what the result of not having a spatial and complete understanding of the Trinity of Personality produces in Systematic Theology. Mr. Grudem cautions the reader to never attempt to solve the "mystery" because all attempts to do so have produced theological error.

> "We should be warned by the errors that have been made in the past. They have come about through attempts to simplify the doctrine of the Trinity and make it completely understandable, removing all mystery from it. This we can never do."(255-256)

Then Grudem says we can at least believe the three statements about God but never be able to put them together.

> "But what we cannot understand fully is how to fit together those distinct biblical teachings. We wonder how there can be three distinct persons, and each person have the whole being of God in himself, and yet God is only one undivided being. This we are unable to understand."(256)

We shall see shortly what results from not being able to join these relationships together. In fact, one might say that the doctrine of the Trinity is not really understood at all, or in the slightest, unless all three statements are joined mentally into an understandable oneness. It is not sufficient to leave the Trinity in three parts as Grudem and modern Christianity has done, much the same as the Modalists of antiquity had done. It is accurate and simple to say and understand that God's singular essence is eternal space and the Son and Holy Spirit share it completely and as a result the disciples share it completely and perceive completely the Triune God and praise God for it! Grudem goes further to tell us how it would even be **spiritually unhealthy** to define or understand fully the Trinity.

> "In fact, it is spiritually healthy for us to acknowledge openly that God's very being is far greater than we can ever comprehend. This humbles us before God and draws us to worship him without reservation."(256)

Again, we see that there is another doctrine going on today that we could identify as the **Doctrine of Ignorant Worship**. The most powerful worship experiences come from the revelation of what God is and our unity with such magnitude. Is it not the whole of our missionary endeavor to teach the ignorant how to worship God? And have we done this by teaching them how to be ignorant of what God is, or how great and magnificent he is? The heathen has always worshipped God humbly in ignorance of his essence. Was not Paul teaching the ignorant how to worship God in knowledge of Him at Mars' Hill? If there is any reservation in worship, it comes from incomprehension and ignorance and such worship is spiritually shallow and sickly. Let's look at the fruits of no resolution or solution to the "mystery" of the Trinity in Mr. Grudem's section on the application of the doctrine of the Trinity. Grudem reduces the Trinity to a perception of unity and diversity.

> "Because God in himself has both unity and diversity, it is not surprising that unity and diversity are also reflected in the human relationships he has established."(256)

How does one move from the Triune nature of God to a dual application of unity and diversity? This sounds like a cheap campaign slogan, not a perception of the theological meaning of the Trinity! Grudem goes on to tell how the Trinity is important to our understanding of marriage of two becoming one and then the gift of children. He then uses the Trinity's reduction to unity and diversity to understand how the church can have many members, yet one body. This unity and diversity, he says, applies to the Jews and the Gentiles, the union of the church and Christ in which we are called the bride of Christ. And now Grudem concludes that even the whole universe will partake of the unity of purpose with diversity contributing to the worship of God the Father, Son and Holy Spirit.

Talk about error! Is it any less error to reduce the Trinity to some vague notion of unity and diversity than to deny one of the three statements regarding the triune nature of God? Now, there's a solution! Throw the entire thing out, and claim it means something totally different! That way you haven't violated the sacred doctrine of the MYSTERY of the Trinity.

The real application of the Trinity lies in its explanation of the power of Christ Jesus to translate the dead world into a living cosmos. If Christ contains not the whole of space then we cannot be sure if we have passed beyond the perimeter of his influence. But he did contain the whole cosmos and therefore all that he experienced was experienced by the cosmos and all therein for all time until he operates upon it again, i.e., the judgement to come and the closing of the door to the Kingdom of Heaven.

The type of thinking by modern Christianity and recited by Grudem results in the following statement he makes in his section entitled "The Knowability of God."

> "Even in the age to come, when we are freed from the presence of sin, we will never be able fully to understand God or any one thing about him. This is seen from the fact that the passages cited above attribute God's incomprehensibility not to our sinfulness but to his infinite greatness. It is because we are finite and God is infinite that we will never be able to understand him fully. For all eternity we will be able to go on increasing in our knowledge of God and delighting ourselves more and more in him, saying with David as we learn more and more of God's own thoughts, "How precious to me are your thoughts, O God! How vast is the sum of them! If I would count them, they are more than the sand" (Ps. 139: 17-18)."(150-151)

Now we see the full fruit of willful doctrines of ignorance that glorify incomprehension as the only worthy worship and praise of the Lord, not to mention the question of the process of transformation. This quote from Grudem contradicts his position on the Trinity. If the Holy Spirit be fully God and we are in Christ and born again and transformed, are we not infinite just as Christ, The Holy Ghost and God the Father are infinite? How then can we say we are finite? And if the mind of Christ, the Son of God, who is fully God be in us, how do we never understand even one thing about God? Has Grudem and all Christiandom forgotten what Ecclesiastes, 1:17-18 says:

> "And I gave my heart to know wisdom, and to know madness and folly: I perceived that this also is vexation of spirit.
>
> "For in much wisdom is much grief: and he that increaseth knowledge increaseth sorrow."

Is there not more to salvation and redemption and transformation and translation into the Kingdom of God and the Kingdom of Reality then the mere learning more and more about God endlessly forever? Well, you bet there is. And that is the oneness you experience in God with your full quaternion capacity of heart, soul, mind and body. This is not a mere learning job. This is living eternally in liberty and glory with the Father, Son and Holy Ghost sharing all things with them in full.

Notice how Grudem ends up missing the power of conversion and transformation into a new creature, wherein all things are made new in this known world, through the operation of Christ's death, resurrection and ascension. How can Grudem say that we are finite when we have clearly become the children of God with eternal life in our possession? How can we obtain eternal life and remain finite? And clearly, ignorance of God is the fruit of sin and the fruit of salvation is being (Ephesians 3:18-19):

"able to comprehend with all saints what is the breadth, and length, and depth, and height; And to know the love of Christ, which passeth knowledge, that ye might be filled with all the fulness of God."

Paul's comprehension of the full magnitude of the love of Christ surpasses knowledge obtained without the Holy Ghost but is not obtained by probing the non-existent "other world" with the "spiritual" mind. Therefore, we see in modern Christianity that ignorance is protected as doctrine and the fruit is powerless words and confusion resulting in no definition of God or man or what happens to us or anything else as a result. This is the fruit of the false sociological equilibrium wherein Satan lives for a short period of time. It is clear that St. Paul did not suffer from this delusion.

PART II - ALIEN PHYSICS / COSMIC OPERATION

CHAPTER 9 - IMPLETION AND ENVELOPMENT –

The Two Complementary "Image" Capacities of Man

The two complementary image capacities of mankind are the essential characteristics that make him the unique creature that he is on earth and in all space and time. It's not "opposing thumbs" alone that make mankind unique. It can be said that the image capacities are the properties of mankind because Christ had them and alienated his followers and believers with the same. This is precisely why Jesus referred to himself as the "Son of Man" rather than the "Son of God." Jesus wanted all men to know that the powers and capacities he possessed were to be given to all men. Jesus did not call himself the "Son of Man" because he feared the Jews or the Romans.

It was more important for Jesus to identify with man rather than God who they knew not. People would listen to him more readily if he claimed to be what all men are and can become rather than what men had no idea of. But in reality, Jesus also knew that men did not know what mankind was or what their potentials were. So, in fact, Jesus further proves his deity by revealing that he knew more about mankind then men knew about themselves, much less God. Men today just assume they know about mankind and believe that it is common, reasonable and expected to be ignorant of God. It is presumed that one who claims to know God behind the "impenetrable curtain" is an arrogant liar. The fact must be that they know nothing about mankind until they know all about God and what He has done through His Son. Without knowing Jesus and what he has done to the cosmos, we are ignorant of the relationship of all things.

Today many scientists report that we operate with only about 10 percent of our brain capacity. But they don't tell you what the other 90 percent is for nor how to access it. Jesus is much more clear about what man's capacities are and what his full potential is, regardless of the amount of active brain material is used to reach it. If a man obtains the capacities of Christ Jesus, he has reached his maximum potential as a man regardless of other anatomical functioning. If a person can grasp the Image Capacities and the resultant power Christ has upon the entire cosmos with only one percent of his brain then he doesn't really need the other ninety-percent. One could list many brilliant men and women who fail to grasp the power of Christ and therefore never really reached their maximum potential even though they possess great intellect. This fact, however, does not mean that Christian principles are not discerned intellectually.

The Two Complementary Image Capacities make mankind spatial rather than terrestrial or spiritual rather than "of the flesh." We derive these two capacities from the Biblical account of the baptism of Jesus given in Matthew 3: 16-17:

"And Jesus, when he was baptized, went straightway out of the water:
and, lo, the heavens were opened unto him, and he saw the Spirit of
God descending like a dove, and lighting upon him:

"And lo a voice from heaven, saying, This is my beloved Son, in
whom I am well pleased."

Notice first, the referral to heavens in the plural rather than singular. This
passage refers to the created heaven below the clouds as one, the created heaven
above the clouds and including the stars, and the remaining eternal heaven above
the exploded matter (eternal, unchanging, unshakable, space). Now notice that three
things occur in this baptism event:

Impletion:

First, Jesus perceives all the heavens opened unto him. How does he perceive
this? Something went up "straightway" out of the water. This was Jesus' space,
spirit or soul. Where did it stop? It stopped upon complete union with all of eternal
space or God's singular essence. This can be called impletion. Jesus filled all space.
The definition of impletion is given in Funk and Wagnall's: As a noun it is "The act
of filling, or the state of being full; also that which fills."

Envelopment:

Secondly, as a result of this impletion something else occurred. Jesus saw the
Spirit of God descend like a dove and rest upon himself. This was the filling of
Jesus with all of eternal space. Now Jesus was filled with the space or Spirit of God.
This can be called envelopment. The space, Spirit or Soul of God or eternal space
descended upon Jesus and filled him up. Therefore, Jesus contained or enveloped all
of eternal space or the Singular Essence of God.

Oneness confirmed by God:

Thirdly, this state of being was then confirmed by a voice that Jesus heard from
Heaven saying, "this is my beloved Son, in whom I am well pleased." This state of
being must be called complete union between God and Christ Jesus. Therefore, we
have the *impletion* of all space by Jesus and the *envelopment* of all space inside
Jesus and a verbal confirmation of that as completed unity with God and Christ. We
will see later how we are complete also.

Impletion and Envelopment are termed Image Capacities because of what they
confirm about mankind and about what God said about man in the Old Testament.
Notice what the voice confirmed. The voice that was heard confirmed Sonship, or
likeness or "in the image of." Refer to Genesis 1: 26-27:

"And God said, Let us make man in our image, after our likeness: and
let them have dominion over the fish of the sea, and over the fowl of
the air, and over the cattle, and over all the earth, and over every
creeping thing that creepeth upon the earth.

"So God created man in his own image, in the image of God created he him; male and female created he them."

God's image is both male and female. Yet He or God is called Father because He created all things within Himself. We see that the Singular Essence of God is again Eternal Space and its only shape is the male and female human. Therefore, the image that God and Jesus and all mankind shares is the unity of the Spirit or Eternal Space the Singular Essence of God. Christ's experience at his baptism is confirmed with Sonship and Image identification. Jesus became the image of God by the union of their Spirits or Space. This is the same space that scientists observe daily.

These two image capacities are spatial concepts and are complementary meaning that one cannot have one without having the other. Through Jesus all men have access to these two capacities. Mankind therefore has the power to fill all of eternal space and to envelop all of eternal space within his finite physical body. This, in fact, is the definition of the possession of eternal life that is promised to us by Christ Jesus in John 3:16.

These are new theological categories that define the image of God and why Christ Jesus has power to operate upon the cosmos and all therein. Now to assemble some of the scriptures that support these new theological terms. Some scriptures will support the impletion, some the envelopment and some both.

St. Paul tells us that the body of **Jesus contains the fullness of God** who fills all and is in all in Ephesians 1: 19-23:

"And what is the exceeding greatness of his power to usward who believe, according to the working of his mighty power,

"Which he wrought in Christ, when he raised him from the dead, and set him at his own right hand in the heavenly places,

"Far above all principality, and power, and might, and dominion, and every name that is named, not only in this world, but also in that which is to come:

"And hath put all things under his feet, and gave him to be the head over all things to the church,

"Which is his body, **the fulness of him that filleth all in all**."

(Emphasis added)

Now we see that Christ contains God who fills all that there is or the cosmos and the galaxies and beyond. This would mean that Christ also fills all things, as we will see more clearly in other scriptures. How would God accomplish all that was just said unless Christ himself be made to fill and contain the cosmos? These powers are not merely made possible by legal decree from God. This did not take place in some otherworldly courtroom but in our observable cosmos. The power to give eternal life to all flesh that believes on Christ Jesus is an actual power over physical observable reality as a result of the spatial totality of Christ Jesus. It's not just because "the Bible says so." It's because a real physical being has performed a real physical operation upon all that is in the cosmos. That which is experienced by Christ, is therefore experienced by all things. All things are new. All things are transformed and translated. All things are reconciled to God. All things are dead, buried, resurrected and ascended.

Therefore we see that the baptism event of Christ Jesus also verifies the fact that God himself is eternal space and eternal space is God's singular essence that unites with "God the Son" and this essence is the Holy Spirit.

The baptism event also puts Christ Jesus at the 0,0,0,0 of the Net coordinate system of the cosmos. The net coordinate system is the real coordinate system for mankind's true evolution. Zero in the X, Y and Z axes for volume and 0 in the T coordinate for time. Natural physics uses various coordinate systems to describe the motions of particles and their relativity to time and position. But for mankind the key to space travel resides in his understanding that the net coordinate system contains him and can operate on him and his world. This is called the net coordinate system because of the resulting power of Christ to gather men from all time and place to judgement at the end of time, as he said in Matthew 13:47-50:

> "Again, the kingdom of heaven is like unto a net, that was cast into the sea, and gathered of every kind;

> "Which, when it was full, they drew to shore, and sat down, and gathered the good into vessels, but cast the bad away.

> "So shall it be at the end of the world: the angels shall come forth, and sever the wicked from among the just,

> "And shall cast them into the furnace of fire: there shall be wailing and gnashing of teeth."

Jesus is that great net that was cast into the sea that gathered every kind in himself. All are affected regardless of their belief or concern for him. Those that love Jesus and are transformed into his image are safely delivered into the Kingdom of Heaven or Eternal Space to inhabit the galaxies. Those that reject him will be cut out of eternal space and cast into eternal darkness where there is no space nor time nor light, where one only has the knowledge that they, once were, and are not now, and never will be again. This is hell or the other world, the world separate from reality or the cosmos that we observe around us today.

Scientists regard intellect and adaptability as the unique properties that make man superior to his animal companions. That is incorrect. It is the power to fill and envelop all eternal space that makes man unique and make him into the image of God. This is why animals don't talk to man. This is also why man is not bound by the natural laws of particle physics. Men are the possessors of Alien Physics or the power of space over all the matter created within it. Ephesians 4: 10 relates to the **impletion of all space by Christ Jesus**:

> "He that descended is the same also that ascended up far above all heavens, **that he might fill all things.**)"

(emphasis added)

It is clear in this passage that Jesus did not go into another dimension but above all heavens above us to fill all of heaven or eternal space. This clearly refers to spatial impletion. John 14: 20 refers to the **impletion and envelopment** of all of God or eternal space by Christ Jesus:

> "At that day ye shall know that I am in my Father, and ye in me, and I in you."

We are in Christ because he had all of space within his physical body and therefore we can never at any time escape or venture beyond his spatial parameter. Christ was then in his Father completely by filling the cosmos (impletion). Then Christ Jesus is in us when the Holy Ghost reveals the spatial nature of Christ and God to us. Our own space or spirit unites with Christ and God. Therefore, we contain God and all things and we have obtained this by undergoing the operation that Christ performed on the cosmos. Colossians 1: 19-20 refers to the **Envelopment Capacity** of Christ Jesus:

> "For it pleased the Father that **in him should all fulness dwell**;

> "And, having made peace through the blood of his cross by him to **reconcile all things** unto himself; by him, I say, **whether they be things in earth or things in heaven**."

(Emphasis added)

It is amazing that "Christians" are carried away by the notion that aliens from other planets can save us from our ways when the greatest event in the cosmos has taken place right here on planet earth. For this reason there cannot be a more superior race of beings through out all of the cosmos to the ends of the galaxies. We see from this passage that it pleased God that all of himself or eternal space (all fulness) would dwell in Christ Jesus. And then by the operation of Christ's death, resurrection and ascension, all things on the earth and all things in the cosmos are reconciled back to God. What creature has or can perform any greater operation and what would it be? If it were possible (which we will see later that it is not) that a creature from another terrestrial ball could visit our planet, I would be compelled to tell him how he has been operated upon by the most superior being to ever exist or that will ever exist. I would also be compelled to tell them of the operation that Christ has yet to perform but will in the future. This will be the closing of the door to the Kingdom in which no other creature will be able to open. Colossians 2: 8-10 refers to the **Envelopment Capacity** of Christ:

> "Beware lest any man spoil you through philosophy and vain deceit, after the tradition of men, after the rudiments of the world, and not after Christ.

> "For **in him dwelleth all the fulness of the Godhead bodily**.

> "And **ye are complete in him**, which is the head of all principality and power:"

(Emphasis added)

Indeed modern Christianity has let modern science spoil the church through philosophy and vain deceit after the rudiments of the world. What are the rudiments of the world? The idea that mankind is merely a thinking rock or a particle subject to the laws of light speed and decay. These rudiments are not applicable to mankind.

The concept of a empty infinite space that is dead, and where God and his Son exist in some other world impenetrable by the human mind, is more sinister than any other falsehood in the history of the church. The view of the earth as flat was nothing by comparison. God was still above their heads in the Kingdom of God or Heaven. The view of the earth as the center of the solar system with the Sun rotating about it pales in comparison to the notion that God and His Kingdom lie outside the observable infinite cosmos. Satan dwells in this new philosophy and is deceiving the nations once again with it. What modern industrial nation does not hold this deadly and incorrect Dual World cosmology? This is exactly what is called the false sociological equilibrium in this book. And the Christian church has once again been conned by cleaver "scientists falsely so called." The church is defending these erroneous scientific truths as they did with the erroneous geocentric views of Ptolemy.

Does this Scripture not speak of Christ containing all the fulness of God in his own physical body? What is this fulness if not the known observable cosmos? What human mind can hope to come up with any viable thing outside the limits of eternal space? There does not exist another world outside the cosmos! Things may be imperceptible at a certain time, or invisible, but they do not exist in another dimension. The other world and other dimensions are the false fabrications of the devil making himself a safe place to live in this observable world.

Notice, also, that **we are complete in him**, which is the head of all power. What is the state of being "complete," if it is not the containment of all that Christ has. This completeness would be the possession of our own souls, in confidence, or eternal life? Complete means that we lack nothing in our being that is available to our being. Being complete also means that we too have filled all the cosmos and all of space is in us in union with Jesus and his Father. What is available is clearly shown in the Son of Man, or perfection. We need to dump those bumper stickers that say, "Christians aren't perfect, just forgiven." The truth is we aren't like other human beings at all. We have been transformed into eternal beings in a state of grace or perfection. The truth is that the perfect can be made to look like the imperfect by the evil in unregenerate men. Followers of Christ who have not experienced rebirth as yet may not understand that statement but one day they will. Why then do some that call themselves Christians entertain the notions of life in space that will come to earth and show us how to live better? But many "Christians hold these views right along with some deity idea of Christ. They can justify the notion that the Son of God is somehow inferior to a visitor from another planet only if they hold the erroneous idea of modern science that God and His Son are in another world outside the observable cosmos.

Christ also testifies to the unity and oneness of himself and God, his Father, in John 10: 27-30. This refers to both **impletion and envelopment**:

73

"My sheep hear my voice, and I know them, and they follow me:

"And I give unto them eternal life; and they shall never perish, neither shall any man pluck them out of my hand,

"My Father, which gave them me, is greater than all; and no man is able to pluck them out of my Father's hand.

"I and my Father are one."

(Emphasis added)

Christ knew that once a man would experience the unity with God or the Impletion and Envelopment of all space and time no one would be able to take eternal life from them. It is this unity and possession of all things and eternal life that cannot be taken away by any other force past present or future. Christ is not only at one with the Father but in unity with all those who allow the physical operation of Christ upon the cosmos to operate upon themselves. The Father who contains all mankind forever has given them to Christ in their unity of space, and none can exceed the space of God to pluck them out of His hand.

Christ **Jesus must implete (fill) and envelop (contain)** all that God is in order for Christ to say the following in John 16: 15-16:

"All things that the Father hath are mine: therefore said I, that he shall take of mine, and shall shew it unto you.

"A little while, and ye shall not see me: and again, a little while, and ye shall see me, because I go to the Father."

The "things" that Jesus refers to that belong to God is all things in the observable cosmos. He obtains all things from the Father by first filling the Father completely and then enveloping the fulness of God with his physical body. I often wondered, as a new follower of Christ's teachings, why the baptism account was given, if he had been conceived by the Holy Ghost and at one with the Father at all times. The baptism account of Jesus clearly describes the mechanics of how Jesus unites with the Father and how he obtains power over the observable cosmos to operate upon it.

Now we see just how complete this operation becomes on those that perceive this operation and allow it to change them from one type of creature to another in John 16: 26-28:

"At that day ye shall ask in my name: and I say not unto you, that I will pray the Father for you:

"For the Father himself loveth you, because ye have loved me, and have believed that I came out from God.

"I came forth from the Father, and am come into the world: again, I leave the world, and go to the Father."

The "world" in this Scripture passage is not the "other world" as the theologians and scientists of the false sociological equilibrium would have you believe. The world Christ refers to is the Kingdom of Heaven or the eternal space all around us.

Those that are translated will now have direct access to the Father because they see Him as he is and believe and perceive how Christ came from the Father and returned to the Father. They see both Christ and God as they truly exist in the reality we live in. Christ did not come from another planet nor from another dimension but from the living eternal space itself. And this Space conceived Christ in the Virgin Mary and confirmed their unity in Baptism. **Christ then Baptized the whole cosmos** with his death, resurrection and ascension in which all men have access to unity with the Father or the Living Eternal Space, in which we presently inhabit. God and all the baptized are one. Christ came from eternal space and went back to eternal space where he can manifest himself at any time in any place in the "twinkling of an eye."

The Two Complementary Image Capacities are named such because our culture is very confused today about life in deep space. The modern church actually entertains the idea that superior beings in space will look different from us. We have already seen no beings in space are superior to mankind. This is because the most powerful operation over the entire cosmos has its origin on Earth and was given to men as a ministry and treasure to administer to all flesh whether on earth or in the heavens above us. It is clear that only those creatures that look like us will be able to comprehend the principals and mechanics of Alien Physics resident in Christ Jesus. This is true already on Earth with millions of life forms all around us. Why would we think otherwise for life forms is space?

The Earth we inhabit is packed with evidence of life forms that look different than we do. We don't have to find life on other planets that look different than we do to know that we are uniquely different from other life forms. The difference is not entirely physical other than the strange fact that all those who can grasp the image capacities look remarkably similar to mankind. If a dog could grasp the image capacities we have described here than we would have evidence of the kind of evolution that scientists present. But Christ himself has said that he was given the power to save all flesh. It only requires that the flesh be able to understand what Jesus has performed with his body. Refer to John 17:1-3:

> "These words spake Jesus, and lifted up his eyes to heaven, and said, Father, the hour is come; glorify thy Son, that thy son also may glorify thee:

> "As thou hast given him power over all flesh, that he should give eternal life to as many as thou hast given him.

> "And this is life eternal, that they might know thee the only true God, and Jesus Christ, whom thou hast sent."

There is good evidence all around us today that only those creatures that look like men have the potential to grasp what has just been said. Only men with evil motives and under the domination of the flesh and sin can not understand these words. But no dog or cat or bird or elephant or monkey can perceive what has been written here. Certainly if a building or automobile or robot could understand these principals they would be transformed also. We will see this clearly in the chapters ahead.

Therefore as to this date, only creatures that look like mankind can grasp the image properties of impletion and envelopment. This leads to the conclusion that all projections of modern science concerning alien life forms being more intelligent are wrong. This further suggests that even if we were to contact flesh that could grasp these concepts, we would be under the obligation to propagate this message to them.

In other words, the intrusion of flesh that looked different from us would not alter the knowledge that we possess presently and would put us into a missionary role rather than a recipient mode. We are the possessors of all knowledge that is required to be complete and for continual eternal life and travel in and to the galaxies.

The problem is that we have allowed this knowledge to become occulted by the lies of modern science and their ideas of a dual world. In short, Satan is not bound in this present age and is deceiving the nations. The good news is that he has just about run out of his short season and must go back to the bottomless pit forever. In the light of these principles made known herein locating Satan's hiding place in the world at this present time, Satan will no longer be able to hide. And this exposure of his last hiding place for some two hundred years will complete the prophecy of John the Revelator. Satan only gets out of the pit once for a short period, and he has been out having a field day. But we see where he hides now and it won't be long till he will be chained for the last time. Therefore, we must conclude that the end time is near at hand when the children of God will dwell in the Kingdom and suffer no more violence.

The Image Capacities are the essential properties of mankind and they are spatial qualities that he shares with God. These properties are entirely unknown and omitted from modern natural particle physics that presently define mankind's hope and future incorrectly. It is this omission that has rendered modern natural physics a death trap for mankind.

It is interesting to note that many times a branch of the Christian Church will copy the ways of the lost world to appeal to the lost, e.g., have a rock and roll mass or adopt a Coke commercial for a slogan like "I found it." However, be assured that it is Satan and the lost world that copy things and who are later revealed to be imposters. It is becoming more clear everyday that the entire new American culture that is saturated with outer space and the hope of detection of alien life are running headlong into Jesus Christ. For he is more alien than they have ever imagined and all their attempts to avoid him will end in total acceptance of him or destruction by him.

Our North American so called "scientific" culture has attempted to provide a New Hope for the world and for Americans without Jesus. At long last their imaginations and dreams are not sufficient to surpass the answers provided by the reality of Jesus Christ and His power over the cosmos and His power He gives to His followers.

PART II - ALIEN PHYSICS / COSMIC OPERATION

CHAPTER 10 - MODERN SCIENCE & "CHRISTIAN" UFOs

The scientific community is spending millions of tax dollars trying to locate an alien or an Extra Terrestrial (E.T.). Hollywood has been running into aliens for years while the Christians are singing songs with lyrics like "I am not alien" (from "The Sky's The Limit" album by Leon Patillo, song entitled "Love Calling"). This dichotomy illustrates again the false equilibrium between science and Christian truth.

The correct equilibrium will correct truth for both science and Christianity. Simply put forth, the Gospel (Good News) or the miraculous supernatural power of Christ Jesus has been normalized into boring religious traditions, while Hollywood and the scientific community create the hope for mankind in meeting an extraterrestrial alien. The Biblical use of the word "supernatural" is above or beyond earth or the natural or "hyperspatial," not "other-worldly." Be careful about the definitions. There is a major difference here. But the truth is that Jesus is the most alien entity that will ever visit planet Earth.

The present retreat of mainstream Christianity into age old traditions, without a new theology based upon the truth of scripture and the pressures applied to it from the modern lost world, has made the Church unattractive for the lost and disquieting for the transformed. Be assured that the newness of the things you read herein only sound that way because of the new framework the lost world has made in an attempt to provide a hope for mankind while cutting their bands and cords from God. In other words, what you read here has been known for generations to Christians, except that they expressed it differently because their pressures were different.

It is ironic that men, that built frameworks to be free from the moral condemnation of God and humble acceptance of Christ, have run straight into Jesus. They have for decades been creating their own religion, only to find that Christ Jesus fits their every requirement of their outer space alien savior.

Therefore, God's word is true and this irony is now revealed as He said it would be in Psalms 2 written some 3,000 years ago:

"Why do the heathen rage, and the people imagine a vain thing?

"The kings of the earth set themselves, and the rulers take counsel together against the Lord, and against his anointed, saying,

"Let us break their bands asunder, and cast away their cords from us.

"He that sitteth in the heavens shall laugh: the Lord shall have them in derision.

"Then shall he speak unto them in his wrath, and vex them in his sore displeasure.

"Yet have I set my king upon my holy hill of Zion.

"I will declare the decree: the Lord hath said unto me, Thou art my son; this day have I begotten thee.

"Ask of me, and I shall give thee the heathen for thine inheritance, and the uttermost parts of the earth for thy possession.

"Thou shalt break them with a rod of iron; thou shalt dash them in pieces like a potter's vessel.

"Be wise now therefore, O ye kings: be instructed, ye judges of the earth.

"Serve the Lord with fear, and rejoice with trembling.

"Kiss the Son, lest he be angry, and ye perish from the way, when his wrath is kindled but a little. Blessed are all they that put their trust in him."

For the first time since the space program started Christians are beginning to question the assumptions and hypotheses concerning the existence of other life forms in outer space with superior intelligence. Yet the arguments against these pro alien assumptions are crude because they are not based upon who and what Christ is and how he has operated upon the cosmos and what we become as a result of this operation.

For example Bob Larson, a Christian author that I heard on a radio show one night, suggests that reported sightings of space ships and so called alien abductions are actual Satanic appearances of demons in spiritual combat to deceive the lost. This faulty notion, however, is the result of the same sociological equilibrium that provides for the domain of Satan in the real world while God and Christ are banished to the "other world" beyond the "impenetrable curtain of death." This according to Christian fiction author, Frank E. Peretti, is where evil spirits lurk and swoop down to make attacks on Christians and then disappear again and where angels and demons fight over our well being. Mr. Peretti is author of *This Present Darkness*.

It is just as erroneous to say that demons inhabit another dimension as it is to say that God and Christ inhabit another dimension. Granted, we don't see everything around us but that does not mean they exist in another dimension. It certainly does not mean that the real battle ground is not the perceivable reality we live in. Satan is alive and well, and his followers are with us in reality in plain view everyday, doing their work of lying, stealing and murdering.

One cannot fight Satan or bind him with a chain or lock him up in the bottomless pit without knowing where his domain is located and how he maintains this refuge from the truth of Christ Jesus. The only way of finding and exposing Satan and thereby binding him, is by determining exactly what Jesus is, what power he holds, what he has done to the cosmos and what he will do to it in the future. When Christ Jesus is shown for what he is and what he has done, there is no place for Satan to occupy or hide. This is the power to chain and bind.

It appears that Satan escaped after the 1000-year reign of the Christian West and has made himself a domain in the so-called "observable world of science." Satan has cast God and Christ into the "other world," or "spiritual world," where anything can be true and nothing can be known. This is the actual present state of sociological equilibrium over the industrialized world. This is illustrated in the worldviews of Mr. Morgenthau and Gingerich in the first chapter of this book. This present state of equilibrium is false to both scientific fact and Christian theology.

However, Mr. Larson has made one correct point that few other modern theologians are willing to make and stand by. His point is that the belief in alien life of more intelligence from other planets is not supportable. And further that this notion contradicts historical, living evidence available to us on earth. However, he holds another idea that is just as incorrect. He has attempted to explain UFOs as evil spirits that have power superior to mankind.

It appears that many "Christians" have not only accepted the notions that God and Christ really are beyond the "impenetrable curtain of death," but they have also accepted the idea that there could be superior intelligence on other terrestrial spheres in outer space. The falsehood of these notions will be made clear at the end of this book by having examined Christ's power to translate men from one type of creature to another. The result should reveal a cosmology that is consistent and true for both scientific fact and Christian theology.

Therefore, Mr. Larson has made a correct point about the faulty assumptions of the NASA SETI program and other space programs like it and the Hollywood depictions of aliens. Yet he really did not present a theology that revealed the reason to boldly deny the existence of such life forms, neither did he arrive at a real explanation of UFO (unidentified flying objects) sightings and so called alien abductions. Mr. Larson merely based his argument upon the "traditional Judeo-Christian view of what man is in the eyes of God" What that means is very unclear. If you want to run for office in the United States, just use that contraction and say, "that violates the Judeo-Christian view." But if you are going to explain theology it is useful to avoid that contraction. The translation of that contraction is something like night-day, or East-West, or antichrist-Christ. The term Christian is sufficient to include the Creation, Flood, Ten Commandments, Judges, Kings and all the prophets and the history of the Jews. But Jesus is the end of Judaism and the Old Testament, the author and finisher of faith, full of grace and truth. The term Judeo-Christian is for politicians only, not theologians.

Of course we don't know what man is until we know precisely what Jesus has done to the cosmos and those that inhabit it. Larson based his argument on the fact that "God loves mankind and gave his only Son for our salvation." In other words he said, "mankind as we know him on earth is unique and central in the cosmos." This is correct, but he does not present evidence as to why that is so, nor does this help in determining or explaining the reported sightings of such things. The sightings and abductions are mere mental delusions induced by a real strong desire for more than what modern industrial society presents as the truth. Isn't this the "vain imaginings" as the Psalmist said?

Mr. Bob Larson bought the whole UFO thing and speaks as though they are real creatures living around us, rather than the product of intense mental desire for a better reality for the "believer." For example Mr. Larson says in his book *UFOs and the Alien Agenda*:

> "I conclude that evil aliens, fallen angelic beings, are clearly orchestrating a social and spiritual mind-set. The irregularity, yet periodicity, of their contact with humans keeps earthlings off balance. We know they have appeared before, and they are likely to appear again, but we can't be certain when it will happen. This creates a neurotic expectation in the human consciousness. The psychological consequence is a mental and spiritual preparation for mankind to welcome, rather than shun, an actual global encounter of the third and fourth kind: contact and communication.

> "If mankind is indeed being set up for the ultimate deception, then those who are spiritually vulnerable may become victimized by the UFO cults, which are increasing in number and eccentricity as we head toward the next millennium."[8]

Does Mr. Larson sound like he is vulnerable to the idea of outer space aliens making contact with humans? Yes! In fact he said they have indeed made periodic appearances before. Wow! How can he argue with UFO believers? He is also a believer! It is not good enough to merely believe they are bad. The vulnerability comes in not knowing what they are and how they are and where they come from. Too many "Christians" are caught up in what Satan is and what he's doing to know what Christ is and what he has done to Satan and his domain.

Mr. Larson knows that Christians are buying into the alien thing and he attempts to condemn them while he himself buys into what he calls UFO cults:

> "And believe it or not, some so-called Christians try to fit the idea of UFOs into their biblical worldview, just as Ann did.

> "Salvation, for these unorthodox believers, is reaching the kingdom of God by a mass alien abduction. They teach that heaven is an actual locale, just outside the Earth's atmosphere."(202)

It is obvious that Mr. Larson has trouble with "so-called Christians" who believe in aliens and try to incorporate these notions into their theology. However, he clearly does not know how to rid them of the notions or rid himself of the same. Doesn't Mr. Larson sound like any other UFO believer? Mr. Larson cannot rid himself of the belief in aliens by merely believing they are evil rather than good.

---

[8] Bob Larson, *UFOs and the Alien Agenda* (Nashville, Tennessee: Thomas Nelson Publishers, 1997), 168-169.

Many atheists would agree with him that these beings are evil. Notice, also, that he berates the "unorthodox Christians" who believe that heaven is an actual locale, just outside Earth's atmosphere. We show in this book how respected modern main stream Baptist theologians present this very picture of heaven, in Mr. Grudem's *Systematic Theology* covered in Chapter 15 herein (*The Spatial Model.*)

All of this confusion about aliens, evil spirits, UFO's, angels, and heaven and where it is, is the result of a false sociological equilibrium between Christianity and modern science which must be challenged by real spatial theology establishing the power of Christ to save the cosmos and all therein.

As Mr. Larson condemns so-called Christians for fitting aliens into their theology, listen to his possible conclusions concerning aliens:

> "First, a large body of evidence supports the thesis that something is going on out there. **Some UFOs are real and their existence has an empirical scientific explanation, which may not be in the realm of current knowledge**.

> "Second, discounting the cases that science can (or will soon) decipher, other UFO phenomena cannot now, and will never be, explained by natural theses. These UFOs appear to be a spiritual or nonmaterial curiosity, which warrants serious consideration by those who hold to the Christian faith.

> "Third, after decades of considering the conspiracy theories, there is not sufficient proof to conclude that UFOs are manmade. If some government or human agency on Earth is behind it all, surely the proof would have leaked out by now. If such advanced technology were in human hands, greed for control or financial gain would have caused someone to attempt to use such exotic techniques.

> "Fourth, while the Bible does not explicitly rule out extraterrestrial life-forms, there is sufficient scriptural evidence that life on Earth was created by God as a special act of divine grace, duplicated nowhere else in the universe. **Thus the aliens who contact us cannot be from another planet or solar system**.

> "Having eliminated all natural explanations for the strange occurrences surrounding the flying-saucer phenomenon, one must conclude that **the source of UFOs is extradimensional**. Such appearances do not have the attributes associated with godly angels, so there must be another supernatural derivation.

> **"Biblical logic then concludes that demons, fallen angels, are the creatures behind legitimate UFO occurrences."**(202-203)

(Emphasis added)

Did not Mr. Larson say that he believes "some UFOs are real?" So why is he arguing with other believers? He says some sightings are real UFOs (but not from other planets) and some sightings are extradimensional evil demons. But Mr. Larson terms these as "legitimate UFO occurrences." His only argument with other believers is the nature of their character, not their existence. It will be clear in this book that the conservative main stream theologian today and the fringe Christian dabbling in the occult sound alike and hopelessly confused. This is because neither one has a real spatial model of the power of Christ Jesus to save all flesh.

Let's now use the theological categories that were developed in earlier chapters to help Mr. Larson and the other so-called Christians out of their struggle with UFOs. First, Mr. Larson presents no evidence at all that would support the reality of UFOs. Secondly, because we now know the domain triad of God as I AM, ONE, OF THE LIVING, we know that we cannot nor should we try to perceive what is in a dimension that is not in existence. Thirdly, if any beings want to continue the delusion concerning aliens it would be those in worldly power. Fourthly, the Bible does indeed rule out extraterrestrial life forms that could contact us, due to the two complimentary image capacities. If they can contact us they are human beings, made in the image of God, or Christ and us, subject to the power of Christ Jesus over the cosmos.

Finally, Mr. Larson makes his worst non-Biblical assumption, concluding that the source of UFOs is extradimensional. It is just as erroneous to conclude that demons exist in a nonexistent other dimension than to say that we do not know God until we die for we cannot perceive anything beyond the veil of death into the other world. This is where all religions and many other types of endeavors are made equal in their quest of the unknown "spiritual world."

The only real Biblical conclusion to make is that there are no "legitimate UFO occurrences." These are all the "bizarre and aberrant" vain imaginings of lost people searching with all their might for something to free themselves of the chains of the modern false sociological equilibrium. Some have seen that they gain at least money and power over others by leading their fellowman into these imaginings only for them all to fall into the ditch of ignorance and death.

Mr. Larson makes another unsupported but fascinating statement concerning how to raise your children in such a way as to protect them from the occult:

> "Parents must also make their children aware of the dangers surrounding occult curiosity. The paranormal must be off-limits, no exceptions. Explaining the difference between the supernatural power of God and the demonism behind occult feats will remove the fascination some children might have for such acts."(209)

Where in all the quotes above did Mr. Larson explain the difference between the supernatural power of God and the supernatural power of demons behind the occult? He has in fact made no such distinction. And, had he done so, he would have arrived at the simple truth that all UFO stuff is the product of lost human beings seeking something better and suffering the wrath of God without Christ Jesus. In fact, if he had only explained the supernatural power of Christ Jesus he would have automatically ruled out any power whatsoever of aliens, UFOs and superior intelligence in outer space. But Mr. Larson did not, and as a result, he could not free himself or anyone else of the delusion that UFOs exist. Is it time, at last, for a real explanation of the power of God to save all flesh in the cosmos through his Son? This is the sole purpose of this book.

Now what can we say about modern perceptions of UFOs that is consistent with this proposed new Christian theology based upon the power of Christ to transform the cosmos from death into life? St. Paul says it well in Colossians 2:6-19:

> "As ye have therefore received Christ Jesus the Lord, so walk ye in him:

> "Rooted and built up in him, and stablished in the faith, as ye have been taught, abounding therein with thanksgiving.

> "Beware lest any **man spoil you through philosophy** and vain deceit, after the tradition of men, after the rudiments of the world, and not after Christ.

> **"For in him dwelleth all the fulness of the Godhead bodily.**

> **"And ye are complete in him, which is the head of all principality and power**:

> "In whom also ye are circumcised with the circumcision made without hands, in putting off the body of the sins of the flesh by the circumcision of Christ.

> "Buried with him in baptism, wherein also **ye are risen with him** through the faith of the **operation of God**, who hath **raised him from the dead**.

> "And you, being dead in your sins and the uncircumcision of your flesh, hath he quickened together with him, having forgiven you all trespasses;

> "Blotting out the handwriting of ordinances that was against us, which was contrary to us, and took it out of the way, nailing it to his cross;

> "And having **spoiled principalities** and **powers**, he **made a shew of them** openly, **triumphing over them in it.**

> "Let no man therefore judge you in meat, or in drink, or in respect of an holyday, or of the new moon, or of the sabbath days:

> "Which are a shadow of things to come; but the body is of Christ.

> "Let no **man** beguile you of your reward in a voluntary humility and **worshipping of angels, intruding into those things which he hath not seen**, vainly puffed up by his fleshly mind,

"And not holding the Head, from which all the body by joints and bands having nourishment ministered, and knit together, increaseth with the increase of God."

(Emphasis added)

If we are not to be "intruding into those things which he (we) hath not seen" namely angels, why should we be intruding into those demons who they and we have not seen? And where does all this philosophy of angels, demons and UFOs come from? It comes from men after the rudiments of the world. Just listen to Mr. Bob Larson expound on how UFOs get around:

"UFO sightings must be some kind of matter/energy manipulation understood by the archenemy of God. The forces of darkness must have understood the theory of relativity, $E=mc^2$, which explains the interchangeability of energy and matter, long before Einstein stumbled upon its secrets. Thus the UFO occupants are demons, and their craft some sort of materialized energy."(204)

Does Mr. Larson sound like he is complete in Christ Jesus, the fulness of the Godhead bodily? Why attribute to demons the power of anything? Are they not, clouds without rain, figments of a vain imagination, beguiling philosophies made after the rudiments of the world by men? Certainly the theory of relativity is a rudiment of the world found by a man.

Notice that the source of demonic deception comes from men, according to St. Paul. Now let us examine how to deal with demons as Jesus did in Mark 5:1-20:

"And they came over unto the other side of the sea, into the country of the Gadarenes.

"And when he was come out of the ship, immediately there met him out of the tombs a man with an unclean spirit,

"Who had his dwelling among the tombs; and no man could bind him, no, not with chains:

"Because that he had been often bound with fetters and chains, and the chains had been plucked asunder by him, and the fetters broken in pieces: neither could any man tame him.

"And always, night and day, he was in the mountains, and in the tombs, crying, and cutting himself with stones.

"But when he saw Jesus afar off, he ran and worshipped him,

"And cried with a loud voice, and said, What have I to do with thee, Jesus, thou Son of the most high God? I adjure thee by God, that thou torment me not.

"For he said unto him, Come out of the man, thou unclean spirit.

"And he asked him, What is thy name? And he answered, saying, My name is Legion: for we are many.

"And he besought him much that he would not send them away out of the country.

"Now there was there nigh unto the mountains a great herd of swine feeding.

"And all the devils besought him, saying, **Send us into the swine**, that we may enter into them.

"And forthwith **Jesus gave them leave**. And the unclean spirits went out, and entered into the swine: and the herd ran violently down a steep place into the sea, (they were about two thousand;) and were choked in the sea.

"And they that fed the swine fled, and told it in the city, and in the country. And they went out to see what it was that was done.

"And they come to Jesus, and see him that was possessed with the devil, and had the legion, sitting, and clothed, **and in his right mind**: and they were afraid.

"And they that saw it told them how it befell to him that was possessed with the devil, and also concerning the swine.

"And they began to pray him to depart out of their coasts.

"And when he was come into the ship, he that had been possessed with the devil prayed him that he might be with him.

"Howbeit Jesus suffered him not, but saith unto him, Go home to thy friends, and tell them how great things the Lord hath done for thee, and **hath had compassion on thee**.

"And he departed, and began to publish in Decapolis how great things Jesus had done for him: and all men did marvel."

(Emphasis added)

What do we learn about demons from this passage? We learn that even demons do not want to perish. We learn that people become very attached to their notions no matter how demonic they may be. We learn that people have a hard time giving up these ideas and they must have something more powerful to replace them. We learn, also, that once they perceive something more powerful they do not want to suffer from the newness and what it might do to them. Legion was afraid that the new truth of Christ would not only destroy his notions no matter how painful they were but would also destroy his own body. Legion was not altogether wrong about this; as Jesus says we need a new body to hold the eternal life he gives us. We learn that Jesus did not argue with the demons concerning their nature or their character. The presence of his truth alone was sufficient to cause them to leave their host.

Notice that Jesus permitted the demons their own request not to suffer being without a host. Even being in swine was better than being without a host at all.

We learn that ideas, emotions connected with them and their power take on a life of their own within a person and control him. We learn that Jesus had compassion on both the host and the demons. This however had to be a violent and scary moment in the Gadarene's life. The result of the completeness and obvious power of Christ was that the host was restored into his right mind.

We learn that the **possession of a right mind is possession of correct and clean ideas**. The unclean ideas had left the man and the man had watched them enter into swine and drown in the sea giving evidence that he was clean again. This evidence was needed in the case of Legion. We learn most of all that incorrect ideas and emotions that are connected with them are uncomfortable in the presence of truth and power. They would leave if they only knew how.

Notice also, Christ did not argue with the demons but merely commanded them to leave **nor did he torment them** as they feared but **had mercy on both the man and the demons**. What a lesson on demons! **Demons only acquire power when a person or group of persons assigns it to them.** The **confidence and completeness of Christ cast fear and helplessness upon the man and the demons.**

Therefore, we learn how to deal with demons and other demonic ideas in society from this example. We learn that we should not fear demons for they are weak and have exceeding fear of the truth. We also learn that demons and their host many times do not know how to escape torment on their own. We learn that demons are destroyed and banished by mercy and permission and display of knowledge and confidence in possession of the truth and power of God. This confidence and power is missing in modern day Christian theology.

We need to resist the assignment of power to demons, aliens and UFOs, contrary to what Mr. Larson has done. We also need to demonstrate the power of Christ Jesus to transform the cosmos into life eternal so that demons have a route of escape and their hosts can be saved without torment and shame. We have all been demonic in our youth and ignorance, but now we live forever by the operation of Christ Jesus.

It is one of the purposes of this book to present the truth of Christ Jesus as the most unique and miraculous thing that has ever happened or ever will happen on Earth or the cosmos beyond. Religious tradition will be avoided except in the most fundamental necessities. It is another mark of this false sociological equilibrium that presents Christ in a familiar and ordinary way while dream weavers capture the imagination of man with euphoric illusions and promises of science and space travel in obvious disregard for scientific facts to the contrary.

Therefore, the concept of an alien will be presented herein that will exceed the hopes and dreams of modern scientific man. It will be shown, further, how Christ Jesus fulfills and exceeds every alien definition created by those who would resist this 2000-year-old means of human evolution.

PART II - ALIEN PHYSICS / COSMIC OPERATION

CHAPTER 11 - THE HYPERSPACE ALIEN

An examination of the false assumptions made by modern science concerning an alien reveal that aliens must look different from us because of their different atmospheric conditions. They also must be born on another terrestrial object. These are the so-called practical views of scientists. But some assumptions offer the hopes of science in that they predict that more superior, "compassionate" aliens come to earth or contact us by radio and tell us how to survive, and give us power to save our planet and ourselves. These assumptions and hopes are not the notions put forth by "cults" but the notions propagated by modern tax supported "science".

Hollywood has exploited the scientific "alien" assumptions in their creation of Silver Screen aliens in a wide array of beings. These creatures include; a dog at the family dinner table in the TV show *Alph;* a parasite in ones human body; a little boy with super powers and silliness in ET; as well as the many creatures and characters in the movie *Star Wars.* Both Hollywood and modern science hold that aliens must look different from us. But, the truth of the miraculous power of Christ Jesus as alien to our world must be avoided to maintain Satan's domain in the real observable world. These false assumptions about aliens have been effective at distracting the people from the truth of Christ Jesus. The report of sightings of spaceships is unnecessary to the maintenance of Satan's domain. Any so-called sightings are the result of the delusions and desires of individuals wanting to be redeemed by a more superior power. This desired redemption is available in Christ Jesus, but not in the alien lore of today as spun by scientists like Carl Sagan, and government agencies like NASA SETI, and private organizations like SETI Institute.

The Funk and Wagnall's dictionary is referenced below to provide an outline of a most supreme alien. All forms of the word "alien" are defined below which reveal Christ Jesus as more alien than Hollywood or NASA ever dreamed. *Lien* is the root word.

The word *alien* as an adjective means: from or of another country; foreign. The word *alien* as an adjective can also mean: foreign in character or not similar. The word *alien* as a transitive verb means: to transfer to another, as property. The word *alien* as a transitive verb can also mean: to estrange. The noun, *alienage*, means: to be in a state of being alien. The transitive verb, *alienate*, can mean: to estrange or to make over or transfer or sell. The noun, *alienation*, means: the act of alienating or the state of being alienated or the legal transfer of property, or title to another. The noun, *alienee*, means: the one who takes over transferred property. The noun, *alienor*, means: the person who alienates property to another.

There are five distinct components of what any alien, of use to modern man, would have to have from these definitions:

1. An alien would have to be **from another place**, perhaps outside our planetary system;
2. An alien would have to be **foreign in character**, perhaps not having the same human flaws that we possess;
3. An alien would have to **possess some property**;
4. An alien must have **power to transfer** some type or types of property to us;
5. An alien would have **power to alienate** or estrange us, perhaps into a new creature.

Now let's examine what has been said and done in the Bible to show the fulfillment of every alien component above. An additional property shall be illustrated that the Hyperspace Alien, Jesus Christ, possessed.

1. Christ is from another foreign place:

First Jesus confesses to Pilate just prior to the crucifixion in John 18:33-37:

> "Then Pilate entered into the judgement hall again, and called Jesus, and said unto him, Art thou the King of the Jews?

> "Jesus answered him, Sayest thou this thing of thyself, or did others tell it thee of me?

> "Pilate answered, Am I a Jew? Thine own nation and the chief priests have delivered thee unto me: what hast thou done?

> "Jesus answered, **My kingdom is not of this world**: if my kingdom were of this world, then would my servants fight, that I should not be delivered to the Jews: but now is **my kingdom not from hence**."

(Emphasis added)

Also Jesus makes the following prayer to his Father about himself and his followers in John 17:14-16:

> "I have given them thy word and the world hath hated them, because **they are not of the world, even as I am not of the world.**

> "I pray not that thou shouldest take them out of the world, but that thou shouldest keep them from the evil.

> **"They are not of the world, even as I am not of the world."**

(Emphasis added)

Jesus confesses that he is not from this world, then where is he from? He was born in Bethlehem. Correct, but how was he born? He was not born naturally by a mother and a father. He had a natural mother but not a natural father. Luke 1:35:

"And the angel answered and said unto her. The Holy Ghost shall come upon thee, and the power of the Highest shall overshadow thee: therefore also that holy thing which shall be born of thee shall be called the Son of God."

Now this may not be enough proof for some readers, that this amounts to anything significant from these scriptures alone, but by the end of this chapter it will be. One of the new theological categories of this book is that of the Domain Triad which locates God by this short statement, "I AM, ONE, OF THE LIVING." This places God and Christ back into the real observable world. Do these foregoing scriptures contradict this domain triad position? When Jesus speaks of another world he is speaking of the eternal space above us not some other unknowable indiscernible world in another dimension. Even Heaven or the Heavens are not in another dimension but they contain us yet are inaccessible to us without Christ. Jesus explains the connection of these places in the real observable world around us in John 3:13:

"And no man hath ascended up to heaven, but he that came down from heaven, even the son of man which is in heaven."

Jesus tells us where he came from, where he is going, and where he was at the time he spoke these words to his disciples. He came from the heavens above us and was going to return to that place and that is where he was when he was speaking. Heaven is the one and only domain for both God and man. There is no other world of any kind! Earth, however, and its many wicked inhabitants that are not alienated into new creatures by the cosmic operation of Christ, create wicked systems and destroy good systems made by the alienees. When scientists speak of the Spirit world, and unfortunately when many Christians speak of the Spirit world, they are thinking of another dimension outside the observable world. This is error that binds Christianity and liberates Satan.

A further example of where Jesus operates, and where he has power, is given in John 2:18-22. Jesus responded to the Jews in the following way after whipping the moneychangers out of the temple:

"Then answered the Jews and said unto him, What sign shewest thou unto us, seeing that thou doest these things?

"Jesus answered and said unto them, **Destroy this temple, and in three days I will raise it up**.

"Then said the Jews, Forty and six years was this temple in building, and wilt thou rear it up in three days?

"But he spake of the temple of his body.

"When therefore he was risen from the dead, his disciples remembered that he had said this unto them; and they believed the scripture, and the word which Jesus had said."

(Emphasis added)

Notice that Jesus himself is recorded as saying that he was going to raise that temple up in three days. He did not say he was going to only raise his own bodily temple up in three days. Jesus was referring to his physical power over the entire cosmos within his body, which included the temple under construction for 46 years.

Jesus did in fact destroy that temple and raise it up in three days. He destroyed it and rebuilt it prior to, what I will now call its second destruction, by the Romans in about 70 A.D. In fact Jesus destroyed every thing in the cosmos and raised it all again in three days. The temple, the earth, the solar system, the stars and the galaxies were all destroyed and raised again on the third day. This is the very operation by which all men from now until the return of Christ are translated from one creature to a new creature. You become a new creature by your death and your resurrection and your ascension. The body of Jesus is the temple and it contained the temple under construction for 46 years.

Therefore, Jesus is not talking about another dimension when he refers to not being from this world. He confirms that he not only is from the observable heavens above us but he operates upon this same reality that we live in and have our being in. And he challenged the corruption in the Temple by whipping the moneychangers and turning over their tables. He challenged the political corruption because that was in his domain. But Jesus was from eternal space and that was not of this world at that time. In the time of the birth of Christ no man had an idea of such an existence and most don't today. Jesus meant he was from a world not known by mankind unless he revealed it to them, as he did. We now know this other world. But it is not in another dimension, it is above and around us infinitely.

As evidence of occulted mainstream modern theology, Dr. Harrison, Th.D., Ph.D., Professor of New Testament, Fuller Theological Seminary, Pasadena, California, says the following concerning Jesus driving the money changers from the temple:

> "Such drastic action quickly brought a demand from the Jews (leaders) that Jesus produce an incontestable sign to show that he had authority for his conduct. He always resisted such a demand (6:30; Mt 16:1). This time he was content to point to the future. Destroy this temple. The **figurative character of the utterance is evident**, not only from Jn 2:21, but from the utter **unlikelihood that the Jews would destroy their own Temple.**"[9]

(Emphasis added)

Dr. Harrison does not indicate that he sees any real connection between the actual physical destruction of the temple and the death, resurrection and ascension of Christ. But this realized connection is critical to the salvation of any man. If Christ did not destroy the temple and raise it again in three days then neither has he

---

[9] Everett F. Harrison, Th.D., Ph.D., *The Wycliffe Bible Commentary* (Chicago, Moody Press, 1979), 1077

done this to anyone or anything. Notice that Dr. Harrison totally misses the point in his continued analysis of this important concept revealing Christ's power over all physical things in space:

> "These words are not to be taken as a command or invitation, but are in the nature of a **hypothesis** "If you destroy, I will raise up." In three days is equivalent to "on the third day."[10]

(Emphasis added)

The presumption made by Dr. Harrison is that Jesus is referring to a case of the Jews destroying the temple themselves. Why would Dr. Harrison presume that Jesus was talking about the Jews destroying the temple? Could it be that Dr. Harrison could not perceive of the concept of Christ having the power to destroy anything and to raise it again? Christ knew the Jews were not considering the destruction of their temple they had worked on for 46 years. Dr. Harrison has already said that it was unlikely that the Jews were going to destroy their own temple. Why would Dr. Harrison then labor himself with an "hypothesis" given the Jews if they destroyed the temple? Further, Jesus is not referring to the defiling of the temple with commerce, because he had, just moments earlier, purified the temple by running them out of it. None of Dr. Harrison's reasoning is accurate. Dr. Harrison continues to try and explain this Scripture passage without success:

> "**Taking him literally, the Jews felt that his statement was ridiculous**, since the Temple had required forty-six years to build. Herod had begun its reconstruction in 20 B.C. Some work still remained to be done, but the structure was sufficiently complete to be spoken of as built. (For the **use of the figure temple of the body**, see I Cor 6:19) This prophecy helped to promote faith on the part of the disciples, but not until after the resurrection of their Lord from the dead (cf. Jn 12:16)."[11]

(Emphasis added)

This concludes all that Dr. Harrison has to say about this event. It is interesting that 2000 years later Dr. Harrison has no more idea of what Jesus was saying then the Jews that Jesus was talking to. Dr. Harrison knew that the Jews could not take Jesus literally but Dr. Harrison cannot take Jesus literally here either! All Dr. Harrison and modern theologians can come up with is that Jesus was referring to his own death, resurrection and ascension. And indeed he was, but Jesus linked that event to the physical destruction of the temple and its resurrection just as he said. Jesus was not speaking figuratively in the slightest, but answering the Jews directly

---

[10] Ibid.
[11] Everett F. Harrison, Th.D., Ph.D., *The Wycliffe Bible Commentary* (Chicago, Moody Press, 1979), 1077

with exactly what he was going to do to show his authority to them. And that is exactly what Jesus did. And that is why we are in the Kingdom of Heaven today. Amen!

2. Jesus has a character that is foreign to mankind:

Now does Jesus have a foreign character that is significantly superior to our own human traits that would drive us to want help from an alien? John 10:7-18:

> "Then said Jesus unto them again, Verily, verily, I say unto you, I am the door of the sheep.
>
> "**All that ever came before me are thieves and robbers**: but the sheep did not hear them.
>
> "I am the door: by me if any man enter in, he shall be saved, and shall go in and out, and find pasture.
>
> "The thief cometh not, but for to steal, and to kill, and to destroy: I am come that they might have life, and that they might have it more abundantly.
>
> "I am the good shepherd: the good shepherd giveth his life for the sheep.
>
> "But he that is an hireling, and not the shepherd, whose own the sheep are not, seeth the wolf coming, and leaveth the sheep, and fleeth: and the wolf catcheth them, and scattereth the sheep.
>
> "The hireling fleeth, because he is an hireling, and careth not for the sheep.
>
> "I am the good shepherd, and know my sheep, and am known of mine.
>
> "As the Father knoweth me, even so know I the Father: and I lay down my life for the sheep.
>
> "And other sheep I have, which are not of this fold: them also I must bring, and they shall hear my voice; and **there shall be one fold, and one shepherd**.
>
> "Therefore doth my Father love me, because **I lay down my life, that I might take it again**.
>
> "No man taketh it from me, but I lay it down of myself. **I have power to lay it down, and I have power to take it again**. This commandment have I received of my Father."
>
> (Emphasis added)

Jesus says that he is indeed different in character from all others before him. And he tells us that he has power that no other man before him has had. This is the power to die and come back to life forever. Would this be different enough for you? Didn't Hollywood think that was a fantastic power to bestow on E.T.?

3. Jesus has property:

What property does Jesus have by his own admission? All the property of the cosmos, the Earth, the stars the galaxies and the universes. Yes, in the cosmos there could be more universes all beginning in a big bang and ending in their collapse, or whatever. But these expanses of space defined by objects therein are all contained in the physical body of Jesus Christ. This is the unique nature of Jesus: A container of all space and time in a human frame with his resulting power to operate upon all space and time with his physical body. And, we have seen how he recognized his own power to give and take his life. This gave him power to operate upon the cosmos to effect people in his time and in all time as he said there shall be **one fold and one shepherd**.

> "Howbeit when he, the Spirit of truth, is come, he will guide you into all truth: for he shall not speak of himself, but whatsoever he shall hear, that shall he speak: and he will shew you things to come.

> "He shall glorify me: for he shall receive of mine, and shall shew it unto you.

> "**All things that the Father hath are mine**; therefore said I, that he shall take of mine, and shall shew it unto you."

> (Emphasis added)

Then Jesus has all the property that belongs to his Father which is all things in the cosmos.

4. Jesus has power to transfer his property:

Another component that would satisfy one of the definitions of the word alien would be the power to transfer the property he has to another. Having shown that Jesus had property to transfer, namely, all the property in the cosmos, does he have the power to transfer it to someone or something (John 17:1-3):

> "These words spake Jesus, and lifted up his eyes to heaven, and said, Father, the hour is come; glorify thy Son, that thy Son also may glorify thee:

> "As thou hast given him power over all flesh, **that he should give eternal life** to as many as thou hast given him.

> "And this is life eternal, that they might know thee the only true God, and Jesus Christ, whom thou hast sent."

> (Emphasis added)

Just in case it is unclear that the power to give eternal life may not be the same as the power to transfer all things or all property that Jesus has to his followers, I Corinthians 3:20-23 shows that Paul knew this to be the case:

"And again, the Lord knoweth the thoughts of the wise, that they are vain.

"Therefore let no man glory in men. **For all things are yours**;

"Whether Paul, or Apollos, or Cephas, or the world, or life, or death, or things present, or things to come; all are yours;

"And ye are Christ's; and Christ is God's."

(Emphasis added)

Jesus expresses to God that he perceives his power to transfer his own life and possessions to others, in fact, all flesh. As a result of the operation of Christ upon the cosmos all things are redeemed including cars, buildings, rocks, trees, and dogs and cats, etc. But not all things or all flesh is able to perceive this operation. Only flesh that has the two complementary image capacities can grasp this operation and thereby be alienated by it. Only beings that look like you and Jesus have these two image capacities. We are inundated with data around us that says that creatures like Elephants, Kangaroos, and Monkeys have a hard time with these capacities. It would not be much of a philosophical leap to conclude that this will be true through out the cosmos. Therefore, the notion by science so-called that says, "intelligence in space may look different from us" is false.

If innumerable life forms around us (in their various states of evolution, if you must) that look different from us reveal their lack of affinity to these image capacities, do we have to search through out the cosmos for life forms that are different? What are the chances of us finding a different-looking intelligence that will break this overwhelming pattern? Must we very methodically begin to list all the life forms around us on earth that cannot grasp these concepts to arrive at the truth that it is only the human being that possesses these capacities?

Can we not therefore agree with one more truth of the Bible that God and Christ created man in their own image, unique in all the cosmos? And what is this image? Look into the mirror and see the outer limits of the cosmos! Is this not the foundation for failure of the modern scientific view of evolution; that science focuses on similar physical appearance instead of the image capacities of mankind to both fill and contain the cosmos? Animals that look similar to men don't count, they must have the exact characteristic of the ability to understand the concept of filling and containing the cosmos in their physical bodies.

5. Jesus has the power to alienate us or remake us:

The fifth and final component of our language dictionary for an alien is the power to "make over or estrange." First it should be noted what Christ said about the necessity of a man to be born again (John 3:1-5):

"There was a man of the Pharisees, named Nicodemus, a ruler of the Jews:

"The same came to Jesus by night, and said unto him, Rabbi, we know that thou art a teacher come from God: for no man can do these miracles that thou doest, except God be with him.

"Jesus answered and said unto him, Verily, verily, I say unto thee, Except a man be born again, he cannot see the Kingdom of God.

"Nicodemus saith unto him, How can a man be born when he is old? can he enter the second time into his mother's womb, and be born?

"Jesus answered, Verily, verily, I say unto thee, Except a man be born of water and of the Spirit, he cannot enter into the Kingdom of God."

This process is not the mere baptism of some child in water at a church house somewhere nor is it sprinkling or submersion. This process is the realization and revelation of the operation of Christ upon the cosmos by his physical body. Jesus related to this phenomenon as childbirth again in John 16:21-22. Christ in this passage is the woman whose hour has come. The passage, via the death, resurrection and ascension, is the **alien birth canal** or **Star Gate**.

"A woman when she is in travail hath sorrow, because her hour is come: but as soon as she is delivered of the child, she remembereth no more the anguish, for joy that a man is born into the world.

"And ye now therefore have sorrow: but I will see you again, and your heart shall rejoice, and your joy no man taketh from you."

John clearly understands the foreign nature of Jesus, the alien power of Jesus to create, and his power to transfer his property, and to estrange his followers in John 1:10-13:

"He was in the world, and the world was made by him, and the world knew him not.

"He came unto his own, and his own received him not.

"But as many as received him, to them gave he power to become the sons of God, even to them that believe on his name:

"Which were born, not of blood, nor of the will of the flesh, nor of the will of man, but of God."

Paul now plainly tells us what has been done to us and to the entire cosmos now and forever (until Christ operates upon it again on his return) in Colossians 1:12-17:

"Giving thanks unto the Father, which hath made us meet to be partakers of the inheritance of the saints in light:

"Who hath delivered us from the power of darkness, and hath **TRANSLATED us into the kingdom of his dear Son**:

"In whom we have redemption through his blood, even the forgiveness of sins:

"Who is the **IMAGE** of the **invisible (SPATIAL) God**, the firstborn of every creature:'

"For by him were all things created, that are in heaven, and that are in earth, visible and invisible, whether they be thrones, or dominions, or principalities, or powers: **all things were created by him, and for him**:

"And he is before all things and **by him all things consist**."

(Emphasis and parenthesis added)

Notice the comprehensive rehearsal of "all things" did not include a non-existent "other dimension" or "other world" that Mr. Larson and mainstream Christian theologians refer to. Where are we and what are we then as a result of this operation of death, resurrection and ascension? The answer is reiterated in Ephesians 2:4-6:

"But God, who is rich in mercy, for his great love wherewith he loved us,

"Even when we were dead in sins, hath quickened us together with Christ, (by grace ye are saved;)

"And hath **raised us up** together, and **made us sit together in heavenly places** in Christ Jesus:"

We are in the Kingdom of Heaven right now as the operation of Christ Jesus has created this reality. And what have we become? II Corinthians 5:17:

"Therefore if any man be in Christ, he is a **NEW CREATURE**: old things are passed away; behold, **ALL THINGS ARE BECOME NEW**."

(Emphasis added)

We have been alienated, evolved, translated and transformed into new creatures. What has happened to the cosmos? It has passed away and become new. Yes, all things, Earth, our Solar System the Milky Way, the other galaxies and other universes (universes meaning other balls of exploded matter throughout eternal space) have all been made new by this one and only most unique alien operation anywhere. What is this operation? It is the death, resurrection and ascension of Jesus. Where does this put other forms of life on Earth and other "alien life forms" in outer space? It puts them under the operation of Jesus Christ! Ephesians 1:9-10:

"Having made known unto us the mystery of his will, according to his good pleasure which he hath purposed in himself:

"That in the dispensation of the fulness of times he might **GATHER TOGETHER IN ONE ALL THINGS IN CHRIST, BOTH WHICH ARE IN HEAVEN, AND WHICH ARE ON EARTH; EVEN IN HIM:**"

(Emphasis added)

Therefore, fellow Christians and those who want to know the secrets of outer space, why do we waste time and money looking for aliens defined by Hollywood and modern lost scientists? This quest is a Satanic distraction and cheap imitation of the real alien savior that has already provided your means of salvation and made provision for your continual life and travel in deep space. Yes, you, no matter how poor or rich, occupy the most advanced space ship ever devised to travel to all the galaxies within and beyond the reach of our most powerful telescopes: your human body! But it can only travel and live in space if the occupant is aware of this operation and allows it to have its effect upon them. If one is able to perceive this operation, they are also able to undergo the operation and be translated into the Kingdom of Heaven or God.

That concluded the definitions of aliens in the dictionary. Now, let's add one other alien power found in the Bible, which we have just covered. Show me a movie where a being in the form of a man creates a galaxy and then goes to it. Show me a scientist that proposes that human form has the power to create solar systems in space and then visit them.

6. Jesus is the co-creator of all things in heaven and earth:

Neither Hollywood, NASA scientists, Washington D.C., the SETI Institute nor the UN has ever suggested the following component of an alien that is omitted in the dictionary but included in the Holy Bible. This is the creation power of Jesus Christ. Jesus was a co-creator with God. Would not this qualify a man for alien status? Have you ever heard anyone say that they had created the Earth and the stars? This fact was stated by several apostles and by Jesus himself. John 17:4-5:

"I have glorified thee on the earth: I have finished the work which thou gavest me to do.

"And now, O Father, glorify thou me with thine own self with the glory which I had with thee before the world was."

Also see John 1:10 that was quoted earlier in this chapter. Also see Colossians 1:12-17, quoted earlier in this chapter. It is clear that Jesus is the co-creator with God of all things. What does this information tell us, even if the faulty hypothesis about alien civilizations in space were true? It would tell us that Jesus created them for himself and that Jesus sustains them as he sustains us because by Jesus all things consist.

Is there something more fantastic presented in Hollywood or by modern scientists? I think not! Christians must quit buying into the lies and cheap imitations of alien saviors yet to come and proclaim the reality of what Jesus has done to all things and us. However, the Christian community must treat this modern quest of an alien savior as a real sincere hope regardless of the erroneous premise behind it and present the real Jesus as that entity who indeed exceeds all their requirements for such a being. We should thank the Lord Jesus for bringing this social phenomena to pass: that when man abandoned God, their own definitions for an alien spatial savior are more than fulfilled in God's own Son, Jesus Christ.

We have now covered six components of Jesus as an alien savior that operates upon the cosmos and upon mankind to **translate** it all into the Kingdom of Heaven. Jesus called himself the Son of Man and only upon several occasions referred to himself as the Son of God. Mankind will never progress or evolve beyond a primitive life form without this definition of man that Jesus gave us. This is why we cannot allow scientists to determine the hope of mankind based upon particle physics alone. We are not thinking rocks or projectiles. We are entities that fill and contain all space.

The following are some of Funk and Wagnalls definitions of the word *translate*: to "**change in form; transform. To convey or remove from one place to another, as a human being from earth to heaven without natural death.** To transport; enrapture. To impart to (any body) motion in which all the parts follow the same direction."

Then from what we have discovered here it would seem logical to say that Jesus, the alienor, has transferred all his property and character to his alienees. He did this by his capacity of impletion and envelopment of all things while on earth and by his operation upon them by his death, resurrection and ascension. We can also say that our alienage may not help us in the modern business climate. This is because Jesus has alienated us to be different from those around us. We can also say that we have an obligation to alienate our fellowmen on earth who seek to be evolved into new creatures to live in deep space forever.

Can it be said that Jesus is the Hyperspace Alien? Several chapters herein have shown the spatial image capacities of Jesus to implete and envelop all of eternal space. Then a mere use of the term 'hyper' applied to space is logical. Funk and Wagnalls defines **Hyper** as, "(prefix) Over; above; **above measure.**"

John the Baptist said in John 3:31-36:

> "he that cometh from above is above all: he that is of the earth is earthly, and speaketh of the earth: he that cometh from heaven is above all.

> "And what he hath seen and heard, that he testifieth; and no man receiveth his testimony.

> "He that hath received his testimony hath set to his seal that God is true.

"For he whom God hath sent speaketh the words of God: **FOR GOD GIVETH NOT THE SPIRIT BY MEASURE UNTO HIM.**

"The Father loveth the Son, and hath **given all things into his hand.**

"He that believeth on the Son hath everlasting life: and he that believeth not the Son shall not see life; but the wrath of God abideth on him."

(Emphasis added)

God, therefore, gives the Spirit unto Jesus without or above measure. This is **HyperSpirit or HyperSpace**. Obviously this is the same operation that gave Jesus all things into his control by his physical body which we have already explored. It is your God given capacity to perceive this power and to let it operate on your person to create a new immortal creature capable of eternal space travel. So be it!

Ronald F. Avery

PART III - CLARIFICATION OF
THEOLOGICAL TERMS

CHAPTER 12 - HEURISTIC VALUE OF ALIEN PHYSICS

The understanding of the spatial relationships of the Domain Triad, the Trinity of Personality, the Singular Essence of God, the Image Capacities result in heuristic logic that can discern the truth of any proposition made by natural science, Christianity itself, and other "religions." Who would argue that interpretation of the Biblical Scriptures must be based on its harmony with other Biblical Scriptures? But now we must not violate the spatial relationships that stand behind the words of the Scriptures. This also means that in searching the "unsearchable riches" we must not violate the manifold wisdom of God revealed in his spatial relationships behind Scripture.

New understandings of Scripture must reinforce the glorification, magnification and revelation of Christ in a way that does not violate the spatial power of Christ to work in the real world around us. The spatial relationships defined in this book can act as a guide in the discovery, articulation and transmission of further theological categories used to describe the power of God and to spread the Gospel.

This should be exciting to all those who now and will study the Holy Bible. Do not think that because we don't know everything about God or His creation that we don't know anything, or that we don't know enough to be transformed and be at one with God. Because we do possess the manifold wisdom of God right now, we are able to assert this reality with boldness.

We must be skeptical of those who try to redefine all the terms of Scripture merely in order to establish or reinforce their own church group that they gather their substance from. This however must not be confused with the attempt to glorify and reveal the reality of Christ Jesus in this world and his power over it to save and one day judge it.

My pastor, Mr. Bob Odom, said one time that his most frustrating semester in seminary was the study of the late Paul Johannes Tillich. Mr. Odom, said that "Mr. Tillich redefined all the terms wherein no one could understand what he was saying without reading all his definitions." What is the purpose of the definition of terms? Is it to occult, obscure, mask, deceive, confuse or diminish the power of Christ? Or, is it to de-occult, or illustrate clearly the reality of God and reveal the power of Christ to operate on the cosmos?

It is clear that many 20th Century theologians were trying to adapt Christianity to science without analyzing or formulating the real power of Christ in scientific terms. They merely were modifying, reducing and diminishing Christianity to be in conformity to some notion of science, falsely so-called (1 Timothy 6:20). That is to say the theologians were accepting the doctrines of science and modifying Christianity to be in conformity to the propositions falsely made by leading scientists such as Einstein. These modifications resulted in the destructive dual world cosmology and the "putting away" of the faith. Rather than warring a good warfare with the scientists falsely so called, Christianity waned and individual

Christians recoiled into a "personal religion," relevant to the individual only. Even the admonition or invitation to obtain a "personal relationship" with Jesus or God can be taken to also mean a relationship that is relevant to you alone, or therefore, unquestionable by modern "scientific" society. (1 Tim 1:18-19):

> "This charge I commit unto thee, son Timothy, according to the prophecies which went before on thee, that thou by them mightest war a good warfare;

> "Holding faith, and a good conscience; which some having **put away** concerning faith have made shipwreck:"

(Emphasis added)

This "putting away" is still, however, part of God's plan wherein Satan is allowed to escape to deceive the nations for a short season and where men fall away from the truth of Christ and believe a strong delusion (2 Thessalonians 2:11-12):

> "And for this cause God shall send them **strong delusion**, that they should believe a lie:

> "That they all might be damned who believed not the truth, but had pleasure in unrighteousness."

(Emphasis added)

But this season is just about over, and now that we know where Satan lives and how he lives, he shall be put back into the bottomless pit forever.

The alien spatial relationships mentioned are not confined between the covers of the Bible but impact every proposition concerning the life of mankind. It is the natural job of every human being to resolve all the data that one collects concerning reality, what it is, and how we should respond to it. When one discovers a higher or general law that explains many phenomena, or orders a whole set of things, it can be said that this law has heuristic value. Einstein said this of his special theory of relativity. The same could be said concerning the spatial relationships discussed earlier. The truth of this statement will be illuminated by the clarification of theological terms that many people use improperly which lead to confusion and disputes between members of the Body of Christ and slows the spread of Christianity in contemporary America.

Einstein suggests that the theory of relativity acts as a test, or heuristic aid, in determining the truth of any natural theory or experiment. He said, if a newly presented theory meets the requirements of the special theory of relativity, which all natural laws should meet, then the theory would be true.

Alien Physics, consisting of the spatial relationships of salvation mechanics, provides the same heuristic aid to interpret the Holy Scriptures and test all propositions for mankind as the theory of relativity does for particle behavior. Einstein, and our modern scientific cosmology, errs by limiting mankind to a mere thinking collection of compounds subject only to the laws of particle behavior. These ideas ignore the reality of man as a container and filler of all space.

Just as the special theory of relativity should apply to any natural inanimate phenomenon, the foundational spatial elements of Alien Spatial Physics should govern the truthfulness of any proposition made for human beings. If any creature has the capacity to grasp these rudiments of spatial relationships between God and mankind then that creature, by definition, is a member of mankind and is created in the image of God. However, it also appears as discussed earlier, that this creature, over a five-thousand-year period of all human history, is a creature that resembles what we visually recognize as mankind. They come in colors and with different features but all undeniably possess the main human features. Do we need to search the galaxies for otherwise, when our own planet is teaming with innumerable life forms and none but what we recognize visually as mankind can speak of these spatial properties?

Alien Spatial Physics governs both the non-man and the man-related theories. This is because God's singular essence of eternal space contains all things and is in all things infinitely small and large. Man is involved with God and has the capacity to share with God these spatial characteristics which make him a special creature like none other in the cosmos.

Until now Christianity has not had a means of testing theories or propositions from science or other religions. That is because the essence of God has always been argued philosophically as "existence" and character, i.e., justice, love, design, creator, etc., rather than living eternal space that shares its domain with man.

The qualities like love, size, wisdom, righteousness, truth, etc., or the creation as evidence of design by God, do not tell us what God is. Nor do these things point to His essence or entity. Men can now understand God in terms of an entity with unique essence and quality that is seen all around us and that we are subject unto while we are yet able to share His Domain. I do not maintain that this fact has not been known intuitively since the beginning but that it has not been stated as clearly in history.

To some it may appear that the act of defining God is synonymous with diminishing God or trying to limit God, or worse, become God. The act of defining God does none of those. It could be said that the sole purpose of Christ was to define and reveal the truth of mankind and God in terms of Space or Spirit. If it is "not robbery to be equal with God" it certainly is not robbery to define God. Paul said to "let this mind be in you" (Philippians 2:5-11). The purpose of the definition of God's essence given herein is to illustrate his power. Which is better, to pretend that we love God and his care for us while we are ignorant and incapable of expressing his power, or to know him, and his power fully in our heart, mind, and soul and attempt to express that to others with all our strength?

St. Paul prayed unceasingly that we would have knowledge of him and "what is the exceeding greatness of his power to usward who believe" (Ephesians 1: 15-23). Knowing and explaining God's power in Christ is the answer to Paul's prayer. It is an insufficient answer to tell others that theology is simple, or "you either get it, or you don't." This is not being ready to give an answer to all those that ask what our hope is in Jesus Christ (1 Peter 3:15).

God has always had the same essence. But, God is also in the process of creating His experience and reality that both He and mankind become together. For instance, prior to Jesus, the knowledge of God had always been on the outside of man except for certain express purposes as recorded in the Old Testament. But after the operation of Christ on the cosmos, God can now be inside mankind. Furthermore, in the future, Judgement will occur for all the nations and Christ will close the door of transformation forever. These events are major transitions in history that change the whole nature of how God and mankind exist together, i.e., God has planned, designed and wanted, but never existed, as He will in post Judgement times.

Armed with the heuristic spatial principles of the power of Christ Jesus to transform the cosmos, we can see the source of errors and contentions, which arise among Christians. Contentions can arise by the mere reading of Scripture without the theological spatial model of the power of God to save the world. This is a fact of modern times, that men have the form of Godliness but deny the power of God (2 Timothy 3:5).

To demonstrate the usefulness of this spatial model several examples are given based upon real conversations held between the author and others. Notice that the present confusions, concerning Christ's power to transform, cut through all denominations. The author has not studied the literature of the Mormons or Jehovah's Witnesses or the Episcopalians nor has it ever been his intent to diminish their strength, as may be the intent of some. The author's only intent has been to respond sincerely in one-to-one discourse between him and others concerning the reality and power of Jesus Christ. The occultation or vacancy of these theological and essential steps to salvation is revealed clearly in the following examples. These examples are to show the importance and usefulness in finding truth in anyone's theology or understanding of reality.

1. Two Mormons:

Two Mormon young men came to my house on a summer Saturday morning and I invited them to the back porch for cold water and a listening ear. Their definition of the "image of God" was the Supreme Being that looked like the Daddy of Jesus and that in heaven we would see him like Jesus. This is a worldly image based upon our own father/son relationships. The image of God is not someone who looks like Jesus with a longer and grayer beard and who flies around with a lot of power. If that were the case, how then can it be said that Christ is the image of the invisible God (Col. 1:15) if God looks like the daddy of Jesus? And, how can it be said that God is invisible if he looks like the daddy of Jesus? When I said that God was eternal space, and that no other entity is larger than He, they could not believe that. They could not leave their idea of God looking like the daddy of Jesus. The famous oil painting entitled "Creation" by Michael Angelo (index fingers about to touch) comes to mind here, and is also very misleading. This is a case of great painting but inaccurate concept.

Only one explanation seems to satisfy this problem. God is the invisible eternal space we live in and Christ Jesus is His "image," the first born of every creature.

This means that Jesus is the first to have this image and that others will also obtain this "image of God" through Christ.

They said, "One day we will see God when we go to heaven." I replied, "I already have seen God and I am in heaven now." They could not believe that either. They said, "We are saved by the death and resurrection of Jesus Christ upon our death." I replied, "We are presently dead, resurrected and ascended by the operation of Christ Jesus." They did not believe this. If this be not the case, how then do we explain Ephesians 2:6? They suffered from the same dual world view of modern scientific man. They were going to be saved at death. They did not perceive the Domain Triad, locating God in the eternal one world of the living (I Am, One, Living) They did not perceive that Christ has already operated upon the cosmos.

They also did not believe that all things were inside the body of Christ nor that Christ had filled the cosmos. This is an essential element of the power of Christ recorded in His baptism. The Two Complimentary Image Capacities establish Christ's power to operate on the cosmos. I said, "Jesus is everywhere and he can manifest his physical being anywhere in the cosmos in the twinkling of an eye." One replied, without argument from his associate, "I don't believe that!" It is a fundamental rule that one cannot live in a place that his mind does not perceive. Where were these young men living?

2. My non-denominational church Brother:

A fellow church mate of mine argued that God cannot be eternal space because it says in Genesis 1:1 that God created the heaven and the earth. I asked him, "Is God bigger than eternal space?" My friend seemed to hold with the young Mormons that God was a force and a character in space, but not space itself. All their views of God were somehow smaller than space but yet they thought God had the created Eternal Space. They certainly rejected the idea that space was alive and had a personality and was God. I presented the following problem to my friend: "If God is not eternal space then that very entity, space itself, is bigger than God." A non-spatial God also places God on a more even plain with Satan, as just another spirit, instead of The Supreme Spirit of Eternal Space.

All those spoken to seem to comprehend that space is eternal, except for my friend who somehow thought that something might be beyond the limits of space. Then I asked, "What lies on the outside of space, is it Jell-O or what?" The difficulty that arises from the non-spatial descriptions of God is that none of these men could explain the concept of the Trinity. And as a further result, they were unable to explain the operation of transformation. None of them perceived the idea that the entire cosmos had been redeemed and that they were presently ascended into heaven at this time.

The only explanation to resolve these complications, and failures to link the power of salvation with the clear understanding of the Trinity, is that God created two layers of space with objects, but the third layer of space is His own boundless Singular Essence of Eternal Space.

3. Jehovah's Witnesses:

Two Jehovah's Witnesses at the San Antonio Airport had a booth and were attempting to pass out magazines and they asked me to take some and I told them that I was already translated and they looked surprised. They asked me if I knew the purpose of God for mankind and I asked, "What do you say it is?" They answered, "God created the earth as a possession for man (Genesis 1:28) and we are to remain on earth forever." I said, "I have inherited much more than the earth by the very operation by which we are translated." They again looked surprised. I continued, "Christ is the container of all space and fills all space, and when he died and was resurrected and ascended, all things did likewise." I added, "Even the airport we're standing in is transformed by the same operation but it is unable to perceive it."

One said in return, "Then this airport and us standing here are in the physical body of Jesus?" "Yes," I replied. He exclaimed, "I can't believe that!" I went on, "If that is not the case, no one can be saved at any time, past, present or future." He asked, "Have you experienced ascension?" I replied, "I have." He said, "I've never heard of that experience reported by anyone else." I replied, "This is the process of rebirth and we are to drink of all that Jesus drank of including his death, resurrection and ascension." He said that he could not accept ascension and that he had trouble believing that Christ ascended. I then told them that Christ had indeed destroyed the Temple and raised it again in three days, just as he said he would do. I said that the San Antonio Airport and all other things including the galaxies were included in that operation.

I continued, "Jesus clearly said that he would destroy the temple and in three days raise it up again." (John 2:19). And I said, "If Christ did this to the temple he also did the same to the San Antonio Airport. Some commentaries say that the reference of Christ to the destruction of the Temple refers to the destruction of the system of the Jewish religion. And other scholars say that Jesus was prophesying about the destruction of the Temple by the Romans in about AD 70. But if we are to be translated ourselves by the operation of Christ's death, resurrection and ascension, then it follows that this operation applies to all things in heaven and earth." This is clearly stated in Ephesians 1:10:

> "That in the dispensation of the fulness of times he might **gather together in one all things in Christ**, both which are in heaven, and which are on earth; even in him:"

(Emphasis added)

I continued to tell them how the Temple was destroyed and raised again, "This indicates that all things are in Christ Jesus and it follows that whatever Christ then did, the same was done to all things in the cosmos." They were astonished as I went on, "Therefore, Christ's death, resurrection and ascension operated on all things in the cosmos. Many people have no difficulty in claiming that they are saved by the death and resurrection of Christ but fall short of proclaiming his ascension as essential. If we can reckon ourselves to be in Christ for his death and resurrection (Romans 6:11) why can we not reckon ourselves to be with Christ in his ascension?

And how else are we raised presently to sit in heavenly places as St. Paul professed?" (Ephesians 2:6)

This conversation illustrates that there are many people out there in "Christian" circles that "believe" in Jesus and the Bible but don't really know the power of God described in the Bible. They have learned many Bible verses and heard many sermons but don't understand the real principles and power implied in the Scriptures themselves. This is because theologians have abandoned the job of expressing the power of Christ and the good news of transformation to our own modern scientific culture. These people are walking around with a mainstream public scientific interpretation of Christianity rather than a Christian interpretation of modern science. They rely on disconnected Bible verses and are unable to resolve them or explain them to the common man. Every thing is "explained" by them as something unexplainable and beyond human understanding which everyone should "accept as a matter of faith." This is no explanation of anything.

One might ask; how can these people be saved, translated, redeemed, born again, transformed or delivered if they cannot express their supposed condition or how they obtained it? It is questionable. However, there is evidence in my own case that reveals that one can be operated upon yet not know how to communicate this to others. This is especially true if we have grown up thinking about the world in a false way. It is also difficult to explain when the whole culture has no way of discerning what you are talking about. That again is the purpose of this book. I experienced the operation of salvation before I could express it to others in this culture accurately and correctly. The real danger from not knowing what is expressed in this book is that the power to spread the good news is thwarted. Certainly, in many cases, the people are not saved or transformed who say they are. Most people mistake a belief in God for salvation. However, even "the devils also believe, and tremble." (James 2:19).

One cannot wish him self into eternal life without a clear path of knowledge and a realization of a new reality. One cannot "decide" to be "born again." One cannot "decide" to regenerate him self! However, one can "decide" to "follow Jesus," but cannot "decide" to be regenerated. Regeneration and transformation comes only in the passage through the doorway opened by the body of Christ Jesus. Experience shows that one can make that journey, and be saved, but it may take years to express precisely what it is and how it occurred. The evangelical power of the church in this age is lame without a clear understanding of the power of Christ Jesus over the cosmos. Herein is the meaning of the parable of the kingdom of Heaven being like a grain of mustard seed (Matthew 13:31-32).

A man that says he will not see heaven or salvation until death is still dead and has not passed from death into life (John 5:24). This is because the operation of salvation operates in the world of the living and is experienced during a lifetime not in some other non-existent world of the dead. This truth is made clear in the theology of the Domain Triad, which locates God's domain, by the declaration of God's nature by Christ, in the expression; I Am, One, Living.

If a man cannot grasp the concept that we are in Christ in all that he did, then how can he be transformed? Transformation is not a matter of our will to do something. It is a matter of perceiving the method and recognizing our condition without the operation that allows our humble resignation to permit the operation to effect and operate upon ourselves. We thereby experience the torture, crucifixion, death, resurrection and ascension with Jesus. Jesus operated upon the Temple, the San Antonio Airport and all other things in this sequence of events. Amen.

4. My Sister Church Friends:

The fourth conversation involves a married couple who is a close friend of the author and attends a sister church of the church the author attends. I told them that I wanted to buy a small planetarium for a toy gift that our whole family could play with. The husband said that they had bought a telescope with a tracking motor about four or five years earlier for about $4500 to go see heaven with a church group. That statement immediately intrigued me. I smiled and said, "go see heaven?" He said that an astrophysicist had written a book on aliens and had located what he and other scientists thought was heaven. I asked where heaven was and he said in some nebula or galactic system. They told me that this astrophysicist thought that aliens were demons that had obtained technology. I tried not to show my amazement at their confession. They were living proof of my observations about the false sociological equilibrium between Christianity and modern science.

They asked, "Do you believe in aliens?" I said that I believe that only one true hyperspace alien has ever visited planet earth. And I told them that most people adopt the implied definition of aliens, which Hollywood promotes on TV and movies i.e., strange looking foreign creatures that follow the modern scientific version of evolutionary environmental adaptive models. I began to give them the actual definition of alien with all of its root words as discussed earlier in this book. I said that Jesus possessed property in his body in conformance to the definition of an alien. I told them that he could transfer that property to others in conformance to the definition of a true alien. And I included that he was certainly from a far away place (the whole eternal living cosmos itself).

Both husband and wife got quiet as I told them that Christ filled all space and contained all space and thereby all things are in his physical body giving him power to operate upon the cosmos. They remained quiet as I continued, "Christians, not knowing this, come short of the ascension. For some reason, Christians can reckon themselves to be dead and resurrected with Christ but not ascended. How can Christians believe that they are with Christ in the two events of death and resurrection but not with him on the third event of ascension?" They did not answer. I continued, "I think it is because they do not have an adequate definition of heaven. They believe that heaven is in another dimension or in some little segment of space that they will never know until death. If heaven, however, is perceived as the entire cosmos we presently observe around us, then we can know it now and know we are in it by the operation of Christ upon the whole of it. If this not be the case, how then did Christ say, he that would believe on him would never see death?" They did not answer me.

I told them that God's essence is eternal space. And that His Kingdom is this same space which contains all things, and that Christ contained this same space as well, and the union of God and Christ is documented in the story of the baptism of Jesus. The husband said that he did not believe that God was space, "because it says in Genesis that God created heaven and earth." I said, "Yes, but, it also says in Genesis that the heaven was the firmament between the waters above and the waters below." He agreed, and we discussed the three layers of heaven and agreed. Yet, when it came to believing that the third heaven was eternal, and above the created or exploded matter, he backed off. He said he thought the third heaven was a place such as he mentioned earlier in some star system.

The husband said, "I don't believe that Jesus contained all space in his body." I answered, "If it were the case that Christ did not contain all space in his body then there is some point in time and space at which one could exceed the limits of the operation of Christ. Alien Spatial Physics is an all-or-nothing principal. Jesus either contains all space and time to operate on all things, or he contains no space at all and is powerless to operate on anyone or anything anywhere at any time." The husband said that Jesus did not contain all space because he had trouble and pain. I said, "Trouble and pain do not and cannot exclude the potential and reality of Jesus containing all space and time, especially in a world of other unregenerate creatures that do not understand what has occurred or is occurring."

They replied, "How do you explain angels and demons and their appearance and disappearance if there isn't another dimension?" I explained, "The power of manifestation is dependent upon having the powers of Christ to fill and contain all space and that this did not require another dimension." I continued, "just because Christ can appear and disappear does not mean he went to another dimension. If we allow for a moment the notion that there is more than one dimension then we doom ourselves to a God that is unknowable making Him King of nothing right along with Satan and his servants." They both could not see why that was true, but thought instead, that God could be master of all dimensions. I agreed but said that we would not and could not know that. I said what makes Christianity powerful is that it deals with the truth in the real known world not some unknown and unknowable world.

The husband explained that demonic aliens were in another dimension because they could move in craft that could change directions instantaneously, something that we cannot not do in this dimension. His wife said, "Yes, that explains that..., I've never heard that explained before!"

5. An Episcopalian Friend:

I told my friend that I was writing a book proving that I was a hyperspace alien. He asked if I believed aliens have come to Earth. "Yes," I replied, "I know one alien has come to Earth. The only alien to ever visit planet Earth and return to deep space is Jesus Christ." He jumped, "No Way!" I asked if he believed any aliens had come to Earth. He said, "No!" And I asked him, "Why not?" He said, "Earth is too far out of the way." I was curious about how we could be too far out of the way in a cosmos where no one seems to know the way to anywhere.

I wanted to know what place was "in the way" or "on the way" and where aliens would be going if they existed. I asked, "Are they going to the mall or the center of town or where? Are we on the edge of town or in the corner of the mall or what? Would it be better to be by the restrooms are the food court?" Isn't it interesting that his reason to deny aliens coming to Earth is founded upon a presumption that they would not want to come to an out of the way place rather than some cosmic or physical law that prevents their existence completely. He believes they haven't come to Earth, because we are in a 'jerk-water' solar system on the edge of a metropolitan galaxy! If we were only near the center of the galaxy, we would have all the aliens coming in to shop or at least stopping for gas on the way to the game!

I said, "Isn't that just like God to use the 'out of the way places' (like Bethlehem) and the small and weak things to confound the great places and the powerful central places? Why could not this little out of the way place called Earth, be the place that affects and impacts the rest of the entire cosmos?" I continued, "I know that Christ Jesus and now all mankind is the most advanced form of life in the cosmos. If I learned that intelligent life existed in some star system I would be compelled to tell them the good news that Jesus has operated upon them to make them new creatures capable of eternal space travel."

I then laid out the whole design to my friend: "God is eternal space. Space is not just empty volume. Space is alive, thinking, creative, with a plan and design and power to implement it. The Ten Commandments show us what we are. God overshadows a virgin with the Holy Ghost, or eternal space, and a child is conceived and the Son of God is born. The baby grows up into Christ Jesus who fills and contains all of eternal space at one with his Father. Jesus physically operates on the physical cosmos contained within his physical body through his death resurrection and ascension. After we experience this operation for ourselves, we also fill and contain the cosmos at one with our Father and with Christ Jesus in the Holy Ghost. We become new creatures with eternal life, and in the future, ability to travel in eternal space. We are transformed from mortals to immortals."

My friend replied, "You think you have this figured out don't you?" I said, "Yes, I do, I know I do, and I testify that I am in the Heavenly Places with Christ Jesus at this present time."

My friend replied, "Then what causes sugar to eventually cause the break down of the human body?" I replied, "I don't know, I'm not a chemist. I didn't even know that sugar did that." He said, "See, our brain power is so weak and we use so little of it that we have to merely have faith. We can't know. We'll never know! And God made us that way so we would need faith and be dependent on faith."

I replied, "Not so! Jesus is the author and finisher of faith. He attracts us by creating a vacuum to draw us to him then he finishes faith by transforming us into immortals possessing grace. If we possess what we searched for in faith how do we continue to hope in faith for what we have already received? (Romans 8:24). I used to have faith and believe that Jesus had done something and that he was truthful. Then I experienced his Death, Resurrection and Ascension and passed through the door into the Kingdom of Heaven and sat down with him in the Heavenly Places as St. Paul has said. On the other side of the door I had faith. On this side of the door I have grace."

My friend replied, "I just believe that the importance of Christ is based on his 'becoming a man' and not 'remaining God' rather than in what he did while he was here..., this gives me hope." I answered, "Yes, but what if his whole purpose of 'becoming a man' was to transform us by his actions he performed on Earth? It is clear in Scripture that we are to be 'born again' and transformed to enter into the Kingdom of Heaven."

He replied that he did not feel like he had been born again or transformed. He said a Pope in seeking rebirth commanded that he be chained to a post and not fed until he was born again and died of starvation. I said, "This is not the way to seek God or rebirth. God is not a tempter or a teaser. God guarantees that you will find him and be changed—Knock and it shall be opened, Seek and you shall find, Ask and ye shall receive."

He went on and said, "I'm a Christian, but if not, I would be a Jew or a Sikh or something..., all need an anchor." I replied; "Yes but I hope you're not saying; anyone will do! For a Christian to say that is like saying; I have been delivered and transformed by Jesus, but Buddha will do just as well..., seek him if you want. This is not true and would mislead others. You are saved, not by faith in anything, but by the operation of Christ upon the cosmos which you had faith in before you experienced it for yourself." My friend finished by saying, "Faith is enough, we are not smart enough for more." Grace and truth is wasted here, faith was enough for my friend.

6. An atheist:

The following is a conversation with a married woman who was an atheist. I had been talking with her a few minutes and she asked, "Why has no one told me about Jesus and what he has performed on the cosmos? Even my Lutheran friends have never said anything like this." I replied, "Fear of modern science has restrained the study of Christ's power over the Earth and galaxies beyond and all things in space and time."

She asked why do you believe the Bible? I answered, "If you read a book's directions on how to make a loud noise and you did what it said and it went 'bang' real loud, would you believe the book?" She continued, "But the Bible was written by men and translated, how do you know it's true?" I answered, "If by reading the book you become a new creature transformed from death into life, who cares who or how many wrote it or what their state of mind was?"

She went on to say, "I feel like I'm a good person and just because I don't know about what you have just described about Jesus, do you think I'm going to burn in Hell?" I replied, "If you do not possess all space and time as Jesus did then you are dead now. Life is the possession of all space and time. You cannot transform yourself from death into life by being good. It is an operation performed by Christ upon all the cosmos including all space and time. Goodness and badness are irrelevant."

I continued, "That's why Jesus could say Love your enemies and do good to them that hate you for your Father in Heaven sends the rain and sun upon the just and the unjust, the good and the evil." I added, "If you die physically prior to perception and transformation by the operation of Christ, you shall never live."

She then asked, "Why are there so many religions, aren't all of them OK and true?" I said, "There are many religions mainly made up of rules and regulations and many have good ideas derived from men of great wisdom that observed great worldly lessons. But what I have just described about the physical operation of Christ upon the cosmos is not a 'religious' process. It is a physical operation revealed by the writing contained in the Bible. What other religion describes a process by which you are translated from one type of creature to another and where all things are destroyed, raised again and ascended filling all space and time?"

She said, "Why can't I understand what you have told me? I'm mad about that!" I replied, "You do not have the words of Christ in you nor have you experienced what I have described. If you want this you must read the New Testament in the Bible then you will know what I'm talking about." She said, "I want this!" I answered her, "Then start reading in Matthew and read through Revelations and you will be transformed. And save my diagram and you will know all I have said is true and all Christ Jesus said is true. You will be a new creature and live forever and travel to the stars."

Now then, how does the Alien Spatial Physics and the relationships discussed earlier, apply to these problems in theology and the world views just illustrated?

First, the **Domain Triad** will stop men from thinking that God saves them in the world of the dead. The Domain Triad will also stop men from thinking that God and Satan drop into the world now and then from an "other dimension." The Domain Triad will reinforce the truth that salvation occurs in this present observable world by the operation of Christ's death, resurrection and ascension. The Domain Triad (I Am, One, Living) and the Singular Essence of God fixes the location and realm of the interest and power of God to impact the world we live in.

Second, The **Singular Essence of God** as eternal space prevents man from confusing God with lesser powers and describes how God permeates our world in every object from the smallest to the largest. This spatial essence establishes the uniqueness of God and the power of God to affect all things even to be the Father of Jesus and to become ours as well. This spatial entity cannot be duplicated nor can any other equal exist. This spatial essence allows for the sharing of its space with the space or soul of mankind. This prevents men from assuming that God is just another invisible spirit flying around in equal competition with Satan and his angles. It is this very essence that makes God superior to Satan and his angels. **Satan cannot rob God of His own unique essence of eternal space!**

Third, The **Trinity of Personality** relating God the Father and God the Son and God the Holy Ghost establishes the connection between God, Jesus and all mankind in and through the Holy Spirit, or that shared eternal spatial essence. God has three personalities, to create, redeem, and be at one with mankind. Jesus operated on the Kingdom of God or Eternal Space making a way for Mankind to become the children of God at one with Him. The Holy Spirit is that common shared essence of eternal space. All three are in agreement and all three are at one with each other. This establishes the fact that God's will for all men is their salvation through this one operation. Salvation can no longer be thousands of different things, feelings, visions and events to different people.

Fourth, the Two **Complementary Image Capacities** of **impletion and envelopment** of all space by Christ Jesus establish his ability to operate on the cosmos and all things therein. This prevents the omission of components of mankind and matter of the cosmos that are saved. The translated items include inanimate objects i.e., Temples and Airports etc. The Two Complementary Image Capacities prevent the partial 'salvation' of man's heart only while his mind, soul and body are left stranded in the deadly confines of particle physics. These theological principles demonstrate that this operation cannot be selective for individuals. They are true for all men for all time until the judgement. These principles of transformation power rule out "degrees or levels of salvation" as a result of its comprehensiveness. All men get the same salvation. All are paid the same wages according to the parable of the laborers (Matthew 20:1-16). This physical operation upon the cosmos prevents the notion that some will farm the earth while only 144 thousand go to Heaven, etc. It is the revealed power of Christ to save anyone at any time that determines the harmony of Scripture.

The operation performed upon the cosmos by Jesus Christ is a **physical operation performed upon physical property by a physical body**. Christ's power to translate and transform us by that same operation makes us new creatures. This is clearly stated by Christ in Matthew 9:17:

> "Neither do men put new wine into old bottles: else the bottles break, and the wine runneth out, and the bottles perish: but they put new wine (new eternal life) into new bottles (bodies), and both are preserved."

(Parenthesis added)

This is something that is done on the Earth while we read this book, not in some unknown, unknowable world of the dead. Jesus knew that the old man who had sinned could not contain the cosmos that Christ was going to deliver to him without a new body. The old body of sin and death would burst. Jesus also knew that the same operation that would give us the galaxies would also give us new bodies that could fill and contain all things. Finally, these principles taken together deoccult the means of salvation and provide a way to interpret the meanings of Scripture.

PART III - CLARIFICATION OF THEOLOGICAL TERMS

CHAPTER 13 - FAITH & GRACE / Essential Difference

Actually, there are two kinds of faith that men talk about frequently and that are mentioned in the New Testament. The first kind of faith is the kind that attracts mankind to Jesus or God. The second type of faith is the kind that we speak of when we go out to do something, e.g., one that has the faith as a mustard seed can move mountains. But the first kind of faith is the kind that we are concerned with in this chapter. This is the kind of faith that leads to a transformation in the type of creature that one is, e.g., a mortal to an immortal.

Men cannot be translated into new creatures by mere faith or belief or opinion. Man must possess a physical channel or means by which he can evolve. This channel is Grace, or the Power of God, to operate over the known cosmos to translate or evolve us into eternal life.

There is a problem in modern theology, again originating in the contemporary sociological equilibrium preventing, Christianity from having any claim on the mind or physical reality. This, however, as has been said before herein, is not a correct equilibrium but merely an unchallenged position, until now!

One effect of this incorrect equilibrium is that the terms "faith" and "grace" in Christianity are used interchangeably and synonymously as if they meant the same thing. This is done because many Christians do not realize that they can obtain anything from Christ except hope and a pure regenerated heart. This is true, of course, but not the whole truth, thank God! In a theology that cannot perceive of a physical transformation of the cosmos, there is no way to discern the difference between faith and grace. But upon understanding what Christ actually did to the cosmos we not only perceive, but become subjects of, the operation that Christ performed. Many Christians do not believe that salvation is a physical event but merely a "spiritual" event.

The channel for salvation is the death, resurrection and ascension of Jesus Christ. This is most accurately described as a physical event for it was the act of a physical person in reality some 2000 years ago operating over the physical cosmos and everything in it. Jesus makes it clear to us that mankind cannot be saved in the heart, mind or soul only but must have a new body to contain what he gives us (Matthew 9:17):

> "Neither do men put new wine into old bottles: else the bottles break, and the wine runneth out, and the bottles perish: but they put new wine into new bottles, and both are preserved."

How else do we get a new body except it be killed with Christ on the cross, it be raised from the dead, and it ascend with him to fill all and contain all? This is a physical and a spiritual or spatial event. It is a physical event in that Jesus was able to accomplish this operation because his physical body contained all things in the cosmos. It is physical because of what the body of Jesus endured and experienced in his crucifixion, death, resurrection and ascension. It is a spiritual event because the space he contained and filled (as shown in earlier chapters) gave him this physical power. In other words it is space or the Holy Spirit that gives power over all physical things within itself. This is also why the spiritual world is not outside the dimension that we live and move and have our being in. We observe the spiritual world all the daylong. This is clearly expressed by St. Paul in his evangelical speech to the Athenians in Acts 17:28:

> "For **in him we live, and move, and have our being**; as certain also of your own poets have said, For we are also his offspring."

(Emphasis added)

Christianity is not learning something about another dimension or having faith in something unknowable but learning how to understand what we see all about us. Faith is important because it takes a while to understand these things and to surrender to the operation of Christ and to communicate what has happened to this culture and generation. In other words, faith keeps tugging on us until we obtain what attracts us.

It does appear that the New Testament writers seem to use the two words, "faith" and "grace" together and sometimes in a somewhat synonymous fashion. But upon a full application of the power of God in Christ to save men, we can discern what the difference is and if there needs to be a difference. This is the job of theology to clarify biblical terms that are not so clear merely upon simple reading. It is not until we experience both faith and grace that we can discern between them and define them. As has been said in a previous chapter, the spatial model that explains the power of God to save mankind acts in a heuristic way to define the difference between faith and grace. We need to review some of the major scriptural texts to determine any difference between them.

First, the gospel of John opens with a significant summary of the epic of Christ and all of history. John states in John 1:17 that the law was given by Moses, but "grace and truth" came by Jesus Christ. Faith is a necessary component of the life of men recorded in both the Old and New Testaments. Clearly Jesus did not bring mere faith to the world, but grace and truth - something new and real. Faith in the Old Testament is explained fully by Paul in Hebrews 11:

> "Now faith is the substance of things hoped for, the evidence of things not seen.
>
> "For by it the elders obtained a good report."

But Paul finishes this soul stirring review of the prophets, patriarchs and harlots who obtained favor in the sight of God by their faith in something they had not seen with a profound proclamation. Paul makes it clear that these who had accomplished great things, suffered all things and received a good report with God **did not** receive a better thing, which we now possess (Hebrews 11:32-40):

"And what shall I more say? for the time would fail me to tell of Gedeon, and of Barak, and of Samson, and of Jephthae; of David also, and Samuel, and of the prophets:

"Who through faith subdued kingdoms, wrought righteousness, obtained promises, stopped the mouths of lions,

"Quenched the violence of fire, escaped the edge of the sword, out of weakness were made strong, waxed valiant in fight, turned to flight the armies of the aliens.

"Women received their dead raised to life again: and others were tortured, not accepting deliverance; that they might obtain a better resurrection:

"And others had trial of cruel mockings and scourgings, yea, moreover of bonds and imprisonment:

"They were stoned, they were sawn asunder, were tempted, were slain with the sword: they wandered about in sheepskins and goatskins; being destitute, afflicted, tormented;

"(Of whom the world was not worthy:) they wandered in deserts, and in mountains, and in dens and caves of the earth.

"And these all, having obtained a good report through faith, received not the promise:

"God having provided some better thing for us, **that they without us should not be made perfect**."

(Emphasis added)

Now Paul even makes a more profound statement regarding the effect of Christ Jesus upon faith. One who obtains grace is no longer in a state of faith but his faith is finished in the possession of grace. (Hebrews 12:1-2):

"WHEREFORE seeing we also are compassed about with so great a cloud of witnesses, let us lay aside every weight, and the sin which doth so easily beset us, and let us run with patience the race that is set before us,

"Looking unto Jesus the **author and finisher of our faith**; who for the joy that was set before him endured the cross, despising the shame, and is set down at the right hand of the throne of God."

(Emphasis added)

It is clear from what Paul has said that Christ brings something better than faith into the observable world. It is this revelation of the power of Christ, and its effect, on the perceiver and observer. And it is this perception or revelation that finishes faith. Jesus Christ at one with the Father and Holy Ghost became the author of faith by attracting men to seek God and believe God. But it is also the appearance of Christ in the world almost 2000 years ago that finished faith.

Peter agrees with Paul in 1 Peter 1: 9-10:

> "Receiving the **end of your faith**, even the **salvation** of your souls,

> "Of which **salvation** the prophets have inquired and searched diligently, who prophesied of the **grace** that should come unto you:"

> (Emphasis added)

Is it not clear in this passage that one's faith is completed in the salvation of their souls, which is the possession of grace? Why then do we continually refer to Christianity as a faith? Why are we as Christians content to have the lost world refer to our state of being as a faith? Why do we allow the world to lump Christianity into the class of blind faith fumblers? We live in an age that equalizes all religion and scientific searches into the broad class of faiths. In case you still wonder about this reality let us finish with what St. Peter goes on to say in 1 Peter 1: 11-13:

> "Searching what, or what manner of time the Spirit of Christ which was in them did signify, when it testified beforehand the sufferings of Christ, and the glory that should follow.

> "Unto whom it was revealed, that not unto themselves, but unto us they did minister the things, which are now reported unto you by them that have preached the gospel unto you with the Holy Ghost sent down from heaven; which things the angels desire to look into.

> "Wherefore gird up the loins of your mind, be sober, and hope to the end for the **grace that is to be brought unto you at the revelation of Jesus Christ**;"

> (Emphasis added)

Many pastors have erroneously taken this to mean some revelation of the return of Christ, or our observation of the returning Christ, or our revelation upon our death. Grace, however, is not a stage of the "afterlife." The revelation of Christ is our perception of what Christ is and what he has done to the observable cosmos that we presently inhabit. Upon this revelation we are under the influence of the operation that Christ Jesus performed with his physical body in his death, resurrection and ascension. We, too, experience these and are baptized into the Kingdom of Heaven while we are yet walking on this earth. Mark 10: 38-39:

> "But Jesus said unto them, Ye know not what ye ask: can ye drink of the cup that I drink of? and be baptized with the baptism that I am baptized with?

> "And they said unto him, We can. And Jesus said unto them, Ye shall indeed drink of the cup that I drink of; and with the baptism that I am baptized withal shall ye be baptized:"

This baptism is not the last supper, or his own baptism by John the Baptist, but his death, resurrection and ascension back to eternal space or the Father. This act by Christ for us reconciled all things in heaven and on earth back to God who is the one and only eternal living infinite space above us.

What is that "something better" that Christ Jesus brought into the world that perfected it? Is it just more hoping and faithing around in the darkness? No it isn't! It is the transformation of the cosmos in which we live and the resultant state of grace. We receive this state of grace by allowing this operation, performed by Christ almost 2000 years ago, to act upon us. This is the **possession of grace**.

In other words Christ is revealed to us when we realize that Christ contained all space, and as a result, all time. There is no time in which the earth or galaxies could travel beyond the limits of the Spirit or Space of Christ. Therefore all space, time and matter are crucified, buried, resurrected and ascended to fill all space. This is the **power of God** or Eternal Space to operate and transform all matter within itself.

So Paul and St. Peter are in agreement that faith is "finished" and at an "end" at the salvation of your soul. St. Peter said the salvation of your soul was upon the revelation of what Christ has done. St. Peter said the Prophets had preached the good news of the glory that was to come at the end of Christ's sufferings on the cross. That glory is now everywhere in the body of Christ. Christ transformed the whole cosmos from death into life eternal. Amen.

Now "faith" has been shown, without contradiction from any source, to be as Paul said; the substance of things hoped for and the evidence of things unseen. But "grace" is the possession of the Kingdom of God (or those things once unseen) and one's own soul as a result of the operation of Christ Jesus upon the cosmos. Grace then is the result and finish of faith. Faith is the seeking and the attraction to grace and truth. But grace is the possession of a state of perfection. Grace, then, is the object and great end of faith.

Paul uses the term grace most distinctively in Ephesians 2:4-10:

> "But God, who is rich in mercy, for his great love wherewith he loved us,

> "Even when we were dead in sins, hath quickened us together with Christ, (by grace ye are saved;)

> "And hath raised us up together, and made us sit together in heavenly places in Christ Jesus:

> "That in the ages to come he might shew the exceeding riches of his grace in his kindness toward us through Christ Jesus.

> "For by grace are ye saved through faith; and that not of yourselves: it is the gift of God:"

In the above verses Paul states that you are saved by grace twice and then once that you are saved **by grace through faith**. It probably makes as much sense to many to say you are saved by faith through grace. However, the statement "you are saved by grace through faith" makes more sense only if we have experienced both faith and grace and know their respective roles in salvation. Clearly, however, these two terms should not have the same definition, or we lose the explanation essence and power of Christ to save men in a way that is beyond the Old Testament means. We merely have to ask the question; "If we are transformed by faith, what then is grace?" And if men were saved, in the Old Testament by their faith in God, why did Christ come into the world?

Notice that neither Paul nor John ever talks about Jesus Christ or God being full of faith. Why? Because God, as we all can agree, would not need faith as he himself is the thing or end that is hoped for. And Christ being at one with God in a perfect state of grace needs not faith either. Remember that John speaks of Christ as being full of grace and truth. Then truly what Christ brings into the world is not faith but grace and truth. But Paul did not define grace as he did faith. It is up to us to define it, now that we know the mind of Christ Jesus, Paul, Peter, John and the other Apostles. It should at least be evident by now that faith and grace are not synonymous, as used by many theologians.

Now, we have learned from Scripture that the great patriarchs of the Old Testament did not receive the promise but received a good report by their faith. We have heard Paul say that Christ is the author and finisher of faith. We have heard Peter say that the end of our faith is the salvation of our souls. We have also heard that we are saved by grace through faith. Faith then obviously has an important role in salvation. But, it is not the means of salvation, nor is our hope the means of salvation. For Paul clearly says in 1Corinthians 15:19-22 that if we only have hope in Christ we are of all men most miserable:

> **"If in this life only we have hope in Christ, we are of all men most miserable.**
>
> "But now is Christ risen from the dead, and become the firstfruits of them that slept.
>
> "For since by man came death, by man came also the resurrection of the dead.
>
> "For as in Adam all die, even so in Christ shall all be made alive."
>
> (Emphasis added)

What then has Christ brought into this world that finishes and brings an end of faith and fulfills our hope and transforms us into a new creature? He brings the knowledge of the power of space over material things within it. He reveals the power of God over all that he has created. Christ takes upon himself all things in heaven and earth and carries them to the cross where they are killed and buried with him. On the third day, Christ, who has been given the power to lay down his life and take it again does so. All things are alive again. And 40 days later he takes all things with him as he fills the cosmos. This is the reconciliation of all things to God. All things are at one with God through Christ Jesus. What things does Paul refer to, the heart? No, not just the heart! But everything in the cosmos including your physical body, the building you work in, the home you live in, the earth you walk on, the air you fly in, the water ships sail upon. All these things are reconciled unto God through Christ Jesus. But who knows this? It is known by only those to whom have had the revelation of what Christ has done to the observable world, i.e., unto whom Christ has revealed it to.

Is there any evidence of the power of Christ over the physical elements of the world, while he walked upon earth? How about raising the dead, feeding 5000 people with two fish, walking upon the water, causing Peter to walk upon the water? Could not Christ walk upon the water if the ocean was resting in the body of Christ and had its foundation therein? Did not Jesus actually calm the wind and sea at the sound of his voice? There is an explanation of these miracles. And it lies within the theological understanding of the Singular Essence of God and the Trinity of Personality and the Domain Triad.

God is eternal space and contains all things. Jesus, God (his father) and the Holy Spirit are at one and share completely the Essence of God, Eternal Space. The perception that God, Christ and the Holy Spirit are not in another dimension but operate upon the known observable world that we live in everyday assures our minds that they did indeed perform miracles or operations upon the material world and that they can continue to do so. God is the great I AM, ONE, OF THE LIVING. Thus we should not think we can seek God after death but seek him in this world, the only reality. When we find him, we obtain eternal life and shall never see death. This is the good news. God has made a way for us to be at one with Him, to possess our own souls in confidence, and live now in the Kingdom of His dear Son. Christ has given us the power to become the Sons of God, as John has said, not upon death but upon our surrender to the power of Christ to translate the entire cosmos and everything in it from death into eternal life. Amen.

Grace or our perception of Christ's operation upon the cosmos is the gift of God unto us. It has been said by many that grace means "unmerited favor." So it does, but this never really explained much about what it really was or what it did or how it was different from faith. "Unmerited favor" only explains our helpless condition prior to the arrival of grace. Faith is also a gift and one that is not merited. How could we seek God or His will if we had not a vacuum placed in us by God? Did God place this vacuum within us because of some great thing we did earning this desire? It should be evident that unmerited favor applies to both faith and grace and is therefore insufficient to describe or discern the difference between the terms.

Therefore, Faith is the attraction to the God we know not, or the attraction to what God will do, that we have not yet experienced. But Grace is oneness with the God we come to know and the possession of what God grants to us through Christ, which is all things. **Faith then is seeking but Grace is possessing**. Therefore, we are saved by what Christ has done to the cosmos and our attraction to this idea until we possess it fully. We then are saved by the gift of the operation of the Grace of Christ through the gift of Faith to seek it.

It should be clear from the preceding presentation that the operation of Christ is a physical one and this should alter the position of the modern Christian churches stuck in the false sociological equilibrium. For the last 50 years or more the extent of the operation of Christ has been limited to the "spiritual" that only effects the "heart" of mankind and nothing else. This of course results from the reduction of the term "spiritual" to mean "other worldly." This is not the meaning implied by the apostles or Christ himself. The meaning they were implying was spatial or non-material or the heavens above us as we have discussed in earlier chapters. Nor has any theologian or scientist ever suggested that **space has power over all that is in it** or that the power of Christ results from his containment of all space within his physical body. This is the new measure of mankind God has given us in Christ, which results in the power to become the "Sons of God." We have established the definition of faith and grace that is consistent with Scripture and the power of Christ to save mankind through the heuristic value of Alien Salvation Physics and the spatial model. We can now prove how necessary it is to have an accurate and separate definition of terms based upon real things.

William Barclay, a famous theologian embraced by the Methodists, wrote a book entitled *The Mind of St. Paul*. In this book he wrote a chapter on "faith" and a chapter on "grace." In the chapter on faith he writes the following, concerning **God treating bad men as good men—He writes concerning "unmerited favor:"**

> "How can we be certain that these amazingly incredible things are true? The answer is: Because Jesus told us that God is like that. Our whole relationship with God is based on **unquestioning faith** that what Jesus said about God is true…"

> "**But another blazing question arises**. How could Jesus know that God is like that? Where did Jesus get His special knowledge of God? How can we be sure that Jesus was right about God? The answer is that we are certain that Jesus was right because we believe that Jesus is so closely identified with God, if you like to put it so, that Jesus knows God so well, that we can only call Him the son of God. Our whole relationship with God is dependent on the faith that what Jesus said is true, and the faith that Jesus is the Son of God, and therefore not mistaken."[12]

(Emphasis added)

Notice the immediate contradiction of the first and the second paragraph. Barclay bases his whole relationship with God on unquestioning faith in what Jesus said and then goes and does nothing but ask questions about what he said. Christian growth into the full possession of grace and image of Christ is by the asking and answering of questions, not mere blind faith, which Barclay very painfully labors upon above.

Also notice that Barclay never once mentions that one may experience something related to what Christ did or performed. All Barclay's self-forbidden questioning is answered by more forced believing. In other words, he says, we

---

[12] William Barclay, *The Mind Of St. Paul* (New York, N.Y.: Harper & Row, Publishers, Inc., 1958), 142

believe because we believe, or even because we want to believe. This is what Barclay calls faith. This might indeed be what faith is, but that is not what grace is, nor can that alone save anyone.

Not once does Barclay mention that one might see a pattern in Scripture or that there might appear to be a spatial model or rational reality underlying all of the power of Christ. Everything he is or believes goes back to his desire to believe or his faith. He never suggests that one could believe because something happens to the person changing their perception and their very nature from one type of creature to another.

Obviously Barclay is seeking knowledge of something real about Christ. But where is the reality or power or knowledge that he attempts to gain? He frustrates his attraction to Christ with unquestioning responses. Barclay frustrates faith by going back to faith of belief for its own sake. He never arrives at a state of grace because he returns to faith as an unquestionable end in itself. This is not honesty nor does it lead to the finish of faith. Faith that ends not in the possession of a state of grace makes us the most miserable of all men. Barclay identifies faith as complete trust and complete surrender to Jesus, but he does not experience what Jesus has performed. Barclay merely believes in Jesus but is not transformed by Jesus.

Barclay says "faith is the complete trust that that which Jesus Christ has done in His life and His death opens for us the way to God."(144). Notice that Barclay does not speak of taking the trip himself or does he recommend that you take the trip or that anything or person other than Christ took the trip from crucifixion, death, resurrection and ascension. This is amazing! Barclay leads us to the door but he does not go in, neither does he beckon us, nor does he suggest that anyone can proceed through the door to God, opened by Christ. And as a result he cannot discern the difference between faith and grace, or reality from belief.

Christ Jesus says that he is the door and that no one comes unto the Father, eternal space, except through Christ himself in John 10:7-9. On one side of the door we have faith that Christ has something for us, and upon revelation of what Christ is and what he has done, we go through the door of his death resurrection and ascension to sit down with him in heavenly places. On one side of the door we have faith on the other side we have grace. Faith is finished in our transformation from a mortal to an immortal. **This is the Gospel or Good News** that will be preached again **in the revival to come**. Amen.

Barclay quotes Ephesians 2:8: "By grace are ye saved through faith."(145) Then he makes a very good observation and suggests a complex answer to a question. But he fails to adequately answer this complex question about faith and grace when he says: "This is a highly compressed saying. We shall later on in our studies have to think much more fully of what Paul means by grace;.."(145)

Listen to the contrast of what Barclay says about Paul's idea of faith and what Paul himself says about faith. Barclay says:

"In Ephesians 3: 17 it is his (Paul's) hope and prayer that Christ may
dwell in our hearts through faith. His prayer is that we will never at
any time doubt what he says, that we will never at any time question
His offer, that we will absolutely and without argument or doubt take

His word about God, and so enter into this new relationship of fellowship with God."(146)

He suggests that actual transformation occurs from a questionless ignorant blind faith. Now let's hear what Paul himself says in Ephesians 3: 17-21:

"That Christ may dwell in your hearts by faith; that ye, being rooted and grounded in love,

"May be able to **comprehend** with all saints what is the breadth, and length, and depth, and height;

"And to **know** the love of Christ, which passeth knowledge, that ye might **be filled** with **all the fulness** of God.

"Now unto him that is able to do exceeding abundantly above all that we ask or think, according to the **power** that worketh in us,

"Unto him be glory in the church by Christ Jesus throughout all ages, world without end. Amen."

(Emphasis added)

Barclay has missed the power and realities of Paul's words because he injected his own definition of faith, which is intellectually defeating. Where in Paul's own words does he pray that we become people of absolutely no questions or argument or doubt? In fact, Paul's aim of his prayer appears to be that we comprehend the complete dimension of God's love and that we be filled with all that God has. Comprehension and fulness of God come from questions and correct answers. Paul then says that power works in us. And what is that power? It is the power to contain and fill all of eternal space and live forever as the children of God. Where is the power in Barclay's assessment of Paul's prayer?

It appears that Barclay may have gotten the cart before the horse. The kind of confidence and doubtless life he refers to above is the result of the possession of grace after becoming a new creature. But mere belief or faith cannot achieve this kind of doubtless knowledge. It can only be acquired upon passage from death into life by going with Jesus through his life, death, resurrection and ascension. But again the confusion comes from lack of definition about faith and grace and other theological terms.

Barclay summarizes his concept of faith by asserting that there are three steps to obtain faith at its fullest and best: First he **hears the message** of Jesus, then is **confronted with the cost** Christ had to pay to bring the message, and finally the **tremendous obligation he owes** Christ. It is obvious that Barclay is treating faith as a thing to be sought in and for itself. He is treating faith as the end of that which is hoped for. Can we hope for faith? That is like hoping for hope. Barclay does not mention receiving anything real or a change or the acquisition of a single thing other than a message and an obligation. It could be well argued that obligations are often insincere and undone, when derived from self-infliction, instead of a natural response to something great and wonderful obtained. One's good works for Christ are done without the knowledge of the other hand. There, actions spring from unity of mind and spirit rather than duties of obligee and obligor. In the state of grace the left hand does not know what the right hand does. One is no longer double minded about their good deeds.

Barclay starts his chapter on grace with a quote from James Moffatt's book *Grace in the New Testament*: "All is of grace, and grace is for all."(154) And then Barclay sets out two ideas about grace: First, he says it is beautiful, charming, loveliness. Secondly, he says grace is completely free and entirely undeserved and unearnable. Who would argue these points? Barclay continues:

"But accept the position that all is of grace, that all is the generous gift of God, and nothing further is needed. To bring in anything further is to deny the full sufficiency and the full adequacy of grace."(165)

But what follows shows how Barclay (without the heuristic value of alien salvation physics and the spatial model) cannot discern the difference between faith and grace:

"Paul was convinced that we are saved by grace; but Paul would have gone further than that. Paul insisted that we are not only saved by grace, but that we are also called by grace. It is not only the final work that is the work of grace; the first movings, the first stirrings, the first faint desirings in a man's heart, are also the work of grace. The grace of God does not only save a man; the grace of God also shows a man his need to be saved and puts into his heart the desire for salvation."(165)

The first movings, stirrings and desirings of man that Barclay speaks of, according to what we now know, must be termed "faith" not "grace." Or else faith and grace are synonymous. And if grace be full sufficient adequacy (needing nothing further) it cannot be faith. Because faith, as Paul said, is the substance of things hoped for and the evidence of things unseen. Now the first stirrings of something missing cannot be grace. Paul also said that the faith of the forefathers of the Old Testament was incomplete without something better brought by Christ Jesus, which was grace and truth. Paul most convincingly stated in Romans 8: 24-25 that if a man seeth what he hopes for, why does he yet hope?

"For we are saved by hope: **but hope that is seen is not hope: for what a man seeth, why doth he yet hope for?**
"But if we hope for that we see not, then do we with patience wait for it."
(Emphasis added)

What is it that we see not, but wait for patiently? Is it not grace? And after we are saved by grace do we still hope in that which we now see and possess? "Hope" and "faith" are more synonymous than "faith" and "grace." On one side of the door we wait in hope and faith for that which we will one day receive. The end and finish of our faith and hope is in the salvation of our souls in a perfect state of grace on the other side of the door.

Barclay leaves us with explaining "works" in relation to grace and ends the chapter with the usual argument given by James. But it is one that could be made better in light of the heuristic value of Alien Physics. Barclay says of Paul:

> "But Paul's whole position is the lover's position: he cannot make the grace which loved him so of no effect; he must spend all life in one great endeavor to show how much he loves the God who loved him so much. That is the obligation of grace. That is where works come in.

> "Here is the balance we need. We can never be saved by works; but, if our salvation does not issue in works, it is not salvation. It is not first works, and then salvation. It is first salvation, and then works. We do not become saved by keeping the Law; we can only keep the Law because we are saved. All is of love, and a man cannot accept God's grace, and then go on to break the heart of the God who loved him so much."(170-171)

The term "fruit" should have been used instead of the term "works." Fruit relates to the natural product of a type of plant. Works usually relates to anything that people do regardless of their relationship to Christ and God and usually means specific things that people go out and do. Jesus said in Matthew 7:16:

> "Ye shall know them by their fruits. Do men gather grapes of thorns, or figs of thistles?"

And Jesus further said in Matthew 6:3:

> "But when thou doest alms, let not thy left hand know what thy right hand doeth."

Jesus means here that without the grace of God, which is the operation of Christ performed upon the cosmos translating all from death into eternal life and creating new creatures, that no man can produce good fruit. Nor can man do good deeds or alms unknowingly without being translated by Christ. Many people in churches try to do works that show their obligation to Christ. Yet their fruit is exposed, because they do their works not from a joyful born-again being but from a duty bound debtor having received nothing but the burden and yoke of religion and endless rule finding and following.

Faith and grace are truly different and grace is not just some feeling or hearing a message about Christ. It is a physical transformation of the cosmos which operates upon us creating new creatures. Only new creatures can do what Christ has said is possible for mankind. The finish of faith is the possession of the state of grace. Jesus gave us power to become the Sons of God. Jesus said that the prophets longed to see this power and possess it but did not. This was their Faith and our Grace. Paul said in Hebrews 12:22-24:

"But ye are come unto mount Zion, and unto the city of the living God, the heavenly Jerusalem, and to an innumerable company of angels,

"To the general assembly and church of the firstborn, which are written in heaven, and to God the Judge of all, and to the spirits of just men made perfect,

"And to Jesus the mediator of the new covenant..."

(and in 27-29)...

"and this word, yet once more, signifieth the removing of those things that are shaken, as of things that are made, that those things which cannot be shaken may remain.

"Wherefore we receiving a kingdom which cannot be moved, let us have grace, whereby we may serve God acceptably with reverence and godly fear:

"For our God is a consuming fire."

Eternal space is unshakable but everything within it is. We receive the Kingdom of Eternal Space as the singular essence of God in Christ Jesus. This is our state of grace. Things made can shake. Space cannot. Space and grace are not shakable therefore we are not shakable.

This illustrates that we who have been transformed by Alien Physics, established by Christ, have obtained possession of a state of grace or perfection. We have joined the band of angels and come to the city of God, which is eternal space. Our spirit or space has united with eternal space in perfection in the same way that Jesus experienced it and prayed to His Father that we would do the same. Grace is the Power of God that translates men from death into life by Alien Physics performed on the cosmos by Jesus as recorded in the New Testament.

There is one Biblical reference that many theologians would say disputes that a state of perfection can be obtained on earth as a result of the operation of Christ Jesus. This is a hard statement to understand, but its meaning also is revealed by the heuristic power of alien physics. It is Paul's statement concerning his apprehension of perfection (Phil. 3:7-16):

"But what things were gain to me, those I counted loss for Christ.

"Yea doubtless, and I count all things but loss for the excellency of the knowledge of Christ Jesus my Lord: for whom I have suffered the loss of all things, and do count them but dung, that I may win Christ.

"And be found in him, not having mine own righteousness, which is of the law, but that which is through the faith of Christ, the righteousness which is of God by faith:

"That I might **know him, and the power of his resurrection**, and the fellowship of his sufferings, **being made conformable unto his death**;

"If by any means I might **attain unto the resurrection of the dead**.

"*Not as though I had already attained, either were already perfect*: but I follow after, if that I may apprehend that for which also I am apprehended of Christ Jesus.

"Brethren, *I count not myself to have apprehended*: but this one thing I do, forgetting those things which are behind, and reaching forth unto those things which are before,

"I press toward the mark for the prize of the high calling of God in Christ Jesus.

"*Let us therefore, as many as be perfect*, be thus minded: and if in any thing ye be otherwise minded, God will reveal even this unto you.

"Nevertheless, **whereto we have already attained, let us walk by the same rule**, let us mind the same thing."

(Emphasis added)

These verses were indeed hard to understand prior to an establishment of the principles of Alien Physics or Salvation Mechanics herein. For I many times have wondered over the meaning of what Paul was saying in seeming contradiction to his other writings of the same and earlier periods. Now most pastors take verse 12 to mean that Paul was establishing the idea that the "Christian walk" is one of a slow process of "sanctification." Please refer to the next chapter of this book for an exhaustive discussion of "Sanctification." This verse does not refer to the never-ending pursuit of Christian perfection, as many modern theologians suggest. Verse 12 refers to Paul's manner of treating all his failures and successes. Paul forgets them all, both failures and successes. **He forgets all that is past and presses forward** to that which is ahead or before.

Verse 12 also establishes how Paul thought of himself even though he had indeed attained perfection as he clearly states in verse 15. Paul is saying that one, in the state of perfection, does not think of himself as being perfect, but is in fact, nonetheless, perfect through the resurrection of Christ Jesus. Therefore, Paul, who had in fact attained a perfect state of grace at this writing, is saying that he does not count himself as perfect. **Paul, being perfect, does not regard his perfection**. This quality of disregard for obtained perfection is also discussed, as a trait of Christ in Paul's same letter to the Philippians just ahead of this statement (Phil. 2:5-8):

"Let this mind be in you, which was also in Christ Jesus:

"Who being in the form of God, **thought it not robbery to be equal with God**:

"But **made himself of no reputation**, and took upon him the form of a servant, and was made in the likeness of men:

"And being found in fashion as a man, **he humbled himself**, and became obedient unto death, even the death of the cross."

(Emphasis added)

Therefore, chapter two and three of Paul's letter to the Philippians speaks of the character of humility as a trait of Christ and of Christians. Jesus disregarded his Oneness with God to establish the Kingdom of Heaven on earth by being conformed to death upon a cross, which was the will of his Father in Heaven. Paul had obtained the state of Perfect Grace, yet did not count himself as having obtained it but forgot all things past and pressed ahead in the high calling of Christ Jesus. Therefore, we are presented with two examples of humble servants of God, Christ and Paul.

Further, the King James Version of the Bible gives two references relating to Phil. 3:12 concerning attaining perfection. The first reference is 1st Timothy 6:12:

"Fight the good fight of faith, **lay hold on eternal life**, whereunto thou art also called, and hast professed a good profession before many witnesses."

Paul is instructing Timothy to make sure that he possesses eternal life. This is not something that Paul wants Timothy to hope to obtain after life in another dimension. Paul is admonishing Timothy to have the perception of being in the Kingdom of Heaven in possession of his own soul right now. Paul would not instruct Timothy to do that, which is not possible in this life. Paul says to all, "**get eternal life**." If you don't know whether you have eternal life or not, you don't have it. You will know when you have it.

The second Scripture reference given for Phil. 3:12 is Hebrews 12:22-23. And we have just finished covering that scriptural text prior to discussing Paul's disregard for his state of perfection or possession of Grace. These verses speak in present tense of our coming to mount Zion, the city of the living God, the heavenly Jerusalem, **where the spirits of just men are made prefect**. What more can we therefore say? The kingdom of heaven is established on earth and we can enter on this side of the "curtain" and possess eternal life in perfection. This is not to be gambled upon in some afterlife. If you gamble instead of possess, you do not have eternal life nor will you obtain it in any other fashion or method in death. The door is open on this side, not the other side.

PART III - CLARIFICATION OF THEOLOGICAL TERMS

CHAPTER 14 - JUSTIFICATION / SANCTIFICATION ETC.

Modern theology, in its flight from the intellectual explanation of the power of Christ to save all men in all times, has left men with no distinct definition for theological terms that is consistent with the Gospel no with science. Modern theology has made a system of achievement for men to progress through, rather than a clear physical model based upon the revelation of the Scriptures and the power of God and Christ to translate all flesh in the cosmos from death into eternal life. Modern theologians tend to get the power of God confused with the growth of knowledge about God and Christ and what they have done to the world.

Most Pastors, preachers and theologians are not in agreement on the definition of theological terms. The theological terms are used interchangeably with one another without regard for clear definitions. Most modern Christians respond favorably by the mere use of the terms regardless of the truth of what is being said. If enough theological terms are stated and it sounds nice and "religious" then the claim is accepted as "spiritual" insight and understanding. Many times an attempt to clarify or dispute a statement (to expose the truth of the matter in discussion) is looked upon as being argumentative instead of analytical. The desire for precision in terminology, and models, consistent with Scripture and the power of God, through Christ, are viewed with suspicion and sometimes anger and hostility.

The rebuttal (to any attempt to clarify and distinguish between terms reinforcing a correct model of power) is returned; "it's simple!" This is, of course, not true. It's only simple, after you have fully understood what has happened and how. But it is unfair and hypocritical to tell the unregenerate person that the power of God in Christ to save men is simple. If it were simple we would have understood immediately the parables that Christ spoke without his explanation of them. If it were simple we would have believed every word of the Bible (both old and new testaments) as we heard them. If it was simple every man that heard of Christ would immediately be saved. But most people confuse simplicity with truth.

This confusion results in a theology, which says, "simple things are true and complicated things are false." Truth can be complicated and intricate and unfortunately falsehood can find refuge in simplicity as it can in complexity. But in this case, the power of God to save is complicated until the operation has been analyzed and categorized like any other field of intellectual pursuit. This field of intellectual pursuit examining the power of God to transform the world is called theology and has been mostly abandoned in favor of one type of political manipulation or another for desired results. One might say modern theology is "outcome based theology."

To prove that theologians, pastors and preachers are confused concerning theological terms we shall review what John F. MacArthur has written as a timely response to this age of flight from intellectual Christianity entitled **Reckless Faith**. This is an excellent book pointing out the futility of escaping the challenge of humanism by hiding in tradition, community and emotionalism. However, in this profoundly accurate analysis of the dangerous symptoms of this age, MacArthur also struggles with theological terms in regard to an explanation of salvation. This struggle illustrates that a clear perception of the symptoms of this age, do not in themselves, help to provide a solution. The solution to this age lies in the clear perception, not of mere symptoms, but of a theological model based in the real world revealing the power of God to save all men through Christ Jesus. All theological terms must then line up and fit with this model. If not, the terms confuse and diminish the power of God to the human mind, betraying God in one of the quaternion components we are commanded to use in finding and loving God i.e., the mind.

It will be useful, supportive and astonishing to quote a large section of MacArthur's book to illustrate the need for a real model of Christ's power to save all men for all time. First MacArthur quotes the **Catholic view of Justification** from the Council of Trent:

> "If anyone says that by faith alone the sinner is justified, so as to mean that nothing else is required to cooperate in order to obtain the grace of justification...let him be anathema (damned) [Trent, sess. 6, canon 9]. Parenthesis "( )" added.

> "If anyone says that men are justified either by the imputation of the righteousness of Christ alone, or by the remission of sins alone, to the exclusion of the grace and love that is poured forth in their hearts by the Holy Spirit and is inherent in them; or even that the grace by which we are justified is only the favor of God - let him be anathema [Trent, sess. 6, canon 11].

> "If anyone says that the righteousness received is not preserved and also not increased before God by good works, but that those works are merely the fruits and signs of justification obtained, but not a cause of its increase, let him be anathema [Trent, sess. 6, canon 24].

> "If anyone says that the guilt is remitted to every penitent sinner after the grace of justification has been received, and that the debt of eternal punishment is so blotted out that there remains no debt of temporal punishment to be discharged either in this world or in the next in Purgatory, before the entrance to the kingdom of heaven can be opened - let him be anathema [Trent, sess. 6, canon 30].

> "If anyone says that the Catholic doctrine of justification set forth in this decree by this holy Synod derogates in any way the glory of God or the merits of our Lord Jesus Christ, and not rather that the truth of

> our faith and the glory of God and of Jesus Christ are rendered more
> illustrious - let him be anathema [Trent, sess. 6, canon 33]."[13]

The earth has seen several hundred years of the advance of Protestant theology and God has certainly blessed that movement up until a few years ago. Is there anyone that still agrees with the Council of Trent? Upon reading it as quoted above we should be thankful to the Protestant movement for freeing men from the yoke of the politically motivated Catholic Church of that period. It is clear that if MacArthur's theology is vulnerable, that the decrees of the Council of Trent was an attempt to completely occult the door to the Kingdom of Heaven available presently by the Gospel of Christ Jesus. And this door is still occulted to anyone that would still believe the Council of Trent. We know that the Death, Resurrection and Ascension of Christ is that door. We also know that we can go through that door at this time, without the aid of works or any priest or church. Amen! Thank you Jesus!

But, most amazingly, Protestants are returning to these ideas, without force, but out of fear of the world of science and to strengthen ranks in the Protestant churches. Most modern Christians cannot discern the difference between works and grace or faith or justification or any other theological category. This is because, as Christ said, they neither know the Scriptures nor the POWER OF GOD.

MacArthur summarizes the Council of Trent:

> "Trent also declared that the instrumental cause of justification (the means by which it is obtained) is not faith, but "the sacrament of baptism" (Trent, sess. 6, chap. 7). The Council also said justification is forfeited whenever the believer commits a mortal sin (Trent, sess. 6, chap. 15) - clearly making justification contingent on human works. so according to Trent, justification is neither procured nor maintained through faith; works are necessary both to begin and to continue the process."(142)

However, it is just as inaccurate to say justification is obtained by faith as it is by baptism. Justification is provided by the death, resurrection and ascension of Christ Jesus. Further, why are we alarmed over the Catholics procurement and maintenance of Justification by works when Protestants claim they are Sanctified by a life-long growing and conformity into the image of Christ? Does not this life-long growing and conformity suggest works? We shall soon see that this life-long conformity is also error.

Does MacArthur and other Protestants presume to maintain Justification by Faith? How would one maintain Justification by Faith any more than by works? Is it worse to procure and maintain Sanctification by life-long conformity than to procure and maintain Justification by works? This is confusion of theological terms where both violate the truth of Scripture and the real spatial model of the power of God to transform the cosmos. This will be proved shortly in this chapter.

---

[13] John F. MacArthur, *Reckless Faith* (Wheaton, Illinois: Crossway Books a division of Good News Publishers, 1994), 141-142.

At this point MacArthur brings his synopsis of the power of Protestant theology upon the error of Trent. He summarizes the Biblical Reformation doctrine of justification in four parts:

The Error of Trent In Four Parts By MacArthur:

❏ First Part:

> "First, Scripture presents justification as instantaneous, not gradual."(143)

MacArthur proffers support in the parable of the prayers of the proud Pharisee and the repentant tax-gatherer who "went down to his house justified" (Luke 18:14). MacArthur also supports this instantaneous idea upon John 5:24:(143)

> "Truly, truly, I say to you, he who hears My word, and believes Him who sent Me, has eternal life, and does not come into judgment, but has passed out of death into life."

MacArthur continues to say; "Eternal life is the present possession of all who believe Ä and by definition eternal life cannot be lost."(143) This is interesting that MacArthur says this in this particular discussion of justification. It will be shown that this is not an appropriate place to use that Scripture. It is true but not for a support of justification, but as a description of grace. MacArthur, himself, is beginning to be confused about theological terms wherein he later becomes almost incoherent.

To continue his summary of the Reformation doctrine of justification:

❏ Second Part:

> "Second, justification means the sinner is declared righteous, not actually made righteous. This goes hand in hand with the fact that justification is instantaneous. There is no process to be performed. Justification is a purely forensic (court of law) reality, a declaration God makes about the sinner. **Justification takes place in the court of God, not in the sinner's soul.** It is an objective fact, not a subjective phenomenon. it changes the sinner's status, not his nature. Certainly at the **moment of conversion** the sinner's nature is changed miraculously; old things pass away and all things are made new (2 Cor. 5:17). **But the actual changes that occur in the believer have to do with regeneration and sanctification, not justification.**"(143) Emphasis added.

Now MacArthur has added two other theological terms (sanctification and regeneration) to that of justification that are supposed to help us understand justification. The fact is they only confuse us more because no real world model of the power of God to save men has been established with corresponding definitions of the processes involved. MacArthur realizes he is getting off the track and tries to comfort us with the following statement that cautions us of the errors that could be made and to assure us that he is not making those errors. Unfortunately it can be shown that he is indeed making those errors while he cautions us to beware:

> "Again, it is **absolutely vital** to keep these ideas separate. **Regeneration** is a spiritual quickening in which the sinner **is born again with a new heart** (Ezek. 36:26; John 3:3); **sanctification is a lifelong process** whereby the believer is **conformed to the image of Christ** (2 Cor. 3:18). But **justification is an immediate decree**, a divine "not guilty" verdict on behalf of the sinner. This is inherent in the meaning of the word justify."(144) Emphasis added.

It will be shown convincingly that these terms are used in an interrelated (not in a separate) way here that confuse the whole power of God to save men and frustrate those seeking God with all their heart, mind, soul and strength. MacArthur continues with his summary consisting of his four Reformation ideas:

❑   Third Part:

> "Third, the Bible teaches that justification means righteousness is imputed, not infused. Righteousness is "reckoned," or credited to the account of those who believe (Rom. 4:3-25). They stand justified before God not because of their own righteousness, but because of a perfect righteousness outside themselves that is reckoned to them by faith (Phil. 3:9). Where does that perfect righteousness come from? It is God's own righteousness (Rom. 10:3), and it is ours in the person of Jesus Christ (1 Cor. 1:30; cf. Jr. 23:6; 33:16). We are united to Christ by faith - we are "in Christ" - and therefore accepted by God in His beloved son (Eph. 1:6-7). Christ's own perfect righteousness is credited to our personal account (Rom. 5:17, 19), just as the full guilt of our sin was imputed to Him. "He made Him who knew no sin to be sin on our behalf, that we might become the righteousness of God in Him" "(2 Cor. 5:21)…The point is that the only merit God accepts for salvation is that of Jesus Christ; nothing we can ever do could earn God's favor or add anything to the merit of Christ."(144)

MacArthur submits his final reformation idea:

❑   Fourth Part:

> "Fourth and finally, Scripture clearly teaches that we are **justified by faith alone**, not be faith plus works. "If it is by grace, it is no longer on the basis of works, otherwise grace is no longer grace" "(Rom. 11:6)."(144)

Observe here that MacArthur speaks of faith and grace interchangeably and synonymously as we discussed in a previous chapter on faith and grace. He speaks of faith and then quotes a verse that does not have the word faith in it but grace instead. This in itself is error as has been demonstrated clearly in the previous chapter. Also notice that MacArthur has said that justification is not any change in the sinners soul or heart but a decree from the court of God. If we are not changed in our hearts, minds, soul and body by Justification, then how would one know they are Justified? One who is redeemed knows his state of being. If the unsanctified, unregenerate person does not know if he is Justified, who else could know on earth? Who on earth can hear this "forensic declaration?" Who cares if we are Justified by faith or anything else if we can't know if we have it or not? MacArthur and others have made a distinction between a real world physical process of transformation and some kind of esoteric declaration in heaven that no one could possibly know, including the unchanged sinner himself. This is error! God does not Justify those that are not changed. There is no process to redeem a person outside rebirth by the death, resurrection and ascension of Christ Jesus. Therefore what purpose would even God have for Justification without redemption. Modern theologians, including MacArthur, confuse the first stirrings of faith in Christ with Justification and Salvation that come only upon the entrance into the Kingdom of Heaven at the revelation of being with Christ in his death, resurrection and ascension.

MacArthur provides the Catholic contrast to the Protestant idea of faith only, or grace only, by quoting the Council of Trent:

> "If anyone says that by the said sacraments of the New Law grace is not conferred through the act performed [ex opere operato, lit., "the work worked"] but [says] that faith alone in the divine promises is sufficient for the obtaining of grace, let him be anathema (Trent, sess. 7, canon 8)."(144-145)

MacArthur finishes his rebuttal to the Council of Trent with a summary of the four Reformation ideas:

> "In other words, grace is received not by faith but through works - specifically, through the Roman Catholic sacraments. But again, the Bible says, "By grace you have been saved through faith; and that not of yourselves, it is the gift of God; not as a result of works, that no one should boast" "(Eph. 2: 8-9)."(145)

It must be said that MacArthur has done a good job of presenting the contrast between Catholic and Protestant doctrine and the importance of knowing what each stand for. MacArthur also seems to have assimilated the definitions of these theological terms in the way they are used in contemporary protestant theology and Church life. Therefore MacArthur is representative of modern Protestantism and his work quoted here can provide an accurate contrast between modern Protestant theology and the spatial model of the Power of God to save all men.

We have observed that in the fourth point MacArthur moves from the use of the term Justification to the terms Faith, Grace and Salvation. **Yet he was trying to keep these terms separate**. He said it was **"absolutely vital."** All these terms are not synonymous even if they occur as a result of the same process. Now let us try to discern what the real problem is by applying our spatial model of God's power to save men. The application of the spacial model will provide an accurate, yet separate definition to the terms, Justification, Faith, Grace, Regeneration, Sanctification, "Born-Again," and Reconciliation.

Also notice that most all of MacArthur's definitions of justification regeneration, sanctification etc. do not involve a real world operation but something either imputed or reckoned to us that we do not possess, or obtain, but merely have declared about us in "God's court." Even the "born-again" experience is confined to a new heart. And somehow MacArthur gets a mere "not guilty" proclamation confused with the possession of eternal life! Nothing in all of MacArthur's labors point to the operation of the Power of God in Christ to translate, recreate, transform or redeem the cosmos by his death, resurrection, and ascension.

Understanding the difference between faith and grace, as provided in this book, can solve Modern confusion over faith, works and justification, sanctification and regeneration. You will remember that men of the Old Testament were justified by faith but they were also imperfect without us and longed to see and hear what we see and hear but did not. Justification therefore falls short of New Testament transformation from death into eternal life. Certainly we are justified at the end of this process but we don't stop along the way at some point of unknowable justification in our attraction to Christ. But we press on until we possess the perfect state of grace and come into the company of innumerable angels in the heavenly places. Many church going people experience the Holy Ghost but have never been born-again nor gone through the door of death, resurrection, and ascension into heaven to possess eternal life or grace.

We simply cannot use the term justification synonymously with terms like regeneration, translation, redemption and grace. Nor should we be overly concerned with justification as opposed to translation and transformation, which include the lesser concept of justification.

Consider the four scriptural qualities that MacArthur uses to determine the definition of justification. Even the qualities themselves contradict one another, e.g., instantaneous, possession of eternal life; declared righteous (but not made righteous); change in status only (not in nature); done in God's court (not in observable reality); imputed (not infused); in Christ; by faith alone not faith and works. How can we be in Christ possessing eternal life (by the instantaneous transformation experience of the death, resurrection, and ascension) and not be changed into a new creature but merely having faith in something not seen? None of this makes sense because the terms are not linked to a real world model that explains the power of God to save all men for ever in Christ Jesus.

Why do men continue to insert works into transformation? Even today preachers insist upon mixing rules and conformity and life-long work and effort into transformation. **Catholics have works** to be justified. **Protestants have the life-long conformity** to the image of Christ to be saved. Protestants reject the idea that one is changed in their condition upon Justification, so it is conformity that results in the actual change according to MacArthur and most Protestants. Both Protestants and Catholics have a formula to set people to working at righteousness and becoming Godly.

Men are saved, translated, redeemed, and transformed, born-again, regenerated, sanctified and justified by the operation of Christ upon the cosmos in his death, resurrection and ascension. That is the method and there simply is no long drawn out process for men to achieve sanctification and regeneration or justification. These conditions of being are provided by the acts of Jesus Christ. Jesus sanctifies (makes holy) us by his word he has spoken to us. Yes we become holy (the children of God) by the word and operation of Christ upon the cosmos. We are spared from punishment and declared to be just because we were attracted to Christ and believed him until we saw him and understood his power and let it operate upon us.

How and when does Justification occur if it is instantaneous but not a change in the nature of a man? Why would an unchanged man be justified? Is it when a man says: "I think I like this Jesus guy!" Is it when a man prays to God to understand and believe the Bible? Or is it when the man experiences the death, resurrection and ascension of Christ and is born-again with a new body, heart, mind and soul? Justification examples in the Old Testament are not solely sufficient to explain the operation of Christ. Christ's own parable about the comparison of the Pharisee and the repentant tax-gatherer are useful only to show the change in the direction of a man, not how he is ultimately saved by what Christ does to the cosmos. Surely, MacArthur isn't suggesting that New Testament theology is mere justification through repentance, nor becoming a friend of God by the act of willingness to sacrifice your own son on an altar!

New Testament theology must exceed justification and faith. The New Testament theology must possess grace and power. This theology must demonstrate knowledge of the operation of Christ and a complete surrender to its power to be regenerated and transformed into a new creature. Works is the Fruit of this new creature. **Long term conformity to the image** of Christ is not the means to salvation any more than **works**. Both suggest something that men do to achieve salvation or sanctification or justification. We shall see clearly that **life-long works or conformity achieves none of these**. Conformity to the image of Christ and works are the fruit of a regenerated creature. The previous discussion should provide a foundation for the development of the correct definition of the following theological terms:

Justification:

Justification then is a particular and partial character of a person who has undergone salvation or redemption or rebirth i.e., Death, Resurrection, and Ascension. But Justification does not tell the whole story nor describe fully the condition of the possessor of eternal life. The possessor is Justified not upon being attracted to Christ by faith, but upon his entrance into heaven by the death, resurrection, and ascension. It may take years to learn and trust this operation of Christ to allow its operation upon one's self but when ascension is experienced it is instantaneous and everlasting. The possessor now is made Just and righteous before God and man. But being just and justified is not the only character of a born-again person. This person has recognized his condition without God and has studied the process of salvation and surrendered to God's transforming operation through His

Son Christ Jesus. This makes the person honest before God and man wherein he is Just and Justified in God's sight. This takes place in the person and in the real observable world which can be shown to be God's real court.

The term Justification only appears three times in the whole Bible and it appears all three times in the book of Romans. Romans 4:24-25 says:

> "But for us also, to whom it shall be imputed, if we believe on him that raised up Jesus our Lord from the dead;

> "Who was delivered for our offences, and was raised again for our justification."

Notice however the process of Justification is not merely a forensic declaration without a real change to the person as stated by MacArthur in his synopsis of the reformation principles. Notice without the resurrection of Christ Jesus there is no Justification of any man. Christ was delivered for our offences and was **resurrected for our JUSTIFICATION**. This is not something that only happens in MacArthur's so-called court but is a physical operation performed by Christ upon the cosmos and effects the real person in their nature.

The other two appearances of the term Justification are in Romans 15:16 and 15:18. It makes more sense to quote the text from 15:15-15:18:

> "But not as the offence, so also is the free gift. For if through the offence of one many be dead, much more the grace of God, and the gift by grace, which is by one man, Jesus Christ, that abounded unto many.

> "And not as it was by one that sinned, so is the gift: for the judgment was by one to condemnation, but the free gift is of many offences unto **justification**.

> "For if by one man's offence death reigned by one; much more they which receive abundance of grace and of the gift of righteousness shall reign in life by one, Jesus Christ.)

> "Therefore as by the offence of one judgement came upon all men to condemnation; even so by the righteousness of one the free gift came upon all men unto **justification of life**."

(Emphasis added.)

Here again, Justification has noting to do with the act of a sinner, nor is this act one of a "court room declaration by God" about a sinner without a transformation of the person or the cosmos. It is, again, the act of Christ Jesus as a free gift to all mankind (or flesh that can perceive this operation). Therefore, It can be concluded that Justification is just one character received by those who can perceive this act and humble themselves to allow the operation to effect them i.e., to die and be resurrected with Christ and ascend with him to be with him where he is. There are other characteristics that the possessor of this state of grace receives.

Sanctification:

Sanctification is a state of being separated from the world of sin and made holy which is again instantaneous upon rebirth. Just as our own works do not justify us, we are not sanctified by our own works contrary to the teachings of many a clergyman. Sanctification is not a separate process, whereby we work to become more and more like Christ, as asserted by MacArthur and modern theologians. It is a state-of-being acquired by becoming one with Christ Jesus and God our Father. It indeed separates us from sin and makes us holy, but we don't do it. Christ does this instantaneously. We are not Sanctified by our life-long conformity to the image of Christ, as MacArthur suggests. We are Sanctified by the action of Christ Jesus.

Being Sanctified is yet another characteristic describing a born-again Christian. The Sanctified are separated from the behavior of the world. The Sanctified are made holy and complete in oneness with God and Christ. But the process by which we obtain Sanctification is still the same by which we obtain reconciliation, justification, redemption and rebirth, i.e., the Life, Death, Resurrection, and Ascension of Christ. Modern theologians suggest that grace and salvation and redemption is what Christ does but faith and sanctification is our response to that action of Christ. This is error. Justification, sanctification, reconciliation, regeneration, redemption are all the results of the operation of Christ upon the sinner. Faith is the attraction that man has to God, but grace is the free gift of the open physical doorway to the Kingdom of God provided by the operation of Christ Jesus upon the cosmos.

We shall see that Sanctification is what Christ does to himself and his spirit or space for us that we may become Sanctified by his operation. 2 Thessalonians 2:13 says:

> "But we are bound to give thanks alway to God for you, brethren beloved of the Lord, because God hath from the beginning chosen you to salvation through sanctification of the Spirit and belief of the truth."

This Scripture even suggests, accurately that sanctification, is not a process entered into after salvation to grow into the "image of Christ," but is another way to express the operation by which a person becomes saved. God has chosen you to be saved through the sanctification of the Spirit. We shall see who and what is sanctified in order for us to become sanctified. 1 Peter 1:2 speaks of the "sanctification of the Spirit, unto obedience and sprinkling of the blood of Jesus Christ." This is the sacrifice of Jesus or his death and resurrection for us. Ephesians 5:26 speaks of Christ sanctifying and cleansing the church washing it of water and the word. 1 Thessalonians 5:23 speaks of the God of peace, sanctifying the people. Now Hebrews 13:12 makes it very clear who is doing the sanctifying and how it is accomplished:

> "Wherefore Jesus also, that he might sanctify the people with his own blood, suffered without the gate."

It is Jesus that Sanctifies and he does it with his death and resurrection and ascension. Hebrews 9:13-14 says:

> "For if the blood of bulls and of goats, and the ashes of an heifer sprinkling the unclean, sanctifieth to the purifying of the flesh:

> "How much more shall the blood of Christ, who through the eternal Spirit offered himself without spot to God, purge your conscience from dead works to serve the living God?"

Hebrews 2:11 says that the Sanctifier and the Sanctified are one. Let us also hear what Christ himself prays to his Father regarding Sanctification in John 17:19:

> "And for their sakes I sanctify myself, that they also might be sanctified through the truth."

How are we then Sanctified? By the Sanctification of Christ Jesus and the truth about what Christ has done to the cosmos in the real observable world. St. Paul writes to the Corinthians (1 Cor. 1:2) to them that are Sanctified in Christ Jesus. Hebrews 10:14 says:

> "For by one offering he hath perfected for ever them that are sanctified."

And what is that offering but the death, resurrection, and ascension of Christ Jesus? You are then Sanctified when you have experienced the death, resurrection, and ascension of Christ Jesus and abide with him where he is now filling all of eternal space at one with the Father as he prayed that we would. Where then is this life-long work that we do conforming to the image of Christ? **We are conformed upon our death resurrection and ascension with Christ.** We are conformed upon the unity of our Spirits with Christ and his Father in the kingdom of Heaven at this present time. As Christ said, he was in heaven as he walked the earth, so are we when we walk the earth under the transformation of the cosmos by the operation of Christ Jesus. Let us review the Scriptures concerning the conformity to the image of Christ and see if it conflicts with what we have just said. Paul says in Romans 8:28-30:

> "And we know that all things work together for good to them that love God, to them who are the called according to his purpose.

> "For whom he did foreknow, he also did predestinate to be **conformed to the image of his Son**, that he might be the firstborn among many brethren.

> "Moreover whom he did predestinate, them he also called: and whom he called, them he also justified: and whom he justified, them he also glorified." Emphasis added.

Now isn't that interesting! How are we working on conformity if we have been predestined to be conformed to the image of God's Son? How did God predestinate us to be conformed to the image of His Son? God predestined us to be conformed to the image of His Son by His complete plan of salvation. That plan is to save men eternally through the physical operation upon the cosmos and all things therein in Christ's death, resurrection and ascension.

Too many Christians falsely perceive the "Christian walk" as one of constant growth without possession, seeking without obtaining, yearning without fulfillment. This is a constant and frustrating pursuit they call faith and grace. But, in truth, it is neither. This constant and frustrating pursuit is not Biblical Christianity but is the result of the modern false sociological equilibrium between science and Christianity. If nothing else is perceived from this book, let it be that a state of perfection is obtainable and available in Christ Jesus during your life time. Your entrance into the kingdom of heaven is accomplished here and now, not in the non-existent "other world." Do not listen to any one who suggests that you can just feel good or just hope in Christ. Rather, pursue perfection in rebirth until you possess your soul with confidence in the kingdom of heaven. This is precisely what Christ has brought to you in this observable cosmos we inhabit presently!

Reconciliation:

Reconciliation is the state of restoring our oneness with God through the operation of Christ upon the cosmos, i.e., Death, Resurrection and Ascension. This is not some different process, but merely one more way of describing what relationship a born-again person has with God. A walking dead man is now restored to God by the operation of Christ upon the cosmos. Colossians 1:20 says:

> "And, having made peace through the blood of his cross, by him to reconcile all things unto himself; by him, I say, whether they be things in earth, or things in heaven."

What things are Reconciled? All things both on earth and in heaven or the outer limits of eternal space! Does that include the buildings and the cars and the airplanes and all the people of every race and religion? Yes! The only problem is, the truth is only known to those that hear and perceive the operation of Christ for what it is and how it works. Some suggest that there is another way for Jews to be saved in this age. This is folly and falsehood. There is only one salvation for all men: that is in the transformation power of the cosmic operation of the death, resurrection, and ascension of Christ Jesus. To tell anyone otherwise would be to pervert and distort and hide the truth of Christ from them. This would be a wicked act. Christ said in John 8:55 "if I should say, I know him not, I shall be a liar like unto you: but I know him and keep his saying." Therefore to know the truth about the operation of God and to have experienced it and obtained possession of your own soul and tell another to be satisfied with less is to become a liar. Now how are we Reconciled to God? Romans 5:10 says:

> "For if, when we were enemies, we were reconciled to God by the death of his Son, much more, being reconciled, we shall be saved by his life."

Where is the life of Jesus now? It is recorded in the New Testament and it now fills all space and time. And we are in unity with it. How are we Reconciled then? We are Reconciled by the death resurrection and ascension of Jesus Christ. **Is this sounding redundant to you?** It should, yet it is the truth. There is no other operation or procedure to be Reconciled, saved, redeemed, sanctified, etc. 2 Corinthians 5:18-21 says:

> "And all things are of God, who hath **reconciled** us to himself by Jesus Christ, and hath given to us the ministry of **reconciliation;**

> "To wit, that God was in Christ, **reconciling** the world unto himself, not imputing their trespasses unto them; and hath committed unto us the word of **reconciliation.**

> "Now then we are ambassadors for Christ, as though God did beseech you by us: we pray you in Christ's stead, be ye **reconciled** to God.

> "For he hath made him to be sin for us, who knew no sin; that we might be made the righteousness of God in him."

> (Emphasis added.)

What things are of God? All things, the galaxies, the stars, the infinite space, the earth and all things therein. What has he Reconciled? All things! If an elephant from Mars was to ask me to tell him something he did not know, I would tell him of the transformation power of Christ Jesus the savior of all flesh and all things.

Can we deny any longer that Christ is not that hyperspace alien that the whole western, industrialized, scientific, world is waiting for? Does he not have power over the things of the cosmos? Did he not operate upon all physical things with his physical body? Did he not possess property in himself? Did he not transfer that property to us? Did he not give us the power to become the Sons of God? What then is the most powerful event in the history of the world? Is it the dropping of the atom bomb? Or is it the transformation of the entire cosmos from death into life by the operation of Christ Jesus? Who has received this power and this ministry and this word of reconciliation, sanctification, and justification? It is those who perceive it and allow it to operate upon themselves who then become ambassadors aliened and alienated or Sanctified to teach the truth.

Regeneration:

What is Regeneration? This term is used only **twice** in the entire Bible. Matthew 19:28 records the following:

> "And Jesus said unto them, Verily I say unto you, That ye which have followed me, in the **regeneration** when the son of man shall sit in the throne of his glory, ye also shall sit upon twelve thrones, judging the twelve tribes of Israel."

> (Emphasis added)

What period of time is the Regeneration? It is the period from the death resurrection and ascension of Christ until the time of Christ's appearance in the clouds with glory and the angels. We live in the Regeneration! Do we act like it? Do we perceive it? We cannot unless we know what has happened to the cosmos and all that is in it. The entire cosmos has been justified and Regenerated and reconciled and sanctified by the operation of Christ Jesus who sits in the throne of his Father in glory right now. Is there any theologian who can dispute that Christ does not sit on the throne of glory in heaven right now? Christ has ruled over the regenerated already for more than a thousand years and Satan has been loosed to once again deceive the nations. We are now entering the coming to the end of the short time of Satan's deception. Satan will soon be bound for the last time with the chain and cast forever into the bottomless pit. The chain is the knowledge of what Christ has done and where Satan lives in the deception of the nations. What can confirm that we live in the time of the Regeneration? Titus 3:5 says:

> "Not by works of righteousness which we have done, but according to his mercy he saved us, by the washing of **regeneration**, and renewing of the Holy Ghost:"

(Emphasis added)

The washing of Regeneration is the age in which we live. For Paul says that we have been washed in regeneration or the death, resurrection, and ascension of Christ Jesus. The church has lost this idea and wanes under the false sociological equilibrium.

Redemption:

Redemption is just another word for salvation or taking back. A search for this term in the Bible will result in a redundant use of words we have already covered. This reveals, again, that the method of redemption is not our work or effort to be something but the act of Christ Jesus. 1 Corinthians 1:30 says:

> "But of him are ye in Christ Jesus, who of God is made unto us wisdom, and righteousness, and sanctification, and redemption:"

What then can be said about the process of the "Christian walk," other than it is one of obtaining knowledge about what Christ has done for us, and allowing ourselves to be transformed by it. Where are good deeds in this process? No where! Our deeds are the natural fruit of our perception of what has occurred to us. The reflection of the love of God towards us is a natural response to obtaining eternal life (the possession of all things including our own souls). This natural response is the fruit of a new creature a new tree that bears real fruit fit for the kingdom of God.

Doing the work and will of God is just as Jesus said it is: To believe on the one in whom God sent, and to know that it is the will of God that all men come into the knowledge of what his Son has done. This of course has to be communicated to cultures in a way that they understand and in a way that is true.

Predestination:

This is a concept that many have trouble with that is easily explained by Alien Physics. The misunderstanding of this Biblical principle has led to an idea that is new in Protestant theology. A trip was planned by our church to attend a presentation by R.C. Sproul in Austin, Texas. My pastor and others of us heard this great theologian say that he no longer feels compelled to tell some people about Christ Jesus because he has no idea whether or not they are predestined to be in the kingdom of heaven. The huge crowd chuckled at this statement and I smiled as well. However, I realized that this is in error.

Predestination is not a matter of God selecting people by name and address to be members of His elite club in the sky. Predestination is the term given to God's comprehensive operation of salvation through His Son's death, resurrection and ascension. Therefore, all men are predestined by God to be saved by this all-encompassing operation from earth to the furthermost galaxy. However, that still does not guarantee that all people will hear or accept this information and allow it to operate upon them.

Some theologians will maintain that it is this part of hearing and accepting that is called predestination. But that cannot be called predestination by definition. The acceptance or rejection of salvation is a matter of opportunity, presentation and free will. Predestination is a known fact for all people but their opportunity, understanding and free will cannot be known by any of us. Therefore it is evident that we have no choice but to tell all we can of the salvation available in Christ Jesus.

The new element of Protestant theology that comes from a misunderstanding of predestination is the concept that Christians must support Jews in their new state of Israel regardless of their acceptance of Christ Jesus as the messiah. It is taught by "conservative fundamentalist preachers" like John Haggie, of San Antonio, and many others that Israel must be supported against their lost neighbors at all cost by Christians because it is somehow Biblical. But, it is clear that Israel is also lost by their rejection of Christ Jesus.

If Christians are compelled to love all people including our enemies (because of the free love that Christ showed us), how can we support the lost house of Israel over another lost group? Christians cannot and the church of early America knew that. Joseph Sewell, D.D. preached before the Governor and Council of Representatives in Massachusetts-Bay, New-England on December 3, 1740. He said there that the Jews or God's people "by rejecting the offers of the gospel made to them by his apostles; the wrath of God came upon them to the uttermost by the Romans, and they are made an execration and a curse unto this day."[14] This new theology, that says the Jews must be supported no matter what, has proved very

---

[14] Joseph Sewell, D.D., *Political Sermons of the American Founding Era, 1730-1805*, ed. Ellis Sandoz (Indianapolis, Indiana: Liberty Fund, Inc., 1998), 40

expensive indeed for the United States after the attack on the Pentagon and World Trade Center.

It is clear that modern industrialized culture, both eastern and western, has attempted to make its own "religion," with the hope of meeting an alien and the removal of that 2000 year old "story" of Christ Jesus. We have seen that without a firm spatial model of the real observable world (describing the power of Christ Jesus to transform the cosmos from death into life) we have no clear definition of any theological terms. We obtain Justification, Sanctification, Reconciliation, Redemption, and a perfect state of Grace upon our passage from death into the Kingdom of God or eternal space at the experience of the death, resurrection and ascension of Christ Jesus. Amen.

PART III - CLARIFICATION OF THEOLOGICAL TERMS

CHAPTER 15 - THE SPATIAL MODEL

What is at the core of Satan's power in the modern industrialized world? What is the cause of the paralysis of the modern Christian Church? What causes the confusion of theological terms and the obvious contradictions that theologians recite as sound doctrine, even when they painstakingly apply many Scriptures?

What is it that will ignite a new revival of power and strength and integrity in the Christian life and the church? The answer must be in the clear understanding of what is real and what Christ actually performed on the cosmos and how. Further, is there not a model of the real world that lies beneath the mere language of the Bible that unites all the Scriptures?

This leads us immediately back to the spatial model of our knowledge of the Singular Essence of God or Eternal Space as God. And from that flows His ability to be at one with Christ His only begotten Son and with us in the Holy Spirit revealed by Christ Jesus. This is the revelation of God's Trinity of Personality, not the continued mystery of God's existence. All other properties of God and Christ that we have discussed earlier herein also are consistent with this view of God and His triune existence. Even His Domain Triad is in recognition of this spatial model. Man's unique Complimentary Image Properties are in harmony with this model. All of it has to do with Space or Spirit.

This is obviously why a reading of the Bible will give you the idea that you can know, comprehend, be at one with, and become the son of God. But when you read commentaries or theologians on the subject, you get the idea that all is never-ending and that you never really come to a full knowledge of anything or enter into heaven while you are on earth. These theologians have studied in a period when even the reference texts and seminaries and colleges and universities do not comprehend the Bible nor its power. This is why people have a problem with witnessing, other than in the most basic form of testimony. I have not heard an intellectual testimony that stands out in my mind. Most testimony has to do with becoming a better person: "I was a drunk, but now I don't drink at all." What about: "I was ignorant of the world and how Christ could do the things he said he could. But now I perceive that, and when I understood it, I was translated from one kind of creature to another by the operation that He performed on the cosmos. I am transformed by His power to contain the world including the galaxies and then lay down His life and take it again. He was buried and on the third day. He was resurrected and walked with His disciples and then He went up into the heaven above us which contains us. God through His Son reconciled the world and the cosmos unto Himself. By this operation I have died, been resurrected and ascended with Him to the kingdom of Heaven."

It is amazing that modern theologians toy with the notion that Scripture can be decrypted or by viewing Scripture as hidden code. Some have come up with the identity of the Antichrist by taking every tenth letter of the Bible. This reminds me of the days when we would play records backward and slower to find hidden messages. These so-called theologians that look for hidden meaning and prophesy by decoding Scripture miss the clear interpretation of the English language and the power therein. Other so-called Christians and theologians are speaking in unknown tongues, yet can't understand the known tongue of English. These movements are in reaction to a dead and powerless theology that is adopted by the modern false sociological equilibrium between science and Christianity. If Christians perceive the truth of plain Scripture in English they would not need mystery, unknown tongues, and hidden message codes. The whole idea behind Christ is revelation of what once was mystery. Yet today, well-respected theologians are creating mystery from revelation. This is because they still don't have the revelation of what Christ has done and the comprehensive nature of it.

"You are beautiful beyond description, too marvelous for words, too great for comprehension etc...I stand in awe of you." These are the words to a song that we were playing in church one day. One of the musicians said that there was a chord missing. And I said that there was also some theology missing. This statement caused a stir. This is the type of theology that has crippled the modern church. If we think that, you will never attempt to comprehend or express the wonder of Christ Jesus. We will not attempt to use words to describe the power of God or His Son. We will not try to glorify Christ or His Father because we don't know words good enough. And if we don't comprehend, how can we have the confidence to declare His Lordship over the cosmos or how He has been able to redeem it?

Those disturbed by my statement, asked, "what do you mean there's theology missing?" I said that St. Paul prayed that we might be able to comprehend with all saints what are the breadth, and length, and depth, and height of God's love through Christ Jesus. They did not believe me and said they had never heard this. Of course I could not remember the verse number. They said that they could back up their claim that God's love was unsearchable. I replied that we live in an age where we are hated and despised for knowing things and having the guts to declare that we know something and the truth of things. I then said with a teasing smile; "well, let me make all men mad today by saying that I know and comprehend and have words to describe the power of God." Ephesians 3:14-19:

> "For this cause I bow my knees unto the Father of our Lord Jesus Christ,
>
> "Of whom the whole family in heaven and earth is named,
>
> "That he would grant you, according to the riches of his glory, to be strengthened with might by his Spirit in the inner man;
>
> "That Christ may dwell in your hearts by faith; that ye, being rooted and grounded in love,
>
> "May be able to comprehend with all saints what is the breadth, and length, and depth, and height;

147

"And to know the love of Christ, which passeth knowledge, that ye might be filled with all the fulness of God."

Notice how Paul prays that we obtain what he by implication has obtained and expects all saints to obtain - COMPREHENSION; TO KNOW; THAT WHICH PASSES KNOWLEDGE! Paul is not talking about slaving over Scripture all your life and failing to grasp knowledge because it is beyond knowing. He is praying that you obtain knowledge that is not available from any source outside of Christ's power to work on the cosmos. No amount of study of the heavens will produce this knowledge as is evident in modern astronomy and physics etc.. But this knowledge is obtainable, and it is above and operates to correct wrong ideas both in Christianity and science.

Notice the contrast between the amazing comprehensive speech of St. Paul and the dull, mundane and powerless speech of modern theology. Why? Because modern theology is void of the power that describes how Christ Jesus was able to operate over the observable cosmos.

What was the cause that Paul spoke of in the beginning of this powerful comprehensive statement about what is available in the knowledge of Christ Jesus? Friends I begin by saying that chills are running all over my body for the thrill of the greatness of what I am about to quote to you! I am not crying, I am empowered by what I read here! This is the act of the MIND, not the heart! This is not conviction and remorse and broken heartedness. This is power from on high through the Holy Spirit acknowledged by the mind, that human organ forgotten and ignored and abandoned to science by the modern church. Ephesians Chapter 3: 1-14:

"For this cause I Paul, the prisoner of Jesus Christ for you Gentiles,

"If ye have heard of the dispensation of the grace of God which is given me to youward:

"How that by revelation he made known to me the mystery; (as I wrote afore in few words,

"Whereby, when ye read, ye may understand my knowledge in the mystery of Christ)

"Which in other ages was not made known unto the sons of men, as it is now revealed unto his holy apostles and prophets by the Spirit;

"That the Gentiles should be fellowheirs, and of the same body, and partakers of his promise in Christ by the gospel:

"Whereof I was made a minister, according to the gift of the grace of God given unto me by the effectual working of his power.

"Unto me, who am less than the least of all saints, is this grace given, that I should preach among the Gentiles the unsearchable riches of Christ;

"And to make all men see what is the fellowship of the mystery, which from the beginning of the world hath been hid in God, who created all things by Jesus Christ:

"To the intent that now unto the principalities and powers in heavenly places might be known by the church the manifold wisdom of God,

"According to the eternal purpose which he purposed in Christ Jesus our Lord:

"In whom we have boldness and access with confidence by the faith of him.

"Wherefore I desire that ye faint not at my tribulations for you, which is your glory."

How extensive then is our knowledge of God through his Son Jesus Christ? The church is to know the manifold wisdom of God. Yes, Paul speaks of mystery, but how does he speak of it? He says that it once was a mystery, but his new appointed job as a minister is to make ALL MEN see the manifold wisdom of God, which was the eternal purpose proposed in Christ Jesus. And now, not only do we have this knowledge revealed to us, but also we have boldness and access, not only knowledge but presence with God—oneness with Him through His Son! How much wisdom of God do we have access to? We have access to the manifold wisdom of God or **great abundance** and not only great abundance but the kind that is formable into concepts that contain many facets. Manifold can mean not only abundance but also the collection of abundance into a singular system as a **manifold connects** things of a similar type. God not only has abundant wisdom but it is understandable. Now not only is God's great complexity organized into memorable categories but reducible to a singular essence. Not only can we know God's manifold wisdom but also we can be at one with His singular essence.

St. Paul goes on to pray on his knees that we obtain what he has apparently obtained himself. He prays that we may be able to comprehend with all saints what is the breadth, and length, and depth, and height. Fellow saints! That is the whole of it. He prays that we would know the whole of the manifold wisdom of God, which has been kept secret from the creation of the world until now! He prays that you and me and all saints everywhere will know the unsearchable riches of Christ in their full width, length, height and depth. Wow! What once was unknowable and unsearchable is now made known! God isn't unsearchable anymore!

And he doesn't stop there. Paul goes on to say that he prays that we will be filled with all the fullness of God. He is saying that we are to be at one with God, full of all that He is and has. As we have discovered earlier in this book, God contains all and fills all and we are to do the same. This is what Christ Jesus did and that is what Christ said that we were to do. Remember the Complementary Image Properties never so revealed prior to Christ. Jesus contained all space and filled all space and was at one with the Father who begot him by His own space or Spirit. We too obtain the power of envelopment and impletion (or containment, and filling). We receive the power to become the Sons of God at One with Him through Christ's operation upon the cosmos. Now, surely some will say that Paul states that the riches of Christ are unsearchable in verse 8:

> "Unto me, who am less than the least of all saints, is this grace given, that I should preach among the Gentiles the unsearchable riches of Christ:"

Paul is saying that he is by grace teaching what was once unsearchable and hid to the Gentiles. How could one preach what he knows not? That would make for some short sermons! It surely makes for some boring sermons! St. Paul never bored anybody with a preaching job. Paul did not stop with this statement. He went on to say that the intent, or manifold wisdom of God, which was only known by the principalities and powers in heavenly places, is to be known by the church on earth. In other words, Paul is saying that he is now preaching the manifold wisdom of God (in its full magnitude) which was at one time unsearchable and hid from the world. Paul states in Romans 11:32-33:

> "For God hath concluded them all in unbelief, that he might have mercy upon all.

> "O the depth of the riches both of the wisdom and knowledge of God! how unsearchable are his judgements, and his ways past finding out!"

But this is a reference to Isaiah 40:12-14 and others, such as Jeremiah 23:18 and Job 15:8:

> "Who hath measured the waters in the hollow of his hand, and meted out heaven with the span, and comprehended the dust of the earth in a measure, and weighed the mountains in scales, and the hills in a balance?

> "Who hath directed the Spirit of the Lord, or being his counsellor hath taught him?

> "With whom took he counsel, and who instructed him, and taught him in the path of judgement, and taught him knowledge, and shewed to him the way of understanding?"

Now get hold of your chair! This, itself, is a reference to Christ Jesus who was with God and counseled with God in making men in their own image! And what is that image? What are the image properties? The Holy Trinity, three in one, God the Father, God the Son, and God, the Holy Spirit. Yes it is Christ who has done all these things with God and counseled with Him. And guess what we have now! St. Paul makes it clear that we have the mind and knowledge of Christ who was with God from the beginning and is now with Him forever and we are with them both in the heavenly places. 1 Corinthians 2:14-16:

> "But the natural man receiveth not the things of the Spirit of God: for they are foolishness unto him: neither can he know them, because they are spiritually discerned.

"But he that is spiritual judgeth all things, yet he himself is judged of
no man.

"For who hath known the mind of the Lord, that he may instruct him?
But we have the mind of Christ."

(Emphasis added)

Now further let us hear from Christ Jesus himself in John 15:15:

"Henceforth I call you not servants; for the servant knoweth not what
his lord doeth: but I have called you friends; for **all things** that I have
heard **of my Father** I have made **known unto you.**"

(Emphasis added)

Here's what we have in Christ Jesus today:
1. We have the once unsearchable riches of God now openly preached by St.
    Paul.
2. We have boldness and access to oneness with the Father God.
3. We have the knowledge of the width, length, depth and height of God.
4. We are now filled with all the fullness of God.
5. We know all that His only begotten Son knew of His own Father and
    Creator of the cosmos and all therein.
6. We have the MIND OF CHRIST, THE MIND OF THE SON OF GOD!

Modern theology however has avoided the implications of the Scriptures we
have just covered concerning the potential of mankind ever possessing the
knowledge of God. How quickly modern theology skips this by asserting that this
knowledge is never obtained in this life or the one to come for that matter. This is
clearly an error based upon the idea that we really can't know God and that error
flows from the lack of a model that allows our oneness with God or that explains
how it can occur. Even the Trinity that theologians pound on the pulpit that would
normally explain some of this is covered up with mystery. To prove this point, a
quote is provided from Alfred Martin Th.D. (Dean of faculty, Professor of Old
Testament Synthesis, Moody Bible Institute, Chicago) from the Wycliffe Bible
Commentary.

Ephesians 3:18:

"May be able to comprehend with all saints what is the breadth, and
length, and depth, and height;"

This quote from the Wycliffe Bible Commentary is his attempt to explain
Ephesians 3:18:

"May be able to comprehend with all saints. A knowledge that every
believer ought to have. What is the breadth, and length, and depth,
and height. This sort of knowledge would be continually growing, for
we could never measure the dimensions. 19. To know the love of
Christ which passeth knowledge. Some things we cannot know fully;
often we have experiences that we cannot understand or explain.

> However, the same root is used here in the infinitive and in the noun, and the idea seems to be to know that which is essentially unknowable-yet to know it enough so that we can rejoice in it. Filled with all the fulness of God. God is infinite and we are finite. This is of course paradoxical, but it is an attempt to convey in language that will mean something to us, the superabundance of grace available to us from our heavenly Father through our Lord Jesus Christ."[15]

The lack of power and knowledge is unmistakable in those theological words from the upper rooms of the modern Christian Church. This reflects no experience, no idea or notion that any power is even available here. All is continual growing and growing and growing and never really coming up with any real power. Wycliffe makes these unsupportable generalities about mankind because they heard them somewhere and the crowd liked them. How did they arrive at the notion that men are finite? Christ said that he that was born of Spirit is Spirit and he that is born of flesh is flesh. Now, it is agreeable that the unregenerate man is finite but we are talking about what Christians should have in their conversion or transformation. They clearly become infinite. Christ also said that he that would believe on him would never die.

Oh, now we can never measure the dimensions! Where do they get this stuff? It's not from the Bible! Christ measured the dimensions and in fact is the dimension and outer limits of eternal space. This is what makes him the Son of God! The shape of space is the figure of Jesus Christ in the flesh. He measured it, he contains it and he commands it and holds it together and he created all things within it. And that, friends, is in the book of Colossians in the New Testament.

The Wycliffe theologians assert that we can never know the unknowable but we can now know just enough to rejoice. WELL PRAISE GOD for that little tidbit and all those experiences, we can't explain! What kind of theological analysis is this? What Scripture reference is given to come up with that?

To be filled with all the fullness of God, means to the Wycliffe bunch, a paradoxical way of trying to communicate to finite man all the abundant grace that is available through our lord Jesus Christ. What does Martin in Wycliffe mean anyway? Why is it that St. Paul makes more sense than Martin? This is not a paradox to get dummies to understand something about free prizes available in Jesus. No! It is, rather, a straightforward prayer that we will be filled with all the fullness of God. In other words we become infinite like God is. We become changed. We become new creatures, remember! Wow! Many undiscerning Christians read this kind of stuff in big books and believe that it makes sense, but it doesn't. Notice when the author doesn't know how to explain something they will just throw in a big word like "grace" and use a phrase such as; "it's just a way to say how wonderful grace is." This says nothing about anything. Don't ask them to

---

[15] Alfred Martin, Th.D., *The Wycliffe Bible Commentary*, ed. Everett F. Harrison (Chicago: Moody Press, 1979),1309.

define grace either! But the modern church eats this stuff up. Modern Christians do not demand anything for intellectual proof. The reason, of course, is that they have abandoned the mind or one of the quaternion components of mankind required to love God. This Scripture is not talking about anything other than being filled with all the fullness of God. It is not about a particular measure of grace, but an existence with God without and beyond measure—hyper oneness with God!

All of this confusion is again based upon the lack of a real world model of the operation of Christ and the explanation of His power in the real world we live in. Without this we cannot derive a correct alignment and harmony of Scripture. It is not enough to quote all the Scripture with similar words. The Scripture must be supporting or modifying a model in the real world that can verify the power of God with our experience in the Holy Spirit. The mere stacking up of a bunch of Scriptures related to a topic does not in itself generate the correct conclusion. We must look for the real world spatial model behind the words that results in the exaltation of the Power and Lordship of Christ over all the cosmos. No amount of Bible study will substitute for a revelation of this model behind the words contained in the whole Bible.

Christ said that the meek shall inherit the world and that the Kingdom of Heaven belongs to the poor in spirit. How can we assert that in this world, if we do not know how this occurs and when? Most believe this occurs at death. I, however, declare that I have inherited the world as of this present time. And I know how I have inherited the world. And I further know and proclaim that I have possession and have entered into the Kingdom of Heaven. This is not something that occurs in death but occurs on earth. For Christ made it clear that he that would believe upon him would never die. This wasn't clever talk about the second death that many theologians assert, but was a straightforward declaration of a fact. If you have obtained eternal life by the operation of Christ's death resurrection and ascension, how then would you be able to die? When we discover that we were not alive until we were born again, through the process just outlined, then we cannot die even if our bodies are taken from us in this age or any other.

To further prove that it is the lack of a real world spatial model that confuses theology and paralyzes the church, the following contradictions by theologians are provided. The first case is how Wayne Grudem contradicts himself in his description of the term "heaven." Wayne Grudem writes:

> "1. Christ Ascended to a Place. After Jesus' resurrection, he was on earth for forty days (Acts 1:3), then he led them out to Bethany, just outside Jerusalem, and "lifting up his hands, he blessed them. While he blessed them, he parted from them, and was carried up into heaven" (Luke 24:50-51)."[16]

---

[16] Wayne Grudem, *Systematic Theology- An Introduction to Biblical Doctrine*, (Grand Rapids, Michigan, Zondervan Publishing House, 1994), 616-617.

Then Grudem quotes Acts 1:9-11 another account of the ascension again describing his going into heaven. But it is Grudem that jumps from these simple accounts into creating a place rather than accepting just what is being said. Grudem makes a serious mistake by not including other Scriptures, and the spatial model behind them, to arrive at the following conclusion:

"These narratives describe an event that is clearly designed to show the disciples that Jesus went to a place. He did not suddenly disappear from them, never to be seen by them again, but gradually ascended as they were watching, and then a cloud (apparently the cloud of God's glory) took him from their sight. But the angels immediately said that he would come back in the same way in which he had gone into heaven. The fact that Jesus had a resurrection body that was subject to spatial limitations (it could be at only one place at one time) means that Jesus went somewhere when he ascended into heaven."(617)

Notice that the upper room accounts are missing from this analysis or systematic theology. The upper room accounts after the resurrection of Jesus record that they were all in the room and the doors were shut and then Jesus appeared before them. Jesus didn't come knocking and they didn't open the door for him. Yes he had a body, but it was one that was not limited to spatial limitations the way ours are presently. This was the glorified body that can be manifested and then demanifested, which we also will have. John 20:26:

"And after eight days again his disciples were within, and Thomas with them: then came Jesus, **the doors being shut**, and stood in the midst, and said, Peace be unto you."

(Emphasis added)

Notice that Grudem fails to associate all of space with God or Christ Jesus. Grudem searches for a place as many Christians do. Christ was also talking about a place but it was a very large place not a very small place. This place was the Kingdom of Heaven and it is one and the same with the whole of the cosmos. Eternal Space is the Kingdom. With this recognition of Heaven, Hell is automatically defined as that which is outside of eternal space—nowhere. That is why you do not want to remain in hell, because that is a no place, a contradiction of the truth. To be cast out of the Kingdom is a non-existence, cut off from all space and all life and all of God. With out this, salvation is not explainable, glory is not shoutable, exaltation is not possible, and worship is vain and powerless. To Grudem, heaven is a place of a measurable size, floating around in the sky above, like Grudem views God himself. I must also say that travel becomes a real problem with this idea. Travel is not a problem when Christ is the envelopment of eternal space and can manifest himself anywhere in it at any time, including the "twinkling of an eye."

Grudem goes on in an attempt to support his idea that the resurrected Christ is finite and that he went to a finite Kingdom of Heaven:

"It is surprising that even some evangelical theologians hesitate to affirm that heaven is a place or that Jesus ascended to a definite location somewhere in the space-time universe. Admittedly we cannot now see where Jesus is, but that is not because he passed into some ethereal "state of being" that has no location at all in the space-time universe, but rather because our eyes are unable to see the unseen spiritual world that exists all around us. There are angels around us, but we simply cannot see them because our eyes do not have that capacity: Elisha was surrounded by an army of angels and chariots of fire protecting him from the Syrians at Dothan, but Elisha's servant was not able to see those angels until God opened his eyes so that he could see things that existed in the spiritual dimension (2Kings 6:17)..." (617)

I want to point out a glaring contradiction within Grudem's statement. He rejects with confidence the idea that Jesus has passed into some ethereal "state of being." Yet in the same paragraph he insists that Jesus went to a finite place in space, but one in which we cannot see in a spiritual world. Well just how is the ethereal world different from the unseen spiritual world? The very definition of ethereal is non-material. And what is the definition of the unseen spiritual world but the non-material world. Funk and Wagnall's third definition of ether is: "A non-material medium assumed to pervade all of space and to be responsible for the transmission of light, heat, gravitational effects, and all forms of energy and radiation." The fourth definition is: "The upper air." Funk and Wagnall's definition of etherealize is "to make or become ethereal; *spiritualize*."

This statement made by Grudem is support for our present false sociological equilibrium based upon the real observable world of science and the unknown, unseen, unknowable, impenetrable and unprovable world of "religion" that must be groped around in with our probing spiritual minds, as if that were possible. One can see what a deadly notion that produces! Ignorance, and the most far fetched ideas, thrive in this environment. Under such a notion, the power of God and His Christ diminish to almost nothing. Christ and God are thrown into the same category with demons and witches and the like. The study of Christ becomes a study of magic where one must abandon the mind and rely on "faith" only. Thanks be to Christ and His Father that we must love the Lord our God with all our heart, **mind**, soul and strength. Let's continue with our minds to see what is recorded in 2 Kings 6:15-20:

"And when the servant of the man of God was risen early, and gone forth, behold, an host compassed the city both with horses and chariots. And his servant said unto him, Alas, my master! how shall we do?

"And he answered, Fear not: for they that be with us are more than they that be with them.

"And Elisha prayed, and said, LORD, I pray thee, open his eyes, that he may see. And the LORD opened the eyes of the young man; and he saw: and, behold, the mountain was full of horses and chariots of fire round about Elisha.

"And when they came down to him, Elisha prayed unto the LORD, and said, Smite this people, I pray thee, with blindness. And he smote them with blindness according to the word of Elisha.

"And Elisha said unto them, This is not the way, neither is this the city: follow me, and I will bring you to the man whom ye seek. But he led them to Samaria.

"And it came to pass, when they were come into Samaria that Elisha said, LORD, open the eyes of these men, that they may see. And the LORD opened their eyes, and they saw; and, behold, they were in the midst of Samaria."

What if you were in a modern war zone, surrounded by tanks and mortars, closing in on you and all you had were rifles? Would you want to have a vision of chariots of fire and horses? Or would you like to see a host of jets circling the area with stinger missiles? Or would you like to see the world as it is with confidence to fight to the last breath? And what is the world as it is? If one sees it they will indeed have confidence to fight the fight in the almighty power of Christ over the cosmos.

These Scriptures are about confidence and perception. The army of Syrians surrounding Elisha were not blinded to the point that they had to be led so they would not stumble upon rocks and trees. They were blinded in their wisdom and knowledge so they could not perceive where they were or where their destiny would be. Yet they walked in their sight all the way, not stumbling upon one another. Likewise, with Elisha's servant. The servant did not have the confidence of Elisha and could not see the power of God, nor did he have confidence in his own power. Notice that Elisha did not say, "Lord let my servant see the chariots of fire." It is not known if Elisha himself saw the chariots of fire. But Elisha knew the power of God. The vision of horses and chariots was sufficient for his servant's confidence. Also notice that the horses and chariots of fire were not used in any way other than to strengthen the confidence of Elisha's servant.

The prayer that Elisha prayed was sufficient to blind the perception of the Syrians into following Elisha into the hand of their captors. So, why were the horses and chariots of fire there? This was the vision that Elisha's servant would accept as sufficient power when he had no other concept of God's power. As I have asked in the beginning. Would this same vision be sufficient for you when surrounded by modern tools of destruction? Or, would you prefer another vision or truth? This vision of horses and chariots of fire is not the maximum power of God.

Notice further that Elisha says, "for they that be with us are more than they that be with them." The New Testament version of that statement is that of 1 John 4:4:

"Ye are of God, little children, and have overcome them: because greater is he that is in you, than he that is in the world."

Our vision is greater than that of Elisha's servant who required horses and chariots of fire. But today we have a truth that exceeds that of flaming chariots and horses, jets with stinger missiles, or nuclear star war devices. We have the truth of Christ and his operation upon the cosmos as the supreme power in the universe. Now let us turn to the blindness that has stricken the modern theological world. Grudem goes on to bask in ignorance and hypocrisy in this next statement:

> "Of course we cannot now say exactly where heaven is. Scripture often pictures people as ascending up into heaven (as Jesus did, and Elijah) or coming down from heaven (as the angels in Jacob's dream, Gen. 28:12), so we are justified in thinking of heaven as somewhere "above" the earth. Admittedly the earth is round and it rotates, so where heaven is we are simply unable to say more precisely-Scripture does not tell us. But the repeated emphasis on the fact that Jesus went somewhere (as did Elijah, 2 Kings 2:11), and the fact that the New Jerusalem will come down out of heaven from God (Rev. 21:2), all indicate that there is clearly a localization of heaven in the space-time universe. Those who do not believe in Scripture may scoff at such an idea and wonder how it can be so, just as the first Russian cosmonaut who came back from space and declared that he did not see God or heaven anywhere, but that simply points to the blindness of their eyes toward the unseen spiritual world; it does not indicate that heaven does not exist in a certain place. In fact, the ascension of Jesus into heaven is designed to teach us that heaven does exist as a place in the space-time universe."(617)

Wow! Grudem admits that he does not see heaven. He further suggests that we cannot see it either and that Scripture does not tell us where heaven is. This is outrageously bad theology, and just bad Bible study. The Bible is full of the precise location of heaven and where it is, what it is bound by, and where it is located. Not only does Grudem state that he can't see heaven, but then he condemns a Russian cosmonaut for admitting that he could not see heaven either. What we have here is agreement between a (presumed atheist) Russian cosmonaut and an American (presumed saved) theologian. Why does Grudem refer to the "blindness of **their** eyes" rather than the blindness of **our** eyes? **Both men could not see heaven** or know where it is or know its boundaries. Yet I declare to you all now and forever that I know where it is and I see it at all times and I learned it from the Scriptures contained in the King James Bible. Both of these men suffer from the same cultural miseducation concerning Scripture and science. Both suffer from the same false sociological equilibrium. Both seek to lead the other and both are blind and have fallen into the ditch.

This is the reason for the new theological category fixing the domain of God. This we call the Domain Triad. It is summarized by the short phrase; "I AM ONE LIVING." I AM refers to eternal, ONE refers to undivided both in dimension and being, and LIVING refers to the world of the living. Then where is God and His Kingdom? He is eternal space or spirit in which we live, undivided, into unknown impenetrable places, but in the dimension, in which we live and observe all the day long. If you have forgotten the Biblical references for this phrase review the chapter on the Domain Triad. The place that Christ prepares for us is the entire cosmos that he operated upon in order to effect salvation for all men for all time. He did this by his power to contain and fill all of eternal space, which is his Father. They share all of space together. The Holy Spirit is this same eternal space that God and Jesus share with us.

Confidence and power come from knowing the truth in Christ and it is more powerful than a hill covered with horses and chariots of fire. If one is in command of perception and knowledge he does not need armies of chariots and horses! Elisha knew this as well.

What is at the center of this theological confusion? First let us remember that God is not the author of confusion and secondly he wants us to find Him. But we must find Him in truth and reality. And His will is that all men be saved. Now let us define Him as He wishes us to in accuracy rather than confusion. It is amazing that theologians go out of their way to think up the most inapplicable analogies while denying the obvious. Grudem states:

> "God Does Not Have Spatial Dimensions: While it seems necessary for us to say that God's whole being is present in every part of space, or at every point in space, it is also necessary to say that God cannot be contained by any space. no matter how large. Solomon says in his prayer to God, "But will God indeed dwell on the earth? Behold, heaven and the highest heaven cannot contain you; how much less this house which I have built!" (1 Kings 8:27). Heaven and the highest heaven cannot contain God; indeed, he cannot be contained by the largest space imaginable (cf. Isa.66:1-2, Acts 7:48). While the thought that God is everywhere present with his whole being ought to encourage us greatly in prayer no matter where we are, the fact that no one place can be said to contain God should also discourage us from thinking that there is some special place of worship that gives people special access to God: he cannot be contained in any one place."(174)

This statement contradicts what Grudem just laboriously attempted to prove about heaven as being a place fixed in the space-time universe. Why would heaven not be a place where God would be at his fullest? **Why would His Kingdom be less than Himself?** Why cannot He and His Kingdom be the same? Why must Grudem have a little place called Heaven where only part of God's completeness dwelled? Why have God living everywhere and us living on some compound in there somewhere? Not that God could not make it so, but why should that be so? And how does that view impact the power of God in Christ through out the cosmos? If God has acted upon the entire cosmos (to redeem creation through His Son, reconciling all the heaven and earth unto Himself) why is heaven less complete than the cosmos that Christ operated upon? Grudem goes on to deny God's singular spatial essence despite the fact that Christ himself said that God was a spirit, or a non-material, or spatial.

"We should guard against thinking that God extends infinitely far in all directions so that he himself exists in a sort of infinite, unending space. Nor should we think that God is somehow a "bigger space" or bigger area surrounding the space of the universe as we know it. All these ideas continue to think of God's being in spatial terms, as if he were simply an extremely large being. Instead, we should try to avoid thinking of God in terms of size or spatial dimensions. God is a being who exists without size or dimensions in space. In fact God created the universe, there was no matter or material so there was no space either. Yet God still existed. Where was God? He was not in a place that we could call a "where," for there was no "where" or space. But God still was! This fact makes us realize that God relates to space in a far different way than we do or than any created thing does. He exists as a kind of being that is far different and far greater than we can imagine."(174-175)

Then how do we become complete and at one with God and yet can't even imagine his being or greatness? Notice that Grudem is aware of the spatial significance and tendency to perceive God as eternal space. But in fear of modern science, he cautions us to resist this spatial urge. Why should we not think of God extending infinitely in all directions? Why is it bad to think of God in spatial terms? Why is it "simple" to think of God as extremely large? No! He suggests that we think of God as a being without size or dimension in space! Yes, let's think of God as a nothing without size or dimension in space! Is this any different than thinking of God without existence in space altogether?

If God has no dimensions or size, what would give Him any entity at all? Isn't it just as easy to think of God as non-existent as to think of Him as a non-dimensional, sizeless, indescribable something floating around in space? How is God superior to Satan if both are mere forces floating around in space without size or dimension? Satan tempted Christ after his baptism with all that Satan had which was the fear of death and earthly rewards. But Christ was able to resist Satan by the experience he had just had with his father—**spatial unity**. Satan could not match God's power because he does not have the same essence. **God is spatial and Satan is material**. If we do not acknowledge or experience this difference then we do not have any way to claim the superiority of God over Satan, which Grudem and all other theologians, including myself, would insist upon.

Christ Jesus experienced complete eternal spatial unity with God his father and the result was complete power to overcome the whole world and all its temptations. "You shall love the Lord thy God and Him only shalt thy serve!" Amen! What is eternal life if not the possession of eternal space in ones body? Christ said he had his father's commandment—eternal life. If one contains all of eternal space, they contain all time. The possession of all time is the possession of eternal life. If Christ

Jesus and Christians do not contain all space and time, how is it proclaimed that they have eternal life?

Grudem only leaves one thing for God to be and that is moral thought or force. If this were true the baptism account of Christ would have been far different. Jesus did not have a moral experience, he had an experience of spatial unity, filling and then containing.

God did not need to say anything to Jesus at his baptism except to verify that Jesus was his son and that God was well pleased with him. Did God say to Christ any of the following:

❑   You act better than any other man!

❑   Your goodness and mine are together and at one!

❑   You shall overcome Satan's evil with my Goodness!

How do we relate differently to space than God does, as Grudem suggests that we do? What then is the Holy Spirit that we share with Christ Jesus and God in oneness? How can we share moral goodness with God and Christ when we are evil from birth? No! We overcome evil by our undeserved unity with the space of Christ and God in the Holy Spirit. Eternal space is the only link possible for God, Jesus and Christians to unite in.

Why does Grudem think that when no matter or material was around that space was not around either? Space is around regardless of the presence of matter and material. An architect might think there is no space created without things to identify it but it is a mistake to assume that without things there is no space. Space is not dependent upon things in it to exist. It might not be visually perceivable or pretty but that doesn't mean it's not there.

The only Scriptures relating to God creating space or heaven are those that we covered in the chapter of the Singular Essence of God. God created the firmament, which was called the first heaven when He created the earth and waters above to rain upon the earth. But nothing says that God created all the heavens including the ones above the known matter in the cosmos. There is nothing on earth or in Scripture to dispute the idea that God is eternal space in all directions with no other to match His magnitude or essence. He shares it willingly with those who will find Him and do His will. Now Grudem is not through, he's going to give us a good analogy to use in thinking about God:

> "We must also be careful not to think that God himself is equivalent to any part of creation or to all of it. A pantheist believes that everything is God, or that God is everything that exists. The Biblical perspective is rather that God is present everywhere in His creation, but that He is also distinct from His creation. The analogy of a sponge filled with water is not perfect, but it is helpful. Water is present everywhere in the sponge, but the water is still completely distinct from the sponge. Now this analogy breaks down at very small points within the sponge, where we could say that there is sponge at one point and not water, or water and not sponge. Yet this is because the

analogy is dealing with two materials that have spatial characteristics and dimensions, while God does not"(175)

First Grudem gets the material world confused with the spatial world. He says that the sponge and the water have spatial characteristics, which they do not. Both are material at least in their expression as water and sponge. Therefore these are material dimensions not spatial dimensions. God is present in both, in that His Singular Essence is Eternal Space in all directions—world without end. And he can effect both materials, in that He is in the infinitely small areas of the atomic structures themselves, just as He can guide the galaxies in His larger capacity as His will is done in Heaven. I agree with Grudem in that we must not think of God as equivalent to any part of creation. But the key word is ***creation***. God's singular essence is eternal space, which is not part of creation. Our perception of space is created by the insertion of material things, but space is eternal and is present with or with out things placed about in it. It is, in fact, the error of Einstein and 20th century philosophers that the church has accepted as its own, that says space is created only when material is placed within it. And we have shown that God did create the first heaven in the first sentence in the Holy Bible. But this was not the same place Paul referred to in Corinthians 12:2-3. The third heaven was not created, as it has always been, even prior to things created within itself.

Here precisely is another problem if one tries to think of space itself as creation. If space itself was created, it is not infinite. If space is not infinite, what lies beyond it? As you can see the only consistent conclusion is that space is eternal and infinite and is the singular essence of God and it is the Kingdom of God. And as you can see this is why you do not want to be cut off from it. To be cut off would mean knowledge that one existed but cannot exist again and never will exist again and that the place one inhabits is non existent. In other words HELL or the flip side of all there is!

The question arises; why go about trying to create material models and analogies that do not work while aggressively denying the obvious spatial reality of God, Christ and the Holy Spirit? Why is it easier to think of God as two materials than it is to think of Him as the space itself within the sponge and the water? Space, as we know, is in every atom and therefore in every material. That is why Jesus could say; "if these should hold their peace, the stones would immediately cry out." (Luke 19:40). Was Jesus coming up with cute sayings or was he talking about reality? Yes God is in the stones and can cause them to do as He wills. Where in the stone is He? He is the space in the stone, in every atom and electron and neutron etc. All space is infinite and continuous and exists as one unique living entity. Just as God directs the galaxies, He directs the atoms and molecules and electrons etc.

Note that the real spatial model of the reality of God does not breakdown upon analysis of the sponge and water model. Nor does it breakdown as does the model used by Tertullian in Apology XXI in the ray of sunlight. Nor does it breakdown related to any of the energy models (refer to the chapter on the Trinity Of Personality). How can Grudem make the statement that God does not have spatial dimensions? Why cannot God have eternal infinite spatial dimensions? Grudem has no difficulty attributing infinite presence to God and infinite power to God. Why can he not attribute infinite spatial dimension to God? Nothing in Scripture is violated or broken as a result of God being perceived as eternal space. In fact, for the first time in recent history, the real spatial model reveals His Trinity of Personality where He shares His uniqueness with His Son and His disciples. For the first time in recent history, the power of God to save the world for all time is explainable, not in sponges and water and light rays but in shared eternal infinite space.

This problem that modern theologians have in describing God is at the center of stagnation in the spread of the Gospel. Theologians have accepted 20th Century definitions of space as a thing just as materials are things created. Space is not created as materials within it are. Our perception that space is created by the placement of things within it is in error. An architect would not suppose that he created the space in which he designed and built something, but that the space is now perceived in a more interesting and useful way. But did the architect create the space in which the new volumes sit? NO! Neither did God create himself or eternal space but He did create the things and the perception of spaces that are within Him Self.

Why have theologians avoided this obvious conclusion when the term space is almost a direct translation of the word spirit? Up until the last several hundred years, people thought of the space above them was the Kingdom of Heaven, as we should today. This also holds true for what the patriarchs in the Bible thought. They also perceived the **Kingdom of Heaven to be the whole of the space** above them. But moderns do not. The moderns search and probe the unknowable 'other world' and the little room called Heaven in space somewhere. Why is that? It is because the church has accepted a notion that is more dangerous then the belief that the earth is flat or that the sun revolves around the earth. They have adopted the idea that Heaven, God and Christ are in another dimension. Because they cannot describe how the Trinity works, they cannot show how Christ can save them. And because they cannot show how Christ can save all people forever, they cannot prove that heaven is not a little place out in space somewhere.

The moderns have gone to great effort to avoid the simple and tried to explain God in a way that will not describe Him at all. To describe God would violate their theology that God is indescribable. But what they have produced is a God that does not exist intellectually, except by their mere forced assertion, which they call "faith." Their mere insistence upon His existence rather than an accurate description of His existence is their error. They have done this in fear of modern science which claims the observable cosmos as theirs and the "spiritual other world" to be the domain of Christians. God does not exist because we want him to exist. God exists because we discover Him in reality. God is not established on our faith. We might need faith to continue to find him. To find God and describe his entity in reality is not robbery nor arrogance but compliance with the will of God Himself.

God has set the boundaries of our habitation that we might seek Him and "haply find Him." And finding God is not finding the courage to insist that he exists, but finding Him in His real and definable essence. Modern theologians insist that you should find and know God. But as soon as you try to describe the God you have found they insist that you can't describe Him. They insist that He is beyond description, indefinable, unsearchable, and impenetrable. Both of these theological positions are not compatible. We can know God and describe Him or we cannot know Him or describe Him. To know is to describe!

The modern church is trying to avoid contradiction in the scientific world where they work everyday. Science has claimed the cosmos and all that is in it as their observable domain. Yet this place is the Kingdom of God and is only accessible through the door or the Star Gate or the death resurrection and ascension of Christ. Grudem and many others deny the obvious spatial characteristics of God the Father, God the Son and God the Holy Ghost because they live in a theological period that has been occulted by modern science. The church must reclaim its domain in the real world in which Christ Jesus was sent to redeem. The church must claim the observable cosmos as the Kingdom of God that shall never be accessed or explored beyond the immediate future without passage from death into eternal life by the death, resurrection and ascension of individuals in Christ Jesus.

We see that the Trinity of Personality (Father, Son & Holy Ghost) is explainable if God has the Singular Essence of Eternal Space. We have no explanation of the Trinity if God were only an unimaginable entity. We see how Christ operates over the cosmos to save all men for all time through His power to envelope (contain) all space and to implete (fill) all space. These theological categories glorify God and His Son and show how they work in the world we live in.

Where is the power of what the systematic theologians offer if they leave the Trinity as a mystery, and salvation as inexplicable and glory as beyond comprehension, and God's existence as unimaginable, and salvation the will of faith? No! Real systematic theology is that which describes the power of God in the world in which we live in order that men see and understand what has been accomplished through Jesus Christ.

PART IV - "CONTACT"

CHAPTER 16 - COLLISION - ALIEN ANSWERS MESSAGE

"Contact" is what the scioreligionists dreamed up but what they got was a collision. A cultural collision occurs when the two elements of the false sociological equilibrium meet revealing the errors that both science and Christianity have made to accommodate each other. Both fields of study have imposed false changes in the 20th century resulting in a dead and powerless industrialized culture. However, it is the real physical world principles of the power of Christ to translate men which provides the only correct adjustment for both science and Christianity.

The National Aeronautics and Space Administration was funded with $100 million to seek extraterrestrial intelligence. This project called NASA SETI (Search for Extraterrestrial Intelligence) with its philosophical foundation is the perfect embodiment of all the false sociological equilibrium of modern America and industrial civilization. A book written by the late Carl Sagan entitled "Contact" laid the detailed foundation for this U.S. government project. After the project was cancelled a movie came out on the same subject with the same name. The analysis herein of this foundation will prove to be the epitome of the modern false equilibrium between "science so-called" and occulted mainstream Christianity.

The NASA SETI project and the movie deserve review. I wrote a letter **(Exhibit A in Appendix)** in response to a September 1992 Life magazine article about the NASA SETI project to be forwarded to NASA SETI wherein I proclaim to be an extraterrestrial, hyperspace alien with the answers to their questions. A comparison of my letter to the philosophical foundation of the tax funded project reveals the dangerous state of our false sociological equilibrium. My letter was never acknowledged by anyone, nor was it referred to in the movie that was later made about this $100 million project. These modern "scientists" rejected the validity of my letter by withholding a reply. We will see why more clearly in the following analysis.

History of *Contact* and SETI

Carl Sagan copyrighted the book "Contact" in 1985 and it was printed by Pocket Books in 1986. Carl Sagan and his associates created the NASA project called "Search For Extraterrestrial Intelligence" and got it funded by the U.S. Congress in 1992. Life Magazine carried an article on this project in September of 1992 outlining the scientific precepts and goals, which followed closely the goals in Sagan's book printed 6 or 7 years earlier.

However, a very unusual event occurred in October of 1992. Life Magazine received a nine-page letter from a man in Texas claiming not to have seen an alien, but to having become an alien transformed by a physical process. He also claimed to have all the answers SETI had asked in the Life Magazine article. This man asked that the letter be forwarded to the NASA SETI project scientist in charge. Strange as it may seem, the event of receiving a letter that would shock them to the core of their existance had been written about in Sagan's book. The magnitude of the shock was not predicted nor its comprehensiveness but Sagan's conscience was alerting him to the potential of real hyperspace power of human life on planet Earth. Lots of people claim to have seen alien, claim to have been abducted by an alien, claim to have been operated upon by an alien and claim to believe in aliens. But never did the scientists anticipate a man, actually claiming to be an alien born of space, contacting Life Magazine by letter.

The NASA SETI project was to last five years ending in September of 1997. No news was ever reported of contacting an alien or extraterrestrial intelligence by this project team after spending, presumably, twofifths of $100 million or $40 million. This project was cancelled in 1994 by a bill sponsored by Nevada Democratic Senator Richard Bryan. The project scientists promised that they would make this news known to the entire world if a contact were made (See Appendix - Alien Letter - Exhibit A - item 1.15). It can only be assumed that if Life Magazine cared enough about the questions being asked by NASA SETI to write a large article about it, that they indeed forwarded the letter to NASA SETI scientists for their consideration. If they did not, it is Life Magazine that has covered up one of the biggest news stories of all time.

Carl Sagan died in 1996 but in 1997 the movie, "Contact," was made based upon Carl Sagan's book by the same name. The NASA SETI project was also designed based upon the premises of Sagan's book. The actual NASA SETI project was described in the Life Magazine article and parts of the movie "Contact" were based upon the actual NASA SETI project described in the LIFE Magazine article. It was never mentioned in the movie that the scientists or any magazine had received a letter from a man claiming to be more alien than anything they had yet described in their article or their book or their NASA project (Exhibit A item B 2.5 Appendix).

The actual COLLISION and the fictitious *Contact*

Life magazine and NASA SETI actually made contact with a true hyperspace alienee that understands what space is and that it has a plan and power to operate on all things within itself. This alienee has been physically translated or evolved from a mortal flesh centered creature to a spatial creature that will travel the stars forever. This alienee underwent a physical operation performed by the one and only hyperspace alien to visit planet earth, namely the Son of God Christ Jesus. The "scientists so-called" wanted to know the answers to the oldest questions of mankind. They got taxpayer funding to do just that, and, after receiving a contact from the alien with the answers they asked for, they rejected him and his answers. Does this sound remotely similar to another older story?

Therefore, we have an interesting history of fraud and cover-up by "scientists" that reveals the insanity of a culture in industrialized society trying to escape God and create their own salvation. This fraud ends up running headlong into Jesus Christ, the hyperspace alien with power to translate all who study him in humility.

Here's how the history goes: A science fiction book is written in 1985 about a radio telescope project that searches for extraterrestrial intelligence. Based upon this book, a real government grant for $100 million is sought and obtained in 1992 to search the skies for such intelligence with radio telescopes. An actual contact is made in 1992 by receipt of an unlikely letter from a local hyperspace alien living in Texas who is unaware of Sagan's book "Contact." The alienee, at the time of writing the letter, is unaware of Sagan's book that mentions the project scientist receiving a letter that proved they were not yet advanced enough to receive such a letter. Life magazine and/or NASA SETI covered up this fact and never responded to the contact. After two years the project was cancelled in 1994. In late 1997 or early 1998 a movie is released based upon the science fiction book and the NASA SETI project that does not mention the alien letter or contact but instead depicts a contact with an alien which did not happen. This is the final destination of modern science, fraud and deception for the advancement of political and financial world domination. So again the laughter from heaven is heard as recorded by the Psalmist from 3000 years ago of the irony of man's attempt to escape the bands of God and save himself. That is to say, their escape plan leads straight to the one they want to escape from. (Psalms 2):

"Why do the heathen rage, and the people imagine a vain thing?

"The kings of the earth set themselves, and the rulers take counsel together against the Lord, and against his anointed, saying,

"Let us break their bands asunder, and cast away their cords from us.

"He that sitteth in the heavens shall laugh: the Lord shall have them in derision.

"Then shall he speak unto them in his wrath, and vex them in his sore displeasure.

"Yet have I set my king upon my holy hill of Zion.

"I will declare the decree: the Lord hath said unto me, Thou art my son; this day have I begotten thee.

"Ask of me, and I shall give thee the heathen for thine inheritance, and the uttermost parts of the earth for thy possession.

"Thou shalt break them with a rod of iron; thou shalt dash them in pieces like a potter's vessel.

"Be wise now therefore, O ye kings: be instructed, ye judges of the earth.

"Serve the Lord with fear, and rejoice with trembling.

"Kiss the Son, lest he be angry, and ye perish from the way, when his wrath is kindled but a little. Blessed are all they that put their trust in him."

The unjust COVER UP of the ALIEN COLLISION

The following analysis of Sagan's book and the Life magazine article reveals why the NASA SETI team and Life magazine staff cannot justify their cover up of the letter they received from an alien in Texas:

❑   REJECTION THEORY 1 - Message did not come via Radio Telescope:

The team might try to dismiss the contact because it came in the form of a letter in the U.S. Mail, instead of a transmission through a large high-tech radio telescope. But in Sagan's book, Ellie, the project scientist for SETI, receives a letter from her mother revealing more "myths" in her own life than those she was attacking in the lives of others. The letter from her mother contained more truth about herself then the message from Vega received by the Radio Telescopes. The Letter to NASA SETI from the Texas Alien contained more truth then the "scientists" were willing to receive. The analogy between the two letters is clear. Ellie's letter was written by her mother to be given to her after her mother's death informing Ellie that her step dad was her real biological father:

> "Ellie had assimilated the letter in a single gulp, and immediately read it again. She had difficulty breathing. Her hands were clammy. The impostor had turned out to be the real thing."[17]

Sagan here realizes that one can be fooled by appearances and that what may look like an impostor may well turn out to be reality. This is exactly what the letter from the Texas Alien demonstrated when received by Life magazine and presumably NASA SETI. This is evidence that Sagan and his associates are aware of this type of surprise and should weigh all evidence coming in no matter how received by ironic letters or by radio telescopes.

❑   REJECTION THEORY 2 - Contents of Contact were Hard to Believe:

It is also ironic that this letter Ellie received from her mother, relates to false and real fathers.

> "For most of her life, she had rejected her own father, without the vaguest notion of what she was doing. What strength of character he had shown during all those adolescent outbursts when she taunted him for not being her father, for having no right to tell her what to do."(429)

Yet this appears to be exactly what Sagan and his associates were doing in their religious quest for truth at NASA SETI. They are denying their own fatherhood in the Father of Jesus Christ and refusing to enter the very door to the kingdom of

---

[17] Carl Sagan, *Contact* (New York, N.Y.: Pocket Books, 1985), 429.

heaven and eternal space travel opened by Christ Jesus. Therefore they are guilty of committing the crimes of hate and ignorance that they accuse others of.

It is clear that Sagan and his associates and planetary friends can discern the difficulty with messages and signals and the ways to filter out things that they don't want to face. But as scientists they are supposed to control their prejudices and acknowledge the truth when they perceive it. In this they have proven beyond a doubt to be the poorest of scientists and reprobates of their own "scientific faith." For they knew to be careful and not rule out signals coming in from all sources yet did filter it out for their own personal gain and advancement. Sagan has the insight to write of Ellie's shock of the truth:

> "She was not sufficiently advanced to receive that signal, much less decrypt it. She had spent her career attempting to make contact with the most remote and alien of strangers, while in her own life she had made contact with hardly anyone at all. She had been fierce in debunking the creation myths of others, and oblivious to the lie at the core of her own. She had studied the universe all her life, but had overlooked its clearest message:"(430)

Is this not the most straightforward confession of Carl Sagan? Is this not what he will have to confess before Christ Jesus? He knows this and don't all men know this? They spend their lives trying to make contact with that which they fantasize about and ignore those in things in reality that they need to make contact with. They are even warned that they should make contact with reality but they not only reject the warnings but also try to prevent others from contacting God. What do you suppose their reward will be?

Therefore, a letter containing powerful truth was acknowledged as important and significant by one who operates a Radio Telescope in Sagan's book. Why would a letter not be significant that purported to answer all of "our philosopher's most important questions" in the real NASA SETI project? We can only conclude that Sagan and his associates were **"not yet advanced sufficiently"** to receive such a letter. That being the case, they should have immediately abandoned the project and given the $100 million back to the bankrupt taxpayers of America.

It should at least be clear from the analysis of Sagan's mentality that a letter would have significance to the NASA SETI project and not be discarded because it was not a radio transmission. It's equally true that the letter could not be rejected based upon the unbelievable nature of it, because the message contained in the letter from the Texas Alien was clear, to the point and sincerely truthful.

Therefore, Life Magazine and NASA SETI had no right to cover up the fact that they had received a letter from one claiming to be a hyperspace alien with the answers to the secrets of eternal space travel merely because it did not come through a radio telescope. Nor did these scientists have a right to ignore this letter because the contents were hard to believe. These concepts are also well addressed in the magazine article and the alien letter itself. (See Appendix - Exhibit A - item 1.24-1.25)

❑ REJECTION THEORY 3 - Evidence was Insufficient to Prove Experience:

It has been established that the letter could not be intellectually dismissed by these scientists and it is also demonstrable that what the alien said about himself and the operation performed on him and all things could not be intellectually dismissed. Sagan, taking all the freedom of imagination and scientific knowledge that he has in addition to that of his associates, can only produce an experience for his heroine resulting from a stationary machine and the discovery that deep within the transitory numbers of pi is a diagram of a circle. We therefore should all relax in peace in the hope that in the infinite divisions of pi there lies somewhere within another circle, i.e., a circle in a circle. Both of these experiences, if you can call them that, are earth-bound. Ellie cannot go before the public, in Sagan's book, until she has proof that is believable to the public that she indeed had this experience of going to the center of the galaxy:

> They made a bargain. She could go back to Argus, although no longer as director, and pursue any scientific problem she pleased... "You come back with a solid piece of evidence, something really convincing, and we'll join you in making the announcement. We'll say we asked you to keep the story quiet until we could be absolutely sure."(408)

Then Ellie finally gets the evidence she believes the whole world will accept as proof that she and her other four companions took a trip to the center of the Galaxy. On her earth bound trip to Vega the aliens tell her that they are looking for the meaning of pi. Later, after her dubious ride, the Argus computer, having worked for days at light speed division of the circumference of a circle by its diameter, supposedly finds the diagram of another circle. Sagan finishes his book with the confirmation of the reality that a letter from an alien on earth is sufficient to demand investigation for the power of cosmic physical transformation:

> "The universe was made on purpose, the circle said. In whatever galaxy you happen to find yourself, you take the circumference of a circle, divide it by its diameter, measure closely enough, and uncover a miracle - another circle, drawn kilometers downstream of the decimal point. There would be richer messages farther in. It doesn't matter what you look like, or what you're made of, or where you come from. As long as you live in this universe, and have a modest talent for mathematics, sooner or later you'll find it. It's already here. It's inside everything. **You don't have to leave your planet** to find it."

> "The circle had closed.

> "She found what she had been searching for."(430-431)

(Emphasis added)

Here we have Sagan's own philosophy suggesting that evidence for transformation does not have to come from outside the earth to be taken seriously by these scientists at the Cornell University department of Astronomy and Space Science. The same can be said for other institutions that support the philosophy of SETI such as the National Science Foundation, the National Academy of Science and elsewhere in contemporary American academia. Yet these same scientists received a letter that promised much more than mere diagrams hidden in the infinite depths of non-divisible numbers or a mere dream of a trip inside a stationary machine. Consequently, the contents of a letter sent to Jill Tarter, via Life Magazine, couldn't be intellectually dismissed by these "scientists," on the grounds that the evidence was insufficient to establish the reality of the experience of a physical cosmic transformation.

❑ REJECTION THEORY 4 - Earth is Source for Transformation Experience:

These "scientists" could make the argument that the experience reported in the alien letter from Texas was obtained by knowledge available on earth rather than from zooming around in the sky somewhere or from some creature flying around in space and therefore is unworthy of serious investigation. But it is too late to make that argument for Sagan's book is about an earth bound experience obtained by Ellie and four other companions getting in a capsule and falling several stories through a magnetic field. This was supposed to cause a time warp of some kind where the real time experience is nano seconds and warp time is 18 hours. During this 18 hours Ellie and her companions go through Einstein-Rosen bridges to Vega and eventually to the center of the Milky Way:

> "Eda was, considering the circumstances, very relaxed. She soon understood why. While she and Vaygay had been undergoing lengthy interrogations, he had been calculating.

> "I think the tunnels are Einstein-Rosen bridges," he said. "General Relativity admits a class of solutions, called wormholes, similar to black holes, but with no evolutionary connection - they cannot be generated, as black holes can, by the gravitational collapse of a star. But the usual sort of wormhole, once made, expands and contracts before anything can cross through; it exerts disastrous tidal forces, and it also requires - at least as seen by an observer left behind - an infinite amount of time to get through." (406)

> "...I'm not yet sure of any of this. But at least if the tunnels can be Einstein-Rosen bridges, we can give some answer when they tell us we were hallucinating."(407)

Here we have Ellie and her companions having difficulty explaining an experience obtained inside a contraption that fell several stories into a net rather than blasting off into deep space. Their explanation consists of time warp, esoteric Einstein-Rosen Bridges, known only to mathematicians, and to this day, not experienced by anyone including Einstein and Rosen. The feasibility of this type of travel would be similar jumping through your own mouth and coming out in the center of the galaxy.

This point is the failure of the movie "Contact" and the book "Contact." People seemed to like the movie until they learn that the travelers go nowhere. They just have an earth-bound experience to explain and justify somehow. Nobody wants that stuff because that's like a lunatic trying to explain his sanity. Both the book and the movie "Contact" tries to make this type of insanity into the best possible definition of "faith." This is why it is very important that we know the difference between faith and grace.

Faith is seeking, but grace is possession of that which we sought in faith. And no one in the book or the movie "Contact" obtained grace. They only sought but never found and then redefined their endless, fruitless, empty pursuit into the ultimate destiny they sought. Faith for them, is the pursuit and the end of the pursuit, is their pursuit. But they rejected the very source of grace and cut themselves off from reality and eternal space travel. Don't be deceived by the faithful! Faith has an end in the possession of grace made possible by the operation of Christ Jesus upon the cosmos and all therein. Never stop pursuing in faith until you possess that which you seek in faith. That is Grace, the state of perfection in the Heavenly places with Christ Jesus. Amen.

Einstein-Rosen Bridges could better be described as ladders for climbing over the wall rather than going through the door to the kingdom of Heaven or eternal space. This is why it is also important to know where heaven is and what it is. The sciologists think that heaven is in another dimension running parallel to our cosmos to only be accessed upon death. This is error and ignorance. The Kingdom of Heaven is the eternal space that we peer into every night and walk around in every day. Anyone that tries to climb over the wall rather than walk through the door is a liar and a murderer according to Christ Jesus in John 10:1-18:

> "Verily, verily, I say unto you, He that entereth not by the door into the sheepfold, **but climbeth up some other way**, the same is a thief and a robber.

> "But he that entereth in by the door is the shepherd of the sheep.

> "To him the porter openeth and the sheep hear his voice and he calleth his own sheep by name, and leadeth them out.

> "And when he putteth forth his own sheep, he goeth before them, and the sheep follow him: for they know his voice.

> "And a stranger will they not follow, but will flee from him: for they know not the voice of strangers.

> "This parable spake Jesus unto them: but they understood not what things they were which he spake unto them.

> "Then said Jesus unto them again, Verily, verily, I say unto you, I am the door of the sheep.

"All that ever came before me are thieves and robbers: but the sheep did not hear them.

"I am the door: by me if any man enter in, he shall be saved, and shall go in and out, and find pasture.

"The thief cometh not, but for to steal, and to kill, and to destroy: I am come that they might have life, and that they might have it more abundantly.

"I am the good shepherd: the good shepherd giveth his life for the sheep.

"But he that is an hireling, and not the shepherd, whose own the sheep are not, seeth the wolf coming, and leaveth the sheep, and fleeth: and the wolf catcheth them, and scattereth the sheep.

"The hireling fleeth, because he is an hireling, and careth not for the sheep.

"I am the good shepherd, and know my sheep, and am known of mine.

"As the Father knoweth me, even so know I the Father: and I lay down my life for the sheep.

"And other sheep I have, which are not of this fold: them also I must bring, and they shall hear my voice; and there shall be one fold, and one shepherd.

"Therefore doth my Father love me, because I lay down my life, that I might take it again.

"No man taketh it from me, but I lay it down of myself. I have power to lay it down, and I have power to take it again. This commandment have I received of my Father."

(Emphasis added)

I got chills just from typing that passage! That of course appealed to my mind, or the intellectual component, and my soul, or spatial component, of the Quaternion Man. I did not cry so it did not appeal to my heart. Is it more difficult to believe these words of Jesus than the Einstein-Rosen bridge wormhole into some time warp trip to the center of the galaxy? Or is the Einstein-Rosen Bridge just another feeble attempt to climb over the wall and lead the sheep astray? Or is it so feeble? Have not these movies and books and government projects using millions of Christian taxpayer dollars led millions astray? Where are the shepherds? Are they also fleeing at the coming of the wolf? We need shepherds to enter into the Kingdom of Heaven by the door of Christ Jesus and lead the sheep to safety!

We can now see why it is important to know where God's domain is, via the Domain Triad, established earlier and remembered easily by the short phrase: I AM

ONE LIVING. God is not in another dimension that we enter upon death. God has always been alive and always will be alive. God is not divided into various dimensions, nor is his essence duplicated, nor is there any equal to Him. God works in the world of the living, not the dead. This establishes the magnitude and location of God, and His realm of influence and power. This knowledge negates the ideas that one can get to God by merely dying. It also indicates that the Kingdom of God is the same as the eternal space above us and is the "pasture" that is enjoyed in and out of the door of Christ Jesus. This also means that men may have limited flight around in the Kingdom, temporarily, but shall never envelope nor implete space nor begin hyperspace travel without going through the door of Christ.

❑   REJECTION THEORY 5 - Alien Does Not Look Different:

It does however appear that it matters to NASA SETI what you look like despite how Sagan finishes his book by stating: "It doesn't matter what you look like, or what you're made of, or where you come from. As long as you live in this universe, and have a modest talent for mathematics, sooner or later you'll find it. It's already here. It's inside everything. You don't have to leave your planet to find it."

But the real hyperspace alien was from Texas and looked like an ordinary man from planet Earth! This is unacceptable! All aliens must look like strange creatures, e.g., elephants with scales, but have great intelligence etc.

But the most despicable look to these scioreligionists may have been the vision of a Texas redneck welder that sounds poor by his grammar and punctuation and his misspelled words. But even those with a **modest talent for the English language (instead of math)** could determine what was being communicated. Yet no return message was ever received. This verifies another presumption of Sagan and his colleagues revealed by his book.

❑   REJECTION THEORY 6 - The Contents of the Contact Were Offensive:

Here is the most likely reason for the failure of NASA SETI and Life magazine to respond to the actual alien contact made. Life magazine and the NASA SETI personnel followed the philosophy outlined in Carl Sagan's book. His heroine, Ellie, states that:

> "If we find the Message offensive we're not obliged to reply…We're very nicely quarantined from Vega."(103)

Jesus brought a message 2000 years ago and apparently it is still found offensive. Jesus said at Matt. 11:6: "And blessed is he, whosoever shall not be offended in me." Could Sagan, Tarter, Clark, Drake, and the National Science Foundation use the same logic against the Letter from the Texas Alien. If the Letter from the Texas Alien was offensive and dangerous to them, **they weren't obliged to reply**. But that would be a lie according to their own project objectives to make the message known. Not only is this Texas Alien poor by the appearance of his computer printer, grammar and such but the "scientists" could assume that their theological experiment was insulated from the Texas Alien by the U.S. government, U.S. culture, their own wealth and their own prestige and their own sciolism. While these "scientists so called" on a religious quest received $100 million from American tax payers, the Texas Alien is struggling just to hack out a poverty level existence in a society that hates his liberty, freedom and transformation process. The Texas Alien has little chance of reaching their "quarantined" academic upper room.

But the Texas Alien lives in America that was established as a Christian nation with law and order and Christian precepts. It is unlawful for the U.S. government to fund a religious quest of any type including a scientific religious quest, especially one that covers up a message from an alien who claims to have all the answers that the project itself seeks to find out. It is criminal fraud to deceive the American public by covering up an actual contact by an alien who exceeds the parameters of the established project, which was the foundation for a $100 million tax grant. This alien promised to discuss with them the process of evolutionary transformation of humans into hyperspace aliens of which they asked to know. They in turn promised to tell the world if they made such a contact for they claimed it would be a message to the world not to just NASA SETI. And so it was for the world not just NASA SETI.

Therefore, it is only reasonable that the damage done to Christianity by the U.S. funding of the work of Sagan and his fellow scioreligionists be repaired with an equal funding of the Texas Alien for his dissemination of the answers to their questions with $100 million.

Funk and Wagnall's define a **sciolist**, as "one who has a smattering of knowledge, especially a pretender to scientific attainment." **Sciolism** is defined by same as "Charlatanism; pretentious superficial knowledge." Superficial knowledge can also suggests one who has much knowledge or an infinite medley of facts but without a frame for organizing them into an accurate reflection of reality or useful theory or product. These terms are selected to characterize the modern adherents to the religiosity of science.

Religionism is defined by Funk and Wagnall's as "The practice of or adherence to religion; used derogatorily to imply affectation and insincerity— Religionist." The combination of these terms yield a definition that simply describes what many "scientists" have been doing for at least 50 years. Therefore, a **scioreligionist** is one, who without an organizing framework for many scientific facts, attempts to produce a structure, hope and false religion for mankind in place of Christianity. This attempt however requires the intellectual dismissal of many scientific and Christian facts resulting in falsehood, insincerity and self-deception.

These terms are needed to accurately discern the conflict between the two most powerful fields in the modern industrialized world, science and Christianity. Religiosity of science and the deoccultation of Christianity have been discussed in earlier chapters. Now a perfect and contemporary example has presented itself where the author, as a single agent of deocculted Christianity and hyperspace alien, answers the message sent out by a prominent group of scioreligionists, well funded by 100 million U.S. tax dollars. The SETI project is cancelled two years after they received the alien message and they make no mention of such a contact but rather fabricate one that never occurred. The ultimate question is who's more sincere and who has had a real life experience transforming them from one type of creature into another type of creature capable of eternal life in the galaxies'?

❏ REJECTION THEORY 7 - The Contact Never Got to NASA SETI via LIFE Magazine:

The final theory for rejection is that NASA SETI never got the message from the Texas Alien because the Editor of Life magazine, Mr. James R. Gaines, threw the certified letter in the trash on or about the third of November 1992. Would you throw a letter away that was sent to you by certified mail from a person, the subject of an article, addressed to the person you recently published a large important article about? Or would you legally wash your hands of the matter by forwarding it to the person referenced? Would you be the editor of a large national magazine by placing the company in liability for such acts? Would you not care enough about articles you publish in your national publication that you would throw letters away answering questions asked in that article? Yes, it is possible that the contact never got to NASA SETI but as you can see it is more likely that the letter was forwarded as a matter of simple business concerns and liability prevention.

Now that NASA SETI is cancelled as of 1994 by a bill sponsored by Nevada Democratic Senator Richard Bryan, these same scientists so-called have started the SETI-Institute and they have a web site where you can e-mail them. The author did just that and asked if Jill Tarter ever received his nine page letter that answered all their questions back during the NASA SETI project. The author has yet to hear from them (see www.AlienPhysics.com for copy of e-mail sent to Jill Tarter). It appears that they got the letter and know all they want to know about the Alien Avery.

It must be stated again that this author was not aware of Carl Sagan's book "Contact" containing the letter episode until six years after he wrote the letter to Jill Tarter via LIFE Magazine. The similarities between the letter the author wrote them and the letter that Sagan writes into his fictional concept of an alien contact are astonishing. Sagan's own writing validates the authority and scientific admissibility and credibility of the letter sent by this author to NASA SETI and Jill Tarter and LIFE Magazine.

PART IV - "CONTACT"

CHAPTER 17 - FAITH THAT CRIPPLES CHRISTIANITY

It is the expansion and misapplication of the word faith, and the occultation of grace, that works to cripple Christianity. As such, they cause the propagation and adoption of certain bogus propositions of scientists as a real hope for mankind's future. Carl Sagan, NASA SETI, and SETI-Institute have provided us with an excellent body of evidence to prove that some scientists have been at work (for at least fifty years) converting their science into a religious faith and using government tax dollars, paid by many Christians, to do it.

There are **two processes in operation to make science into a religion**. The scientists, at our tax expense, have become the religious leaders of our age and industrial culture. They determine what is moral and immoral and what is good and bad politically. This is true for cosmology as well as microbiology or astrophysics and stem-cell research. First, Christianity is being reduced and categorized as a mere "faith" equal with the faiths of every other "religion" with nothing more to offer or obtain from Christ than the hope of something good after death. Secondly, science is elevated from the mere practice of the "scientific method" and redefined to be the quest for truth concerning the ultimate questions of nature, origin and destiny of mankind. Science itself is then proclaimed a "religious" quest of "faith" to find out the truth about mankind and what is his moral foundation and obligations.

Central to this dangerous trend is the common misunderstanding in Christianity of the difference between faith and grace which allows this delusion to grow. As has been said earlier, faith is the act of seeking, but grace is the possession of that which was sought. St. Paul says that Christ Jesus is the author and **FINISHER of faith**. Faith is the seeking, but grace is the possession of that which was sought in faith. Also, grace is obtained during our lifetime not after our death. Many unfortunate souls have been deceived into the belief that grace is obtained after death, and that in the death of the Christian, immortality is obtained. This immediately renders scioreligionists the winners because we all know: that the scientific view is the only rational way to look at the observable world we live in, right? The scioreligionists gladly concede the "spiritual," otherworld to be probed by the religious faiths of the world. Christianity is also banished to this otherworld to be probed by the "spiritual mind." Under this view the only player is science because all others use emotional voodoo to probe an unknowable impenetrable world of the dead. This is false and dangerous Christian theology.

The Domain Triad discussed earlier shows that God is not concerned at all with a non-existent-world of the dead, but is the Great I Am One Living, i.e., the eternal undivided God alive and working in the world of the living. He has also opened a door into which man, in a state of walking death, can enter into the real observable world around us to dwell in the galaxies forever in Christ Jesus. Therefore, grace is a state of perfection obtained by one's passage through the hyperspace birth canal that Christ Jesus opened by his operation performed upon the cosmos 2000 years ago. A person in this state, after transformation, has acquired truth about the observable cosmos and his relation to it and what the cosmos is. This knowledge can and will challenge the false doctrines of the lost "faith" of the scioreligionists in their quest for the priesthood and domination over humanity. The following quotes from the book "Contact" and the Warner Brothers film by the same name and the article about the NASA SETI project written about in Life magazine will expose and prove the aim of scioreligionists to make a religion of their science. The jacket to the 1997 Warner Brothers motion picture "Contact" says:

> "Foster is astronomer Ellie Arroway, a woman of science. McConaughey is religious scholar, Palmer Joss, a man of faith. They're opposite ends of a spectrum…"

The whole theme of the movie is how Ellie learns that she too must have "faith" as a scientist. The movie implies that a skeptic scientist needs faith, as some things in science cannot be proven. And who better to teach her this than the dropout preacher that shacks up with her and has some how failed to find the truth and reality of Christ Jesus? The preacher seeks some kind of poetic otherworldly knowledge and tries to help Ellie believe in things she does not see.

Then what is the "faith" at the opposite end of the spectrum? The truth is that Matthew McConaughey played the role of a drop-out main-stream preacher and aide to the U.S. President who never mentions the name of Christ much less the power of Christ to save men or to operate upon the cosmos with his body. In other words, this dropout preacher is a non-believer in Christ and a man without grace, who has not been transformed. Yet the movie and the book make the pitch that this man is a man of great faith. And in a way that is correct. For in modern Christianity, faith is the ultimate misunderstood destiny of Christians. But in real Christianity our ultimate destiny, in this life, is the perfect state of grace. If Christians were to perceive this distinction, Palmer Joss in the movie and book "Contact," would be a miserable man attempting to pretend he was a Christian. And in fact, that was indeed the part he played. Both Ellie and Palmer are lost characters when we meet them and they remain lost when we leave them in both the book and the movie. Yet, the author and his promoters are correct in saying they are both of faith.

The result, obviously, is that these two individuals do not really represent two opposite extremes of the spectrum of faith or life. They are, in fact, representatives of the same end of the spectrum. Both are seeking truth in "faith" that there is some. Both are also attracted to the doctrines offered by scioreligionists for the hope of mankind's future. Neither character is attracted to the hope that Christ Jesus has somehow altered the cosmos and has power to make all men and women the children of God.

Therefore "faith" in this movie and book is the faith in the scientific quest for truth they hope will provide a way that mankind can be saved through the work of knowledge and skill as scientists, engineers and craftsmen. Neither of these individuals has Christian faith leading to a perfect state of grace by the revelation of what Christ has done to the cosmos and all things therein. It is therefore no wonder that these two lost in "faith" would fall in love with each other in their common quest for truth. They are in fact identical in their minds. But, unfortunately, this dropout preacher really does represent a great number of lost "Christians" and "Christian churches" today.

Too many modern "Christians" would say that the analysis herein does not hope with those that hope and cry with those that cry and rejoice with those that rejoice as Paul admonished. But Paul would never have admonished us to heresy, where ever there is heresy, especially when the grace that God has instituted for all men is superior to any that Sagan has experienced or dreamed of. This grace is available to us on this side of the "curtain of death" and is worthy of proclamation.

Not only do Ellie and the preacher represent the same side of the spectrum of "faith" (where both seek truth or hope found in science) but only two kinds of Christian characters are permitted in the movie and the book "Contact." We will explore these two characterizations in more detail in the next chapter. The first type is the religious, ignorant, fanatic who is dangerous to a rational and truth seeking society. The second is the Christian who is a seeker of truth in every place but Christ Jesus. The later is depicted as strong, quiet and open-minded:

"Zealotry, fanaticism, fear, hope, fervent debate, quiet prayer, agonizing reappraisal, exemplary selflessness, closed-minded bigotry, and a zest for dramatically new ideas were epidemic, rushing feverishly over the surface of the tiny planet Earth. Slowly emerging from this mighty ferment, Ellie thought she could see, was a dawning recognition of the world as one thread in a vast cosmic tapestry. Meanwhile, the Message itself continued to resist attempts at decryption.

> "On the vilification channels, protected by the First Amendment, she, Vaygay, der Heer, and to a lesser extent Peter Valerian were being castigated for a variety of offenses, including atheism, communism, and hoarding the Message for themselves. In her opinion, Vaygay wasn't much of a communist, and Valerian had a deep, quiet, but sophisticated Christian faith."[18]

As we can see it is the quiet, **lost, yet sophisticated "Christian"** who is most admired by a lost world filled with "faith." Sagan chooses a good word for Valerian and it applies to the modern state of the church. The term "sophisticated" really means unnecessarily complicated, rather than complex. Many Christians are very sophisticated with an overly complicated and ill-defined "faith," but few hold to an accurate or well-defined, yet complex, theology.

An important step in creating a "superior religion" out of the ideas of a few scio-religionists is the nullification of Christianity. Here are the three steps used to nullify Christianity. This is done by lumping Christianity in with all the other

---

[18] Carl Sagan, *Contact* (New York, N.Y.: Pocket Books, 1985), 129.

"religions" of the world and show the turmoil between them, as a group, and apply that turmoil to anyone of them separately. Therefore, first, we call Christianity a "religion" (which it is not) then we say: "look at all the turmoil and destruction caused by all these religions!" Then we can also suggest that: "if any of these religions were correct they would all quit their fighting and follow the truthful one."

Therefore the **three steps to nullify Christianity** are:

❑ Categorize Christianity as an equal "faith" with other "religions."

❑ Show the turmoil that exists between all "religions."

❑ Apply the turmoil as proof that Christianity is erroneous.

These steps are developed well in Sagan's book and the movie. As a result, it is Ellie and her hope of "contact" with a real superior alien that will draw the world of selfish religious people together. It is the religion of science and its technology that will reach the alien who will unite the warring religious factions together. The winning religion is the one that has a claim upon the study of the observable world around us and which seeks truth about the origin and moral destiny of the planet and its inhabitants. This winner is science according to the theme developed by Sagan. This attempt to create the superior religion of science is clearly seen in the above quote.

Now for the compelling evidence that Sagan and his fellow scio-religionists are busy creating a scientific cult. In the following quote we also see the evidence of the **split worldview** of the "observable world of science" and the "spiritual other-world" that is impenetrable except in death. This, as has been said herein, is false both to science and Christianity:

"She imagined a heaven with all those nice moms and dads floating about or flapping over to a nearby cloud. It would have to be a commodious place to accommodate all the tens of billions of people who had lived and died since the emergence of the human species. It might be very crowded, she was thinking, unless the religious heaven was built on a scale something like the astronomical heaven. Then there'd be room to spare."(152)

Ellie is incorrect in her imagination with regard to both the religious heaven and the astronomical heaven, because they are identically the same place. Sagan clearly creates his heroine with his mindset and that of his colleagues. They perceive the tangible world around them as the scientific observable world and the existence of a separate religious world of the dead or the **"religious heaven."** This is incorrect Christian theology and incorrect science created by scientists, with Christian acquiescence, to make scientists the priest over the dominion of the observable world.

Sagan confesses his true religion through Ellie in the following quote from the book, which, by the way, is also the religion of Albert Einstein. In fact this chapter of Sagan's book is preceded by a quote from Einstein:

"I maintain that the cosmic religious feeling is the strongest and noblest motive for scientific research."(143)

On this same note expressed by Einstein, Sagan reveals his real religion via Ellie's self designed and engineered religion:

"She reached toward the bedside table for Volume 16 of an old Encyclopaedia Britannica Macropaedia, titled "Rubens to Somalia," and opened to a page where a scrap of computer printout had been inserted as a bookmark. She pointed to an article called "Sacred or Holy."

"The theologians seem to have recognized a special nonrational—I wouldn't call it irrational—aspect of the feeling of sacred or holy. They call it **'numinous.'** The term was first used by ...let's see...somebody named Rudolph Otto in a 1923 book, The Idea of the Holy. He believed that humans were predisposed to detect and revere the numinous. He called it the misterium tremendum. Even my Latin is good enough for that.

"In the presence of the **misterium tremendum**, people feel utterly insignificant but, if I read this right, not personally alienated. He thought of the numinous as a thing 'wholly other,' and the human response to it as 'absolute astonishment.' Now, if that's what religious people talk about when they use words like sacred or holy, I'm with them. I felt something like that just in listening for a signal, never mind in actually receiving it. I think all of science elicits that sense of awe.

"Now listen to this." She read from the text:

"Throughout the past hundred years a number of philosophers and social scientists have asserted the disappearance of the sacred, and predicted the demise of religion. A study of the history of religions shows that religious forms change and that there has never been unanimity on the nature and expression of religion. Whether or not man...

"Sexists write and edit religious articles, too, of course." She returned to the text.

"Whether or not man is now in a new situation for developing structures of ultimate values radically different from those provided in the traditionally affirmed awareness of the sacred is a vital question.

"So?"

"So, I think the bureaucratic religions try to institutionalize your perception of the numinous instead of providing the means so you can perceive the numinous directly—like looking through a six-inch telescope. If sensing the numinous is at the heart of religion, **who's more religious would you say—the people who follow the bureaucratic religions or the people who teach themselves science?**

"Let's see if I've got this straight," he returned. It was a phrase of hers that he had adopted. "It's a lazy Saturday afternoon, and there's this couple lying naked in bed reading the Encyclopaedia Britannica to each other, and **arguing about whether the Andromeda Galaxy is more 'numinous' than the Resurrection. Do they know how to have a good time, or don't they?**"(152-154)

(Emphasis added)

Well they may be having "fun" but it will soon pass and they will one day know that broad is the way and wide is the gate that leads unto destruction and many there be that enter therein. It is not the numinous that Christians speak of when they talk about religion. Christians talk about the **numero uno alpha and omega hyperspace alien Christ Jesus** who has operated upon the cosmos and transformed them from a death state into an eternal creature with the capacity to travel among the stars forever. This is not to say that Ellie and her shack-up are not capable of having a feeling that there is a God out there. But what really matters is: are they being honest with themselves in regard to who and what God might be and what their actual condition might be without Him and His Operation upon them?

It is obvious that Sagan through the characters he has created believes that his science is a religion and more "numinous" or religious than the resurrection of Christ Jesus. Also notice that "misterium tremendum" has raised its ugly theological head in this story. And why not, it is, after all, one of the main pillars of the false sociological equilibrium between Christianity and science? Remember the "mystery" of the Trinity we must except on "faith?" Again, if the Trinity is a mystery so is Christ, salvation, faith and grace and every other aspect of Christianity. But in Christ the mystery of the ages is now revealed and preached, at least by Paul and the other Apostles. **In true Christianity, there is no "misterium tremendum"—only revelation.**

Notice in the foregoing quote from Sagan's book that any experience of these people becomes a religious experience. Therefore, virtually anything in the world, any experience or interest in the world, is now a religious experience. Looking into a telescope is, no doubt, fun and exciting but that does not and cannot transform a person from one kind of creature to another. In fact, Ellie says that she has a feeling of religious awe when she listens for answers, even without hearing the answers. Wow, just the practice of science is an awe producing experience of the numinous. It's interesting that Ellie and her shack-up preacher don't compare their sex-out-of-wedlock experience as a religious numinous. They do however, consider peering at Andromeda through a telescope to the resurrection, which they have not experienced. These characters are quick to discern when they have no experience at all to base an opinion. They should, at least, have gotten married and cultivated a better opinion of sex!

It is clear which religion bothers them the most. Throughout the book, it is Christianity that receives the worst treatment. The resurrection relates to Christianity and it is compared to the mere thought of another galaxy. These two characters speak of comparing the experience of the resurrection with that of the numinous of looking at Andromeda through a telescope. Yet neither these characters nor Sagan have experienced the resurrection and cannot therefore compare it to anything else. One might also say, that they have not experienced Andromeda either, except from afar.

Also, notice how willing Sagan's heroine is to believe what is written in the encyclopedia. She says "if I read this right." In other words, she has not really experienced what the author of her encyclopedia has called the "numinous" because she's not sure that it "alienates" her or not when she experiences it. In other words, let's believe in anything or any book as long as it is not Christianity or the Bible. That is the one thing these loving truth seekers hate!

The straight and narrow way to eternal life in the galaxies is not acceptable because they want to make their own way! It is Christianity that is castigated most by Sagan and his fellow scioreligionists. Is this because, subconsciously, they perceive that it is Christianity that is most capable of exposing the error of science "so called?" Christianity has the power to discern between real science and so-called science. A person can know this intuitively and subconsciously. Christianity's truth creates a disturbing tension on those who want to reject it. It is too intense and documented and uncontrived to be false. But because it is not understood by casual interest, recreational scanning or unbecoming motives, it is avoided and discounted.

It is also clear throughout the book and the movie that none of the characters, including the dropout preacher, have ever had a transforming experience in which they can explain what they once were and what they have now become. They can only claim an experience that they have enjoyed or learned something from but never an evolution from one kind of a creature into another. Ellie herself defends evolution but never experiences it in the book or the movie.

Sagan also makes it clear to us what was in his mind, it is time to make new structures of religious values that are radically different from those of traditional sources i.e., Christianity. And just what kind of structures, laws and rules and transformation power would he and his band of scioreligionists propose for us? This is scary indeed that a man, even in the wilds of his most creative imagination, cannot come up with an actual transformation experience that alters our nature from one kind of being into another. When real evolution and transformation is available in Christianity, why does the modern Christian church accept the notions of Sagan and his fellow scioreligionists creating new religions wherein we serve them and their telescopes and technology? Sagan has never described a transformation experience that he or any other scientist has experienced in a way in which reveals a change in a cosmic relationship.

Sagan and his scioreligionists were not and are not capable of developing these new religions that will not oppress men with "one-world" political agendas which proliferate throughout his famous book "Contact."

CHAPTER 18 - TWO "CHRISTIAN" TYPES - Two Attacks

We covered the tactic used to nullify Christianity. This was shown to be the reduction of Christianity to a mere "religion" or "faith" equal with all other "faiths," and then to assert that the just tension between these religions is proof that all of them or Christianity is deficient or false. Sagan, in his book *Contact*, speaks through Ellie, the heroine, about his idea of a Christian:

> "The major religions on the Earth contradict each other left and right. You can't all be correct. And what if all of you are wrong?"[19]

Two Types of Christians:

Ah, but guess who is making another religion to add to the major religions on the Earth? Yes, Carl Sagan and his fellow scioreligionist! Well, meet the new-world-order-Christian!

> "I'm a Christian and you don't speak for me. You've trapped yourself in some sort of fifth-century religious mania. Since then the Renaissance has happened, the Enlightenment has happened. Where've you been?"(166)

After Ellie tells her shack-up that she would like to "punch out" that "cocksure, know-it-all, holier-than-thou..." Der Heer responds that she should be satisfied that this Christian she argues with lives in "ignorance and error," which should be painful enough. Sagan gives himself an opportunity to reveal what kind of a Christian he is by having Joss (her shack-up, dropout preacher) ask Ellie, candidly, what she meant when she called herself a Christian:

> "I was struck by one or two things you said this morning. You called yourself a Christian. May I ask? In what sense are you a Christian?"

> "You know, this wasn't in the job description when I accepted the directorship of the Argus Project." She said this lightly. "I'm a Christian in the sense that I find Jesus Christ to be an admirable historical figure. I think the Sermon on the Mount is one of the greatest ethical statements and one of the best speeches in history. I think that 'Love your enemy' might even be the long-shot solution to

---

[19] Carl Sagan *Contact* (New York, N.Y.: Pocket Books, 1985), 162.

the problem of nuclear war. I wish he was alive today. It would benefit everybody on the planet. But I think Jesus was only a man. A great man, a brave man, a man with insight into unpopular truths. But I don't think he was God or the son of God or the grandnephew of God."(167)

Here we have an example of one of two kinds of Christians that will be perceived in the New World Order to come if Sagan and his scioreligionists get their way. Sagan through Ellie reveals that he is comfortable in calling himself a Christian in the sense that he believes **Christ was a nice man** that lived once upon a time. Sagan believes that Jesus said a few nice things and might even have the long-shot fix for the threat of nuclear war.

However, Sagan is forced to also believe that Jesus Christ was a liar and a fraud. To believe in what he said, is to believe that he performed an operation upon the cosmos that has changed it and mankind forever. It's clear that Sagan through Ellie does not believe that. One of the **"unpopular truths"** that Ellie unknowingly refers to is Christ's statement relating to his power to lay down his life and take it again—the resurrection. Even Ellie and Joss don't like this truth and have said as much in their naked bedroom scene. In this scene, covered in Chapter 16 herein, they compare the mere view of Andromeda through a telescope with the resurrection.

Another such unpopular truth is Christ's statement that all would one day see him return to earth in his glory with his holy angels. These things Sagan cannot believe, and therefore, it must be concluded that Sagan believes Christ to be a liar. But even Sagan via Ellie claims to be a Christian. Therefore even Sagan fits into this **one and only acceptable kind of Christianity**. This is the kind that is quiet, deep, sophisticated, strong, and most importantly, **impotent**, without the transformation power of God resident in his only begotten son, the hyperspace alien Christ Jesus. To have this transformation power, to become the adopted children of God, and to possess the resultant courage that attends it, to proclaim it from the roof tops even unto the towers of science "so-called" is repulsive to Sagan and his fellow scioreligious friends.

The only other kind of Christian that is portrayed in Sagan's book and the movie is the dangerous, unstable, ignorant, superstitious **sociopathic terrorist**. This Christian is a threat to society and is willing to kill others and destroy property to stop the righteous pursuit of truth by modern scientists. This erroneous "Christian" typecasting is threatening to the New World order priesthood of scioreligionists concerned with man's origin, destiny and moral obligations by the intelligent. Obviously, this type of "Christian" is dangerous to civilization. While it is maintained that scioreligionists, on the other hand, are caring humanitarians that will save the planet from the ignorance of other less scientific religions, i.e., Christianity.

The movie "Contact" depicts an even more sinister Christian than the book. After the message from Vega is made public by President Clinton's own appearance in the movie, Ellie drives through a gauntlet of ignorant humans on the approach to Argus, the radio-telescope facility. An intense middle aged, well-dressed, hippy with long white hair is standing on a portable stage on the great procession of what is obviously cast as religious lunatics. This white-haired hippy is preaching to the crowd in front of his "midway booth." He is telling the crowd that they should not trust the scientists because they are the ones who are poisoning the air and water. He says that they should not trust the scientists to talk to their God for them and the common man. As Ellie drives by in the government car, it stops for a moment, and she lowers the window to hear him—he looks at her with anger and intolerance and points to her as one of the scientists.

After they decrypt the message and find the set of plans for a vehicle hidden therein they build it. Costing the world a third of a trillion dollars, it is the gross national product of several nations. This amount of money is more expensive than any other project in history. And we thought it was stupid to build the pyramids for the Pharaoh and his wife to go meet the Sun God while the builders were left to starve on the earth, and his servants killed and buried with them!

Some time later but during the unmanned test of the newly constructed machine, Ellie spots, on a surveillance security camera, the same white-haired lunatic preacher dressed as a technician on the launch pad. She screams out in the control room that there has been a security breach. But before security can apprehend the lunatic preacher he ignites the bomb attached to his chest that blows the machine apart sending debris far into the sky, some of which hits the control room several miles away.

Therefore Sagan has revealed the only two types of Christians that he acknowledges or presents in his book and movie. These two types are already visible in mainstream society and so named by the scioreligionists or New World Order spokesmen:

1. The impotent quiet, sophisticated, person willing to settle for "faith" in anything.
2. The hateful, lunatic, sociopathic preacher types who are willing to become terrorists to stop the pursuit of truth which is obviously only perceivable by modern scientists.

Now that we have analyzed the two types of Christians in Sagan's world and the new world order, of which he mentions many times in the book as the UN, we review the two fold attack upon Christianity under way for sometime now by modern science in the industrial nations.

Two Fold Attack on Christianity:

There is a most interesting paradox at work in the two-fold attack on Christianity that has been in operation for at least 50 years and presently culminates in NASA-SETI and SETI-Institute. The full ramification of this paradoxical attack is revealed in the Sagan book and movie called "Contact." This is the difficult position of distracting the American public with the hope of aliens in space with the answers to all our problems here on earth. And at the same time, rejecting the idea that the alien might have already come in the person of Jesus Christ. With the occultation of certain Christian theological perceptions in modern times, these scioreligionists have been successful in maintaining this paradoxical position.

What are these occulted Christian theological perceptions? They are the theological categories discussed earlier herein, namely:

1. The **Singular Essence of God**—eternal space or The Holy Spirit.
2. The **Domain Triad** fixing the location and activity of God to be in the world of the living, which we observe around us at all times.
3. The **Two Complementary Image Capacities** explaining the spatial ability of Christ of physically operating upon the entire cosmos and all therein.
4. The demystification and **deoccultation of the Trinity** of Personality revealing the true sharing of Holy Spirit in God the Father, God the Son (Christ) and God the Holy Spirit (man).
5. The **Quaternion components** of mankind required to love God, namely the Heart, Mind, Soul and Strength.
6. The perception of how Christ Jesus has **physically operated upon the cosmos** and all therein by his Death, Resurrection and Ascension.
7. The perception that **Christ Jesus is the most alien and powerful entity** ever to visit Earth or any other place in the galaxies.

About 50 years ago, at the beginning of the atomic and space age, our perception of heaven was changed. What Christian society once called heaven we began to call space. As a result heaven became a place outside the known and observable cosmos, it became the other world or the "**spiritual world.**" This was a serious mistake both to science and to Christian theology. God, then, was also banished from the cosmos to be the caretaker of the "other spiritual world."

The question concerning the Sonship of Christ Jesus is irrelevant if one doesn't believe that God exists in the observable world. Even the existence of God is of little importance to one that does not perceive the domain of God or Godhood to be in the same world he lives in. The only way left for Christians to consider God and His Son was to focus their anticipation on the final revelation of them in death. This idea made it easier for Christians, for a while, in that no astronomer, physicist or scientist of any field could argue the question of "what is on the other side of death." The Christian began to have faith in salvation in the *after life* rather than seek the Trinity and their power to transform us in this real world we live in. Certainly in death all will perceive a final revelation, but the doorway to the stars and galaxies has been opened in this known and observable world to be traversed now to enjoy from now on. And contrary to modern Christian theology, salvation and completeness is obtained in our lives on Earth, not after the death of our bodies.

Further, the Christian was wrong in thinking that we knew nothing about our being after our bodies die on Earth. We know all that Christ knew and he knew most all of it. Therefore, although the scientist would not argue with the Christian about life after death, he also lost integrity with the scientist. The scientist now could argue that the Christian knows nothing about anything, life or death. The truth is that the real transformed Christian knows all about life and death. This is because a walking, breathing Christian on Earth is dead now and with Christ in heaven at this moment. And nothing can take us from Christ because he is stronger then all. On the topic of our death in Christ while we live on Earth, we have this knowledge as expressed by St. Paul in Romans 6:3-6:

"Know ye not, that so many of us as were baptized into Jesus Christ were baptized into his death?

"Therefore we are buried with him by baptism into death: that like as Christ was raised up from the dead by the glory of the Father, even so we also should walk in newness of life.

"For if we have been planted together in the likeness of his death, we shall be also in the likeness of his resurrection:

"Knowing this, that our old man is crucified with him, that the body of sin might be destroyed, that henceforth we should not serve sin."

On the topic of separation from Christ, Christians know (Romans 8:35):

"Who shall separate us from the love of Christ? shall tribulation, or distress, or persecution, or famine, or nakedness, or peril, or sword?"

Again in Romans 8:37-39:

"Nay, in all these things we are more than conquerors through him that loved us.

"For I am persuaded, that neither death, nor life, nor angels, nor principalities, nor powers, nor things present, nor things to come,

"Nor height, nor depth, nor any other creature, shall be able to separate us from the love of God, which is in Christ Jesus our Lord."

This shift in the way we perceive space and heaven caused Christianity to be understood as a mere "faith" like others around the world, wherein people tried to understand something about what was on the other side of death without using their minds, but only their hearts. This crippled the church because there is no other world outside the observable cosmos and death is not the travel into some other dimension. And, certainly, this non-existent dimension is impenetrable by the human mind, the spirit, heart, soul or any other capacity or power. However, one can be banished to live forever in this non-existent dimension by being cast into hell. Hell is this other world that does not exist. To be damned is to be cast out of the domain of God and his Son Jesus Christ, or all of eternal space, to live forever in the non-existent completely collapsed world. You talk about a black hole! That's it! Who can stand to live in the great and unbearable paradox. Therefore the words of St. John the Revelator (Revelation 17:8):

"The beast that thou sawest was, and is not; and shall ascend out of the bottomless pit, and go into perdition: and they that dwell on the earth shall wonder, whose names were not written in the book of life from the foundation of the world, when they behold the beast that was, and is not, and yet is."

Compare this to the great revelation that St. John had of Jesus Christ and those that will enter the gates of heaven he made with his own body (Revelation 1:18):

"I am he that liveth, and was dead; and behold, I am alive for evermore, Amen; and have the keys of hell and of death."

These two revelations sound identical until it is perceived what is meant and the timing involved. In the first case Satan was in the world and powerful but in the end he will not be. Yet he, himself, will be conscious of the fact that he did live even though he lives no longer in the domain of eternal space, but in the non-existent place, alone, with an impassable gulf between the two. In the second case, Christ Jesus was in the world with Satan but was cast out and killed. But now Christ lives eternally at one with his Father and the Holy Spirit or eternal space which contains all the galaxies and matter of every kind. Therefore, those that perceive the doorway to the stars, made by the operation of Christ Jesus upon the cosmos, will enter. And they too, shall have been, and are no more, but live forever with Christ and his Father in their eternal spatial domain that we observe and live in at this moment.

These occulted Christian perceptions have been given names for the first time herein, but that does not mean that they were not perceived earlier by Christians. Earlier Christians did not need the clarification and of these perceptions for they were not in contest as they are today. Other ideas and perceptions were in contest with their own time period which took the time of the theologian of those periods such as the trinity, the Eucharist as blood or wine or both, the nature of Christ's manhood and Godhood and the resurrection of Christ. The domain of God was known to be the world that man lived in. The destination of Christ in his ascension was not a question until now. All the ancients knew that Christ ascended into the heaven above them which is identical to the space above us today, which we contemplate space travel within.

But Satan was loosed from the bottomless pit for a time to deceive the nations once again by the great falsehood, that God's domain is only known and accessed in death. Mankind is meant to travel to the stars and galaxies and many have already done so. But we shall not go there in the manner in which Carl Sagan and his scioreligionists friends think or wish or hope. We go there in a better, faster and more efficient manner, as we shall see herein.

The following review of Sagan's book and movie illustrates the presence of the paradoxical two pronged attacks upon Christianity in the modern industrialized world. Let's restate this paradox as the great hope that an alien from another planet or galaxy will give us all the answers to our problems and at the same time refute the notion he has already come in the person of Jesus Christ. Sagan's whole book and movie is packed with the depictions of exciting hope for the benefits that will come from meeting an alien:

> "And there were those who sensed a change in the world political climate and contended that the very existence of the Message, even if it was never decrypted, was exercising a steadying influence on the quarrelsome nation states. Since the transmitting civilization was clearly more advanced than ours, and because it clearly - at least as of twenty-six years ago had not destroyed itself, it followed, some argued, that technological civilizations did not inevitably self-

destruct. In a world gingerly experimenting with major divestitures of nuclear weapons and their delivery systems, the Message was taken by whole populations as a reason for hope. Many believed the Message the best news in a long time. For decades, young people had tried not to think too carefully about tomorrow. Now, there might be a benign future after all."(119)

The Life Magazine article also agrees with this notion of the great opportunity that awaits us in **meeting the alien**. The article quotes a blue ribbon panel of astronomers in their conclusion that:

"Intelligent organisms are as much a part of the universe as stars and galaxies. It is hard to imagine a more exciting astronomical discovery or one that would have greater impact on human perceptions than the detection of extraterrestrial intelligence."[20]

The immediately preceding quote was not from a science fiction book or a cheap sensational tabloid at the checkout counter, but from the real world of tax-supported modern science. Now let's not get confused about what they have said above. They are not saying that the detection of life on other planets would have great impact. They are saying the detection of **extraterrestrial intelligence** would have great impact. Well, they weren't very impressed when a true hyperspace alien wrote them a letter! I have asked many people from all walks of life if they believe in aliens from other planets. Most of them, including "Christians" said they did believe in this kind of potential. Most people I have talked to have seen "Contact" and adopted the ideas, or had that philosophy set forth therein prior to the movie. However, they did not like the idea that "Ellie didn't actually go anywhere."

Sagan continues to build the hopeful climate in his book:

"Amidst the continuing frenzy of sectarian commentary, there was also - all over the world, it was now apparent Ä a sense of wonder, even of awe. Something transforming, something almost miraculous was happening. The air was full of possibility, a sense of new beginning."[21]

Wow, a whole new beginning for the whole world! And Again:

"There was a whiff of hope in the air"(181)

Again, notice now that the New World Order is more effective in the quote below. All the little "nation states," as Sagan calls them, are beginning to get along. The little slave states can forget their identities, and their laws, and their protections of individual liberty, and their limitations on government. The slave states can now

---

[20] Dava Sobel, "The Search For A Real ET - Is Anybody Out There?" *LIFE*, September 1992.

[21] Sagan *Contact*, 180.

look forward to unlimited world wide government imposed on all states. We can trust the priesthood of scientists, mediating with the aliens, or at least probing deep space for the alien savior just out of reach with good news for us all:

> "The United Nations found itself unexpectedly effective in mediating international disputes, with the West Irian and the Chile-Argentina border wars both apparently resolved. There was even talk, not all of it fatuous, of a nonaggression treaty between NATO and the Warsaw Pact."(183)

It is the obvious intention of Sagan and Scio-religionists to build the hope of mankind on our quest for the aliens and all they will have for us. However, it is the paradoxical nature of their quest that is most critical to perceive and understand. Because in fact their wildest expectations of the future have already come true in the power of Christ of two thousand years ago. And further, the author herein responded to their message to contact an alien in a serious and open fashion and was rejected and never contacted in return. The physical processes available to transform them are more fantastic then they ever imagined and are contained in the New Testament and explained in detail herein. This author even told these same scientists, who are in the real project and who wrote the book "Contact," that he would explain this evolutionary process to them in detail and in their own scientific language which is laid out herein. You may read the entire letter sent to them in the appendix.

The author of this book promised to meet with them and explain the processes of transformation and was ignored. But they have chosen out of ignorance and fear to discredit the Lord of Lords and King of Kings and the Hyperspace Alien of All Time and Space as a cheap fraud. The following is material from Sagan's book, the movie "Contact" and the Life magazine article about NASA-SETI, establishing the most important and dangerous nature of their quest.

There is a scene in the movie, modified but originating in the book "Contact," where Ellie is driven in a government automobile through a gauntlet of campers that are gathered around the Argus Radio-telescope facility awaiting the news of what the message from the alien civilization might say. They drive through this 'midway' cast as bizarre ignorance in various modes of anger, mockery, merchandising and fear. But at one point there stands, bigger than life size, a **cardboard figure of Jesus Christ with a flying saucer over his head in the place of a halo**. This symbol clearly mocks the idea that Jesus Christ could possibly be the most alien entity in the cosmos. The operation that Christ has performed on the infinite cosmos makes him central to all space and time. Even if earth was visited by another space alien, they would be subject to, and lesser than, Christ Jesus. There is no being in all of space or time that exceeds or is superior to Christ Jesus except his own Father - God - The One and Only Living Eternal Space Entity. Christ is the express image of God. And now Man is the image of God, after his transformation into the Kingdom of God by the physical operation that Christ has performed upon the cosmos and all things therein. Therefore, we have evidence that Mankind is superior to anything or any life form we will find on Earth or in Heaven. We are the image of God in the cosmos. AMEN AND HALLELUJAH! PRAISE GOD!

Many people, including those that claim to be Christians, actually say they believe in God and Christ but have included the scioreligionist idea of the existence of intelligent life in outer space that is equal or superior to human life. How can these people believe that Christ and God and his salvation power coexist with aliens with super powers? They can believe this because they believe that Christ and the Father exist in the "spirit" world outside the limits of the observable cosmos. In other words, it is the dual split worldview of the cosmos established by scioreligionists that permits this error in thought to persist. Their logic says, "If God and Christ are in the "spirit" world, unknowable until death, then aliens with other ideas of God and deliverance and help exist in deep space."

These people have not considered the spatial comprehensiveness of the acts or operations of Christ upon the cosmos and everything in it. The spatial comprehensiveness of Christ's death, resurrection and ascension are required in order for anyone to be saved by his actions. This also illustrates that those holding the idea of aliens with salvation for us do not perceive the operation of Christ that produces salvation for anyone or anybody. How can anyone be saved without perceiving the power by which they are saved?

Salvation requires knowledge of the method and operation of it. Otherwise, salvation is mere wishful faith and this type of wishful faith is practiced by liars in error and ignorance. This again illustrates why it is important to establish the Domain Triad fixing the real location of God and Christ in the real observable cosmos - I AM ONE LIVING. As has been established in earlier chapters, the unique Complementary Image Capacities of Christ give the only real world explanation of the power of God to deliver or transform or translate anyone at any time into the Kingdom of Heaven.

The impact of the operation of Christ upon the cosmos alters our knowledge of all that is out in deep space, no matter if, we see it with a telescope or hear it with a radio receiver or visit it in a space ship, or see nothing at all. The God-Man, Christ Jesus, has changed all things in the cosmos to the limits of infinity. Therefore, there is no greater being in the cosmos that we can expect to ever find except his Father, as Jesus has said, and that is eternal space. Further, as has been shown earlier herein, it is impossible for Christ to deliver any one man in a given age, if he does not have the power to deliver all men in any age, until Christ operates upon the cosmos again. This is because the power of Christ to transform men is resident in his unique power of impletion and envelopment of all space and therefore all time. The impletion and envelopment of all space is an **all-or-nothing** power. Obviously this also applies to all creatures, objects or matter within eternal space as well.

What impact does this power of Christ to transform all men in any age have upon the many "religions" of the world? It tells us that all of them and their central figures have been operated upon and they are subject unto the truth and power of Christ Jesus. Can all the religions of the world get together with a common belief given this knowledge? All flesh that can perceive of the operation that Christ has performed upon the cosmos has moved from death unto life (John 5:24):

"Verily, verily, I say unto you, He that heareth my word, and believeth on him that sent me, hath everlasting life, and shall not come into condemnation; **but is passed from death unto life**."

(Emphasis added)

John 17:1-3:

"These words spake Jesus, and **lifted up his eyes to heaven**, and said, Father, the hour is come; glorify thy Son, that thy Son also may glorify thee:

"As thou hast given him **power over all flesh**, that he should give eternal life to as many as thou hast given him.

"And **this is life eternal**, that they might know thee **the only true God, and Jesus Christ, whom thou hast sent**."

(Emphasis added)

As has been shown earlier, it is God's will that all men come together under his only Son, Christ Jesus. And this is the only *will* of God—that you first **believe on the one in whom God sent** and that **all men be saved**. But the modern Christian church persists in coming up with all kinds of junk as God's *will* for their members, and many ways for their members to probe the unknown, to determine these *wills* of God. Now, just because there is resistance to God's will that all men be saved and delivered to the Kingdom of Heaven, this does not mean that this is not His will or that He does not have the power to do so. It merely means that men are resistant to God's will, because of other distractions, they mistakenly think they want more than eternal life in the galaxies with God.

Even if Christians have been slow to bring this about, it does not mean they will deny their own reality either, when pressed. The New World Order globalists are organizing a combination of all religions into a single one-world religion, for the evil purpose of attacking the power of transformation in Christ Jesus. Christianity will not become part of the one world religion without brute force exerted by the scioreligionists. It goes without saying; that this one world religion without the supremacy of Christ Jesus will not have the power to transform anyone into a new creature with eternal life to travel the stars forever. Therefore, it follows that we should question the purpose for pursuing a one-world religion if it would have no power to do anything other than oppress mankind.

In another movie scene, as Ellie approaches Argus, the music is playing from the crowd the tune "**Spirit in the Sky**." This again alludes to the idea that fools in this ignorant crowd of humanity believe that Space might actually be alive and operating as a whole with a plan and a process in the person of Jesus Christ. The book "Contact" is about eighty percent condemnation of Christianity, about five percent creation of one-world government and religion, and about fifteen percent science of the most boring sort. This is one of the most dangerous pieces of poor thinking around. This book's philosophy is acceptable to most, including "Christians," without critical analysis.

It should be evident that the scioreligionists have a paradoxical problem. They point to space saying; "our hope is in alien intelligence being located by our scientists." But whatever you do, don't look to that man who raises his eyes above and says, "Father." It should also be clear that scioreligionists have targeted their one and only enemy with power to defeat them; the Christian Gospel and its real-world power to transform all mankind without any help from any scientist. In this they are correct that Christianity has power to defeat their heresy, but incorrect that Christianity is their enemy. For no man is the enemy of the love of God in pursuit of exposing their ignorance, therefore liberating them into life eternal. Did we not just prove that? It is God's will that all men be delivered, even the scioreligionists, who hate the idea of Christ Jesus as the hyperspace alien with power to do what they ultimately want to do—**GO TO THE STARS FOREVER!**

PART V - THE HOPE OF NATIONS HAS COME

CHAPTER 19 - THE HOPE OF NATIONS

We all know that the hope of modern astronomy is the detection of extraterrestrial intelligence. We all know that the desire for modern physicists is to travel into deep space and actually visit planets, other solar systems, and other galaxies. And we also know that most people including modern scientists of every field and every nation still find it difficult to believe that we will ever achieve any of this. Yet, they continue to entertain these notions in hope and desire. What does God say about the hope and desire of nations (Haggai 2:5-9):

> "According to the word that I convenanted with you when ye came out of Egypt, so my spirit remaineth among you: fear ye not.

> "For thus saith the LORD of hosts; Yet once, it is a little while, and **I will shake the heavens**, and the earth, and the sea, and the dry land;

> "And I will shake all nations, **and the desire of all nations shall come**: and I will fill this house with glory, saith the LORD of hosts.

> "The glory of this latter house shall be greater than of the former, saith the LORD of hosts: and in this place will I give peace, saith the LORD of hosts."

(Emphasis added)

Was God speaking of a new project, men would build on some real estate in Israel? Or was God speaking of something much greater? Wasn't He speaking of shaking the heavens and the earth, the sea and the dry land and all nations! God is referring to the shaking that Christ Jesus would perform on the entire cosmos including the heavens around us containing the galaxies, including the earth (land and sea) and the nations and their political systems. This shaking is the desire of all nations! It is the revelation of what our present and greatest scientists, world wide, hope for and desire.

What does it mean to shake something like the heaven and the earth? It is clear in the Bible that this type of **shaking is a harvest of people** either to destruction or redemption depending on the kind of person one is. Shaking in this case is how one, including God, removes both good and bad fruit from either a vine or a tree. The agent or force that God uses to shake the heaven, earth, land and sea, and nations is the revelation of Jesus Christ and what he has done. Is this shaking referring to the end of time or the operation of Christ Jesus upon the cosmos in his death, resurrection and ascension? Paul said in Hebrews 12:22-24:

> "But ye are come unto mount Zion, and unto the city of the living God, the heavenly Jerusalem, and to an innumerable company of angels,

"To the general assembly and church of the firstborn, which are written in heaven, and to God the Judge of all, and to the spirits of just men made perfect,

"And to Jesus the mediator of the new covenant

...(and in 27-29)...

"and this word, yet once more, signifieth the **removing of those things that are shaken**, as of things that are made, that **those things which cannot be shaken may remain.**

"Wherefore we receiving **a kingdom which cannot be moved,** let us have grace, whereby we may serve God acceptably with reverence and godly fear:

"For our God is a consuming fire."

(Emphasis added)

This passage is not written in the future tense but in the present tense. **We now possess this kingdom which cannot be moved nor shaken because it is not made**. Eternal Space, the same of which Einstein and Descartes refer to, is not made. It is eternal and independent of all other made or created things. And space travel for the transformed is based upon this fact. One who has been transformed by the operation of Christ's death, resurrection and ascension (made possible by his impletion and envelopment of all space) obtained the power to manifest and demanifest themselves where ever and when ever they chose through out the stars and galaxies as Christ does presently.

Notice that Paul did not say "ye are going" but said "ye are come." This is past tense. Ye then are come to mount Zion or the kingdom of heaven. Paul also said "Wherefore we receiving a kingdom" instead of "We will receive a kingdom." Paul is clearly saying that **the heavens and the earth have been shaken by the operation of Christ Jesus** and all things therein have been reconciled back unto God. Those that refuse this message will not remain in the kingdom, which is all of eternal space, but will be cast out. And where is this place they are cast out to? The flip side of eternal space, which is nowhere, the ultimate black hole where the compression is unbearable yet endured. This is the ultimate contradiction of all things.

If you think this hope and desire of modern science and of the nations is waning, refer to the January 2000 issue of the National Geographic Magazine. The magazine has a cover story about "life beyond Earth," with some of the same characters of the $100 million NASA-SETI project of 1992.

Scientists are trying to think themselves into deep space or the Kingdom of Heaven. Fred Allen Wolf, A physics professor at San Diego State University provides one such attempt by the use of "quantum psychodynamics" and "evolution from parallel worlds," wherein one conceives of other universes where everything imaginable is happening. Reality evolves into our "real physical world," when we select one possibility over another, or even when a group picks one option as the more desirable reality.

I read this work in serious quest for truth that he could present about reality and our perception. But, at times the notions were so preposterous that laughter could not be held back. However, hysterical laughter dies when realized that this stuff is being taught to the youth of America as well as the populations of the industrialized world. This type of thinking is presently in charge of many large corporations and government projects and political movements. Mr. Wolf explains his hope for mankind:

> "The mental worlds are, according to the parallel worlds concept, actually occurring now. What you think here is happening there. The forms of physical reality we experience are not unique. They are formed from harmonies of other parallel realities. This physical existence is just one of many mental existences."[22]

> "The "movement" of time is expressed as evolution. The direction of evolution may be described as making matter conscious. From the parallel worlds hypothesis, this means bringing more worlds into harmony through interactions that lead to the greater acceptance of physical and mental differences. This is its higher purpose, or its higher will."(274)

At this point one cannot escape the implications that a rubber ball, put in motion down a 2 x 8 inch wood plank on incline, suddenly evolves into consciousness and begins to wonder what it is doing and where it is going. The ball is now moving towards a higher form of life accepting the differences of other shapes as equally great; "just because a cube cannot roll does that mean it cannot be equally alive?" Don't laugh! Let us continue with serious particle physics and quantum mechanics and our own future!

> "Thus, according to Quantum Psychodynamics, the true cause of suffering on the material plane is our unwillingness to let go of our babyhood, the babyhood of humankind, the early, reptilian adventure we call our origins. We adhere to it. The proof is the existence of reptiles at this level of being. These reptiles are both physical and mental; they are "out there" and they are in our heads. Our reptilian brain is unfortunately still running the show. Survival comes first.

> "The physical reptiles are there to remind us that we must let go so that they can evolve into us. All physical suffering is due to our unwillingness to let go of our prehistoric parallel world of wars,

---

[22] Fred Allen Wolf, *STAR WAVE Mind, Consciousness, and Quantum Physics* (New York, N.Y.: Macmillan Publishing Company, 1984), 274.

death, and violence - all necessary when humankind first began."(275)

"We say in the language of Darwin, that the ape will evolve into a man.

"The man, who is at an obviously higher level of consciousness than the ape, is also aware of his apeness. He remembers his lower manifestation. He is more aware of his apeness than the ape is aware of his humanity. Both ape and man are equally projected from consciousness. When the man lets go of his apeness, he can evolve. When the man holds on to his apeness, both the man and the ape cease to evolve."(276)

What kind of political policy could one develop from these ideas held by many modern scientists? Not only is mankind an "environmental stressor," according to the United Nations, but he also now is a staller of evolution. Mankind by holding on to his apeness has caused all the evolution in the cosmos to come to a screeching halt! But has motion and time stopped? No! But I thought Fred Wolf said that motion was evolution, and if we are in motion we are evolving, and experiencing the march of time. And if all things are in motion of one kind or another and time is moving on, why can't I hear the ball speaking to me? Why can't the ape tell me something? And just why can't the ape let go of his reptilian babyhood and tell us to take a hike? No! The real problem in the world is that everyone runs into some degree of truth about reality. Just because we think something, doesn't make it real or evolve into reality. We dump old ideas when they lead nowhere. Some wrong ideas about reality lead to personal disaster and some wrong ideas commonly held, lead nations to destruction.

Professor Wolf has difficulty in determining reality in any plane, physical or mental. Professor Wolf is receiving a monthly check and that is all he knows and depends upon. He is supported in his erroneous views because this is the kind of thinking wanted by the New World order to be taught to our youth to make them slaves. The true test of ideas is their consistency and power under persecution. Under persecution, Professor Wolf can merely pick another reality that is more suitable at providing the life style he desires. I presume he will reject the reality where cars are moving on square wheels, and rubber balls are discussing the merits of integration and snakes refuse to live outside his bedroom.

And now what about the legendary Albert Einstein? What hope has he given us in terms of space travel into the stars? First, Einstein says the laws of Gravitation, developed by Newton to predict the location of planets and stars, are not significantly changed by the law of general relativity:

"If we confine the application of the theory to the case where the gravitational fields can be regarded as being weak, and in which all masses move with respect to the co-ordinate system with velocities which are small compared with the velocity of light, we then obtain as a first approximation the Newtonian theory. Thus the latter theory is obtained here without any particular assumption, whereas Newton had to introduce the hypothesis that the force of attraction between mutually attracting material points is inversely proportional to the square of the distance between them. If we increase the accuracy of the calculation, deviation from the theory of Newton make their appearance, practically all of which must nevertheless escape the test of observation owing to their smallness."[23]

Einstein admits that observation of the change of Newton's laws by the general theory of relativity occurs in few places:

"Apart from this one, it has hitherto been possible to make only two deductions from the theory which admit to being tested by observation, to wit, the curvature of light rays by the gravitational field of the sun, and a displacement of the spectral lines of light reaching us from large stars, as compared with the corresponding lines of light produced in an analogous manner terrestrially (i.e. by the same kind of atom). These two deductions from the theory have both been confirmed."(104)

So, without going much further, we as humans still live in a Newtonian cosmos for all practical purposes. But what else did Einstein say that really influenced the way the world is perceived? How did what he say remove God, the Father, and God, the Son, from reality? One of the most important propositions of Alien Physics is the idea that God's singular essence is eternal space, and that God was removed from the observable cosmos by the introduction of the theory of a finite cosmos with the possibility of expansion and contraction. Einstein was the biggest promoter and seller of these ideas, but they came from other philosophers before him. Einstein added a 22 page discussion of "Relativity and the problem of Space" in the appendix of his book. There he agrees with Descartes' idea that there exists no space "empty of field," i.e., without material objects and their extension defining space and location, there is no space. This is nothing, other than starting with materials, while rejecting any other explanation and ending with materials. God or eternal space is not dependent upon any material that He creates to define Himself or prove His spatial reality.

"The assertion that extension is confined to bodies is therefore of itself certainly unfounded. We shall see later, however, that the general theory of relativity confirms Descartes' conception in a roundabout way.

"What brought Descartes to his remarkably attractive view was certainly the feeling that, without compelling necessity, one ought not

---

[23] Albert Einstein, *Relativity, The Special and General Theory* (New York, N.Y.: Crown Publishers, Inc., 1961), 102.

to ascribe reality to a thing like space, which is not capable of being "directly experienced"." (136)

A footnote is added behind the "directly experienced" quotation marks, which said, "This expression is to be taken cum grano salis." Which is to say it should be taken with a grain of salt.

I think it is understood that men can indeed experience space directly and do so with out reference to any particles or material bodies at all. This experience is the unity with God himself, and this spatial experience of unity in Christ is available to all men. This is the "direct experience" of none other than the Holy Ghost or all of Eternal Space, the Singular Essence of God.

> "Strictly speaking, there are no precise laws, even in the macro-region, for the possible configurations of solid bodies touching each other.

> "In spite of this, no one thought of giving up the concept of space, for it appeared indispensable in the eminently satisfactory whole system of natural science. Mach, in the nineteenth century, was the only one who thought seriously of an elimination of the concept of space, in that he sought to replace it by the notion of the totality of the instantaneous distances between all material points. (He made this attempt in order to arrive at a satisfactory understanding of inertia)."(148)

What is going on here? Men are attempting to understand the physical world and how it behaves in a way in which they can predict. This is good for use in various things, but is not useful at all in determining how we will travel to the stars or in determining who will travel to the stars.

We can now see what has happened to the ideas of God and his domain as a result of modern physics and its theories. Let us remember that it is the Trinity and the Image Capacities that allows Christ to save anyone. If he can save anyone he can save all men, in all space for all time, until he operates upon the cosmos again. Einstein goes on to say the following:

> "In this, the essential thing is that "physical reality", thought of as being independent of the subjects experiencing it, was conceived as consisting, at least in principle, of space and time on one hand, and of permanently existing material points, moving with respect to space and time, on the other. The idea of the independent existence of space and time can be expressed drastically in this way: If matter were to disappear, space and time alone would remain behind (as a kind of stage for physical happening)."(144)

This last sentence is a complete rejection of the idea of God as the eternal existing one whom creates and redeems. Why do Christians rave about the greatness of this poor man? Then Einstein explains that the concept of field came along to replace the idea of a particle, which regarded matter as a continuum. These ideas were important in the study of heat transmission in a solid body or a body of water and liquid in motion in a pipe. These ideas considered a field of moving spaces containing these bodies.

> "But in the first quarter of the nineteenth century it was shown that the phenomena of the interference and motion of light could be explained with astonishing clearness when light was regarded as a wave-field, completely analogous to the mechanical vibration field in an elastic solid body. It was thus felt necessary to introduce a field, that could also exist in "empty space" in the absence of ponderable matter."(145)

This treated the empty space as a solid body with particles spread very sparsely and resulted in the idea of the form of matter (thought at one time to be everywhere) called "aether."

> "The aether-theory brought with it the question: How does the aether behave from the mechanical point of view with respect to ponderable bodies? Does it take part in the motions of the bodies, or do its parts remain at rest relatively to each other?"(147)

Einstein then explained that the concept of aether-at-rest, was proved by H.A. Lorentz:

> "The results of all these facts and experiments, except for one, the Michelson-Morley experiment, were explained by H. A. Lorentz on the assumption that the aether does not take part in the motions of ponderable bodies, and that the parts of the aether have no relative motions at all with respect to each other."(147)

Because the discussion of the equivalence of all inertial systems or inertial spaces and the laws of Nature being invariant in relation to the Lorentz transformation equation and the problem of simultaneous events, is so long, we are going to skip to the summation of Einstein concluding that space does not exist outside of field:

> "We are now in a position to see how far the transition to the general theory of relativity modifies the concept of space. In accordance with classical mechanics and according to the special theory of relativity, space (space-time) has an existence independent of matter or field. In order to be able to describe at all that which fills up space and is dependent on the co-ordinates, space-time or the inertial system with its metrical properties must be thought of at once as existing, for otherwise the description of "that which fills up space" would have no meaning. On the basis of the general theory of relativity, on the other hand, space as opposed to "what fills space", which is dependent on the co-ordinates, has no separate existence... Space-time does not claim existence on its own, but only as a structural quality of the field.

"Thus Descartes was not so far from the truth when he believed he must exclude the existence of an empty space. The notion indeed appears absurd, as long as physical reality is seen exclusively in ponderable bodies. It requires the idea of the field as the representative of reality, in combination with the general principle of relativity, to show the true kernel of Descartes' idea; there exists no space "empty of field.""(155-156)

It is also important to mention another idea that Einstein introduced in his book. This is the idea of a finite spherical cosmos. He applies the experience of history of the solid we live on to space itself:

"Let us consider now a second two-dimensional existence, but this time on a spherical surface instead of on a plane... Similarly, this universe has a finite area that can be compared with the area of a square constructed with rods. The great charm resulting from this consideration lies in the recognition of the fact that the universe of these beings is finite and yet has no limits."(109)

Another potential for the construction of space Einstein proposes is an elliptical space:

"It may be mentioned that there is yet another kind of curved space: "elliptical space." It can be regarded as a curved space in which the two "counter points" are identical (indistinguishable from each other). An elliptical universe can thus be considered to some extent as a curved universe possessing central symmetry.

"It follows from what has been said, that closed spaces without limits are conceivable. From amongst these, the spherical space (and the elliptical) excels in its simplicity, since all points on it are equivalent. As a result of this discussion, a most interesting question arises for astronomers and physicists, and that is whether the universe in which we live is infinite, or whether it is finite in the manner of the spherical universe. Our experience is far from being sufficient to enable us to answer this question."(112)

Why are these theories and ideas important to Alien Physics? They are important because the ideas and theories of Einstein and others have been taken out of context of their local usefulness and used to describe the observable cosmos in an incorrect manner. The curved, spherical and elliptical universe Einstein refers to is not one that is perceptible at all in space without a physical platform such as the spherical earth we walk on or an elliptical moon or asteroid we could visit. However, these material models cannot describe space itself, for eternal space has only one shape—that is the shape of the human being. Christ Jesus was the first to take the shape of eternal space as first the filler and then the container of eternal space.

Michael Guillen, Ph.D. and ABC-TV's award-winning and popular Science Editor and instructor of physics and mathematics in the Core Curriculum Program at Harvard University sums up the ideas of Einstein:

"To begin with, in order to be consistent with the relativistic behavior of Faraday's electromagnetic phenomenon, Einstein scrapped the notion of absolute space and time. In his universe, those qualities would be relative, in that people would not necessarily reckon distance and time in exactly the same way.

"After searching for such laws, Einstein finally found them in, of all places, the Fizeau experiment. According to its puzzling results, the speed of light appeared the same to people moving with different speeds; it was only after the people had added or subtracted their own speeds from what they saw that they were left disagreeing irrevocably as to the true speed of light."[24]

Michael Guillen went on to say:

"There was another way of seeing this mysterious constancy, Einstein realized. It was as if the different tourists' perceptions of space and time changed in accordance with their individual motions, in such a way that the speed of light—and only the speed of light—always appeared the same.

"According to this interpretation, Einstein's universe was based on a cosmic-size optical illusion whose confounding effects were universal. No matter how fast a person was moving, his reckoning of an inch and a second always changed so as to leave unchanged his reckoning of the speed of light!"(247)

"What happened, Einstein wondered, when material objects moved as fast as light—that is, when v equaled c? In such a case, Einstein noticed, the precise expression (not merely the approximation) of his original shrinking formula was reduced all the way down to zero:

"This meant that for a person traveling at the speed of light, space and time—indeed, the entire visible universe—appeared to shrink down to nothing. Reciprocally, furthermore, the person's mass energy appeared to expand up to infinity (the reciprocal of zero being infinity).

"Neither of those really seemed possible, an incredulous Einstein concluded. Therefore, rather than take them seriously, he interpreted those outrageous predictions to mean that his new theory was trying

---

[24] Michael Guillen, Ph.D., *Five Equations that Changed the World, The Power and Poetry of Mathematics* (New York, N.Y.: Hyperion, 1995), 245.

to tell him something, namely that it was physically impossible for any material body to travel as fast as an electromagnetic wave—that is, to catch up with a light beam."(250)

"For example, even at speeds of hundreds of miles an hour, the mathematical value of Einstein's shrinking factor remained very close to 1, which meant that the various relativistic aberrations were virtually undetectable: In the realm of everyday life, therefore, space and time and mass and energy appeared to behave normally.

"Even in the future, when astronauts would travel to the moon at 25,000 miles per hour, the discrepancy from normal would amount to a minuscule five parts in a trillion. Compared to people left behind on earth, in other words, an astronaut's impression of an inch and a second was shorter by that absolutely negligible amount."(254)

Therefore we can conclude that Einstein has not really provided anything for modern man to hope for in terms of travelling to the kingdom of heaven on our own mechanical power. We also conclude that Professor Wolf, with his quantum physics and psychology, cannot get us to the celestial kingdom by improving our selections of simultaneous parallel realities. We shall also see that Dr. Sagan and others have not done any better at providing this hope of escaping the earth to live in the stars.

Roger S. Jones, as associate professor of physics at the University of Minnesota at Minneapolis St. Paul, has stated that modern science has become our new **state religion**:

"In a sense, **science has taken over the role of state religion** in modern culture, and it has become a very influential religion at that. Who can deny that the scientific establishment has become a modern priesthood? The pronouncements of scientists are respected and accepted by today's public just as the doctrines of the church fathers were respected and accepted by people a thousand years ago. The rigorous training in arcane mathematics and methodology is no less exacting, demanding, and monastic than was the medieval study of ancient languages and theology. Modern **scientific training today is an insuperable barrier** to the layperson who would question the authority of science, just as the ecclesiastical training of the Roman Catholic priesthood was a great obstacle to the medieval laity with its questions and doubts. If anything, modern science incurs far less challenge and criticism than the church ever did. The church fathers would have given their eyeteeth to command for medieval

Catholicism the kind of obedience and blind faith that we freely lavish on science today."[25]

(Emphasis added)

Mr. Jones goes on to explore some ideas of modern physics that he believes are mere mythology:

"It is fruitful to explore physics from a phychic and mythical point of view and to compare its metaphors with those of alternative systems of knowledge, belief, and wisdom. In many primal and ancient cultures, matter is not inanimate but has spirit or soul. Space is not empty but enfolds within it intelligence and insight. Time is not linear and relentless but has a cyclic, cumulative, and enriching quality. To our peril, we have allowed science to discount and reject this precious lore. Yet science has its own nourishing mythology and spirit, if only we are willing to acknowledge it.

"The desire of power and the fear of death undoubtedly play a role in physics. Sigmund Freud, Brigid Brophy, and Norman O. Brown have emphasized how deeply our psyches and lives are influenced by our knowledge and fear of death...I believe that the most basic concepts in physics-space, time, matter, and number—have a metaphorical character, which, among other things, unconsciously denies death.

"Space, for example, is the very medium of existence itself-a guarantee against oblivion and the loss of being. The word exists comes from the Latin and means to stand out. Space is precisely what we stand out from. It is the background against which we contrast and articulate our being, our individuality, our ego, our existent selves. Physics, in fact, has crystallized and promoted just this meaning of space. The empty void of physical space is the all-encompassing container of things, matter, bodies, beings. It is the platform, the scaffolding, which supports matter and provides it with place, location, extension, room—all the things we take for granted as individual, articulate beings. To treat space as the mere abstract continuum of mathematical physics is to deny its very real metaphorical, psychological, and mythical character." (317)

Jones is getting close to the seed of Alien Physics except that the mythical character of space is not an accurate description of God. Furthermore, the idea that eternal space is God with power to create, redeem and destroy is not lore. Who would like to inject the mythical character of space into the world of physics or

---

[25] Roger S. Jones, *Physics for the Rest of Us, Ten Basic Ideas of Twentieth-Century Physics That Everyone Should Know...and How They Have Shaped Our Culture and Consciousness* (Chicago, Illinois: Contemporary Books, 1992), 134-135.

theology? The idea of injecting lore, mysticism, and occult into physics is just as repulsive as adding those things to Christian theology.

Einstein did an excellent job of making space disappear in the minds of modern man. With the disappearance of space so the disappearance of God himself. We can say that Einstein occulted God or Eternal Space with Matter or that which God created. We could easily say from Einstein's logic, that where there is no field or material points, there is no God. Most men know intuitively and instinctively that God and His singular essence is immutable eternal space. They can sense this because God makes them with this capacity, as discussed earlier.

God is not energy nor mass, but space itself. This space gives rise to all things and life to all living. And this is precisely why God is not energy or mass or time. If God were energy, he would be a component of mass and convertible into mass. This is not the nature of God. God is Space and Space is superior to all things consisting of matter and energy. God or Eternal Space has shared His essence with mankind whereby we obtain the power that Jesus has to travel in Himself. We are united completely with God and Christ.

Another popular physicist today is Stephen Hawking. Has he got good news for us? Mr. Stephen Hawking, who at the printing of his book *Black Holes and Baby Universes* in 1993, held the Newton Chair as Lucasian Professor of Mathematics at Cambridge University, makes a very good observation about the world around us: **We don't know what reality is without a model theory.** This means that man does not hold a flawless detector of reality but latches on to ideas as they come up and defends those that he has adopted without much analysis. We know that Christians do this in theology and scientists do this in physics. Therefore, this seems to support a thesis herein that a false sociological equilibrium can be reached between the whole fields of physics and Christianity that is false to both.

> "Maybe I'm being a bit harsh on philosophers, but they have not been very kind to me. My approach has been described as naive and simpleminded. I have been variously called a nominalist, an instrumentalist, a positivist, a realist, and several other ists. The technique seems to be refutation by denigration: If you can attach a label to my approach, you don't have to say what is wrong with it. Surely everyone knows the fatal errors of all those isms.

> "The people who actually make the advances in theoretical physics don't think in the categories that the philosophers and historians of science subsequently invent for them. I am sure that Einstein, Heisenberg, and Dirac didn't worry about whether they were realists or instrumentalists. They were simply concerned that the existing theories didn't fit together. In theoretical physics, the search for

logical self-consistency has always been more important in making advances than experimental results."[26]

With the following statement Mr. Hawking makes it is clear that physicists are attempting to help mankind by modeling our ideas about how we view the cosmos. But, these strictly inanimate particle relationships do not regard what mankind is and what his potentials are in space and what his actual relationship to space is.

"What I hope I have demonstrated is that some sort of positivist approach, in which one regards a theory as a model, is the only way to understand the universe, at least for a theoretical physicist. I am hopeful that we will find a consistent model that describes everything in the universe. If we do that, it will be a real triumph for the human race."(47)

Mankind is not a mere particle that travels around in space subject to the laws of particle physics and light speed. Rather man is first a filler of space, all of it, and then he is a container of space, all of it. This is how Christ Jesus operated upon the cosmos and that is how he is now able to manifest himself anywhere in it. And this is how he has alienated us into beings with the same power with which we will travel space as he does presently.

It should be evident from both Hawking and Einstein that their theories were developed, not by pure experiment, but from logic and word problems. Their theories have validity with respect to mere electromagnetic waves, but mankind is simply not an electromagnetic wave. The consciousness, that even they agree that we have obtained in some way, disputes our mere particle existence. Einstein's theory of relativity was developed on word problems just as the harmony of the power of Christ to operate on the cosmos was. Consciousness is telling us that we are not mere particles or groups of particles that are subject to mere particle or wave laws. Just as human consciousness separates us from the "apeness" of Darwin theory, our human consciousness also separates us from the particleness of Einstein and Hawking.

In other words, it's not that we should let go of our apeness so that the world and its species can further evolve, but instead, we should let go of our foolishly simplistic views of man as a particle or wave subject to the transformation of energy laws. We are more than rocks! But the physicists are treating themselves and all men as such. The way we model the travel of light is not the way we should model the travel of mankind. The way that particles and waves act is not the way men act. There must be a correct model theory of the universe for particles that is separate from a correct model that describes mankind's consciousness and relationship to all space and time. These two sets of models can and should be true for both particles and mankind.

---

[26] Stephen Hawking, *Black Holes and Baby Universes and Other Essays* (New York, N.Y.: Bantam Books, 1993), 42.

Give credit where credit is due. The respected theoretical physicist, Mr. Hawking, has abolished the idea, promoted by Carl Sagan, that black holes could possibly be a means of space travel to other stars and galaxies. However, it's hard to imagine that anyone ever considered *travel by a black hole* a real option, if they had heard or read anything about a black hole. Our modern scientific priests argue about questions that a reasonable layman would never even consider as real.

> "To sum up: It seems that particles can fall into black holes that then evaporate and disappear from our region of the universe. The particles go off into baby universes that branch off from our universe. These baby universes can then join back on somewhere else. They may not be much good for space travel, but their presence means that we will be able to predict less then we expected, even if we do find a complete unified theory. On the other hand, we now may be able to provide explanations for the measured values of some quantities like the cosmological constant. In the last few years, a lot of people have begun working on baby universes. I don't think anyone will make a fortune by patenting them as a method of space travel, but they have become a very exciting area of research."(125)

So much for Carl Sagan and his book "Contact" and the mythological trip to the center of the galaxy! But, like Einstein, Carl Sagan has been successful in the occult of Christian theology. In this, one might conclude that an implied tenant of modern physics is to keep the public interest away from the idea that there is a real and effective way to be translated, and transformed into a hyperspace alien by the operation of Christ Jesus. It seems to be a drive of modern physics to get rid of the idea of God and man as anything other than a particle in a finite ever changing mechanical system of rigid laws.

A Comparison of Christian Cosmology and Modern Scientific Cosmology:

Modern physics is hopelessly found in want of a way for man to travel in deep space to visit the stars or evolve into anything free of destruction and decay. Let's compare what we have found from a century of modern physicists and the revealed Alien Spatial Christian Physics described in word problems in the New Testament. Our view of space is the key to human survival on planet Earth and travel into deep space forever.

- ❑ The Biblical, three layered space, or heaven is eternal, infinite, powerful and purposeful and longs to share its entirety with mankind.

The view of space by modern physics is that space is expanding and possibly contracting; is finite and curved and hopefully foldable back onto itself to allow us to travel great distances so that the speed limit of light can be broken.

- ❑ The Biblical view of the shape of space is the shape of Jesus Christ. Yes space is curved and shaped in the Bible. All of eternal space has its only shape in that of Christ Jesus and now us. Look into the mirror and behold the shape of eternal space. If you are not yet transformed, then behold one with the capacity to fill all space and contain all space and time.

All real physicists must despair at their findings. They realize that they are no better off then they were before Newton. They cannot get much of anywhere in deep space without breaking or violating the laws they have discovered.

❑ God has indeed set the bounds of mankind's habitation. But the purpose of that was that they might "seek him and haply find him." Yes, God has a purpose in restricting mankind's ability to travel in heaven by his own devices. That is so, that they would be in despair of their own limits and seek God's power of liberation in humility and obedience to his only Son.

So what has Einstein really provided for the hope of mankind? His particle man cannot exceed the speed of light, which is incredibly slow in the expanse of deep space. And that is not to mention what you become at near light speeds. Due to his conversion of mass and energy formula we see that man would become light as he approaches light speed. Men have gone to the moon at a rate of 6.9 miles per second. Einstein's theory of relativity was experienced in five out of a trillion parts.

We see what the late great Carl Sagan has given us in the travel through black holes. In fact, Einstein's theories are no better than the black hole theory of travel. As we have seen from Einstein's shrinking factor, inherent in his conversion formula, one is either in a process of mass or energy conversion. In other words travel at these speeds would render the human perception of being exploded. This is to say that there are space ships all around now for such travel. Just strap a stick of dynamite on your chest and light the fuse. This is Einstein's mode of particle travel.

Carl Sagan attempted to give us another less excruciating method of travel in his black hole. How many of you can look forward to falling into gravity so strong that light can't escape and where your particles are either evaporated and emitted as heat or spit out eventually in imaginary time on the edge of the universe? Well this is all available right now! Go get in your car and drive it to the wrecking yard and ask them to crush your car into a nice little cube and get in and buckle up for the ride of your life! We balk at the "cults" like Heaven's Gate, yet what have these particle physicists provided any better? Are you sure that some of those "cult" ideas don't originate from modern physics?

Oh yes, a man can be made to conform to particle physics, just as a friend of mine said "put a match to your hand and see if you are not subject to the laws of particle physics." But is that what we want? Is that all we are and all we have capacity for? All modern theoretical physics can offer us, is the promise of being ground up and destroyed by the laws of particle physics. Does mankind have other attributes that free him completely from the laws of modern physics? Thanks to God, the answer is yes! The really good news, even today, is that mankind has the capacity to be free from all the laws of particle physics. These capacities rest in the true nature of space, and what it is, and how we are related to it. And this is the same observable space that particle physicists presume to know and study.

What human has ever testified that they traveled through a black hole, or experienced the relativity of time, or entered a time machine etc. etc.? But how many humans have testified to a transformation experience that they became different creatures, wherein they were once physical flesh centered creatures but then transformed into spatial spiritual centered eternal creatures? Thousands of men and women have, over the centuries, experienced this operation and are now in the Kingdom of Heaven. They were transformed by their perception of the operation of Jesus Christ upon the cosmos.

How many human Christians have submitted to the particle physics of tyrants and barbarians in the defense of the good news of freedom from the laws of the same? Christ himself voluntarily suffered the crucifixion in knowledge that the laws of particle physics did not hold for him. And his disciples also experienced the same and many thousands of later converts as well. But today modern physics rules the planet and Satan makes his domain and abode in the deception of the nations. This deception is only for a short season, which is coming to a close at the publication of this book and others to come like it, of which others will write and defend.

Yes, the hope of nations has come almost 2000 years ago, but modern physics and philosophy have occulted this reality over the last 300 years or more. But this age is coming to a close and Satan will again be cast into the bottomless pit for the last time by the revelation of where he lives and what his power consists of. Satan's exposure will result in his inability to deceive the nations. And the hope of nations will shine bright and clear for the rest of time, as Christ will come with his Holy Angels in the clouds of Heaven. Amen! You now presently have access to travel the stars and galaxies through the transformation power of Christ Jesus.

Let us see what has changed in the great scientific minds between 1614 and 1941 some 327 years. The first quote is from a letter to Grand Duchess Christina by Galileo Galilei and the second quote is from an essay by Albert Einstein.

> From these things it follows as a necessary consequence that, since the Holy Ghost did not intend to teach us whether heaven moves or stands still, whether its shape is spherical or like a discus or extended in a plane, nor whether the earth is located at its center or off to one side, then so much the less was it intended to settle for us any other conclusion of the same kind. And the motion or rest of the earth and the sun is so closely linked with the things just named, that without a determination of the one, neither side can be taken in the other matters. Now if the Holy Spirit has purposely neglected to teach us propositions of this sort as irrelevant to the highest goal (that is our salvation), how can anyone affirm that it is obligatory to take sides on them, and that one belief is required by faith, while the other side is erroneous? Can an opinion be heretical and yet have no concern with the salvation of souls? Can the Holy Ghost be asserted not to have intended teaching us something that does concern our salvation? I would say here something that was heard from an ecclesiastic of the

most eminent degree: "That the intention of the Holy Ghost is to teach us how one goes to heaven, not how heaven goes."[27]

It is clear that Galileo perceived the heaven that one goes to by the operation of Christ Jesus as one and the same as the one he studied in science. It is also clear that he saw that the highest and main goal of God through the Holy Spirit was the transformation of a man to the stars of heaven. Galileo also expresses the idea that the motion of the Sun and Earth and all other galactic relationships are irrelevant to this goal of salvation. This indicates that the rudest of men, with no appreciation of mathematics, will travel to the distant galaxies while the most learned of men, knowing the secrets of planetary motion, may never visit anything anywhere. Galileo exhibits a unified view of Christian truth and cosmic science. Now let's review the quote from Einstein:

"Accordingly, a religious person is devout in the sense that he has no doubt of the significance and loftiness of those super-personal objects and goals which neither require nor are capable of rational foundation. They exist with the same necessity and matter-of-factness as he himself. In this sense religion is the age-old endeavor of mankind to become clearly and completely conscious of these values and goals and constantly to strengthen and extend their effect. If one conceives of religion and science according to these definitions then a conflict between them appears impossible. For science can only ascertain what is, but not what should be, and outside of its domain value judgements of all kinds remain necessary. Religion, on the other hand, deals only with evaluations of human thought and action: it cannot justifiably speak of facts and relationships between facts. According to this interpretation the well-known conflicts between religion and science in the past must all be ascribed to a misapprehension of the situation which has been described.

"For example, a conflict arises when a religious community insists on the absolute truthfulness of all statements recorded in the Bible. This means an intervention on the part of religion into the sphere of science; this is where the struggle of the Church against the doctrines of Galileo and Darwin belongs." (92)

Einstein resolves the conflict between Christianity and science by claiming that religion or the Christian religion is super-personal without need of truth nor capable of being proved to be true. And it is science alone, which can determine the relationships of the cosmos. He suggests that Christianity requires no foundation in truth nor can be founded on truth. But if this were true how could we arrive at moral truth that would be worth extending and strengthening in society? Einstein further

---

[27] Janelle Rohr, *Science & Religion: Opposing Viewpoints* (St. Paul, Minnesota: Greenhaven Press, 1946), 20.

suggests that Christians cannot and should not claim that everything in the Bible is true. Therefore Einstein leaves absolutely nothing for a Christian to stand on nor assert in the observable cosmos. Science alone determines all real facts and relationships and Christians are left without even the authority of scripture.

Further, we see that Einstein defended Galileo, but he did so in a way that even Galileo himself would not. Galileo perceived that scripture did not address the way the heavenly bodies moved nor their relationships. But Einstein insists that scripture says something about that and that it is not true. But more importantly Galileo had a unified view wherein both Christian truth and science existed together, or at least perceived that they should be both true. It is obvious that Galileo perceived that Christ delivered one to the place that he studied with science. But Einstein perceived that religion had a position in determining values and ethics even if they could not rely on the source of such in their faulty book (the Bible). Galileo had a unified view of Christian transformation power in the real world and Einstein had a split view where science ruled the observable cosmos and religion or Christianity existed only in the super-personal, unfounded, non-provable world of ethics and morality.

This is, indeed, a major shift in the philosophy of science. Galileo acknowledged a sociological equilibrium between science and Christianity that was true for both, even if he knew that the view of the Christian church was wrong in adopting another erroneous scientific view, wherein the Sun was thought to revolve around the Earth.

Einstein, on the other hand, represents the new false sociological equilibrium between Christianity and science wherein there are two worlds. Science is not to be intruded upon in its fact determination for the observable cosmos and the Christian church is in charge of the unseen, unknowable, impenetrable world that should determine issues of morality. In this, Einstein is a member of the dual-world perception of the real observable cosmos and the unseen spiritual world of the dead. Notice that Einstein has really said, Christianity and religion are of no real use even in the matters of "human thought and action." He has said essentially that a devout "religious person" is stranded on an island unto himself with only super-personal objects and goals which "neither require nor are capable of rational foundation." Therefore, according to Einstein, such a religious person does not ascertain ethics and morals because his religion, if any good at all, is only good for himself. This meant to Einstein that, nothing is discernible concerning the ethics of another because none are capable of rational foundation.

Now, if you think that I am being too harsh on Albert Einstein's views, as I know many "Christians" idolize him and his writings, let me quote another passage from his essay. This quote should clear up any confusion that might be out there concerning his perception of Christianity being able to determine anything in any realm:

> "The **ethical behavior** of man is better based on sympathy, education and social relationships, and **requires no support from religion**. Man's plight would, indeed, be sad if he had to be kept in order through fear of punishment and hope of rewards after death." (93)

Ronald F. Avery

(Emphasis added)

Now we truly see that Einstein had no place for Christianity, or religion of any kind, in the observable cosmos. He said earlier, "religion deals only with evaluations of human thought and action." And now, in the same essay, he says that ethical behavior "requires no support from religion." This was not a contradiction to him but a revelation to us of his real position. To Einstein religion dealt only with **speculation** about the unknowable, impenetrable world **behind the curtain of death**. Einstein was a **true dual world scientist** representative of the type we have now. We now see clearly that Einstein did not see how religion, namely Christianity, was good for anything in the ethical area or the factual area of the observable cosmos. **Einstein resolved his conflict with science and religion (Christianity) by removing Christianity entirely** from the real world or the observable cosmos. This was a radical departure from the view of Galileo who perceived that Christianity had power to transport one to the heavens he observed. Einstein did not see Christianity as a transport to anywhere. He rather regarded it as a speculation on the punishment or reward in the after life in some other world, impervious to the human mind on this side of the curtain of death. This is the view of our present "duel-world cosmology" that we have discussed earlier.

Upon presenting this contrast of Galileo and Einstein to a friend, my friend said that he saw no difference between them at all. I was astonished! I said, "You don't see the difference between the views of Galileo and Einstein? How can you not perceive that Galileo said that the Holy Spirit was interested in how one goes to heaven, not how heaven goes, while Einstein did not even perceive that heaven and the cosmos he observed were the same place? You don't see that Einstein perceived a world of the dead and a world of the living? You don't see that Galileo acknowledged the power of Christianity while Einstein saw no power nor truth to Christianity by saying that it was unsupportable in truth and that the trouble comes when a community suggests that the Bible is true?"

He said, "no, these men both spoke in the times they lived in." I replied, "Sure they did and that's the point I'm making, these times are radically different from 300 years ago, as shown by how men reconciled science and Christianity. One perceived Christianity as powerful and the other had no perception of its relevance or power or truth."

He said, "Well sure, the church was powerful and Galileo would have been killed if he responded any different and Einstein was a Jew." I replied, "Jesus was a Jew, the twelve disciples were Jews and thousands of converts are Jews and I have become a Jew by inheriting the promises of Abraham in the obtainment of eternal life through Christ. Are you trying to say that Jews are automatically excused from the truth and the operation of Christ upon the cosmos, and it is somehow impossible for a Jew to perceive Jesus and his power?"

He said, "I could very easily be a Jew if I lived in Israel and grew up there. We adopt the religious system of our communities." I replied, "What has that got to do with what we are talking about? What does that have to do with the truth of a system? I am talking about the fact that these two men represent a tremendous shift in the perception of reality. Galileo lived in the Christian age where he had a clear perception of both the power of Christianity and science, together in the observable cosmos, wherein one deals with travel to the stars and the other deals with perceiving how the stars move relative to each other. The church had power but it was not fear of that power that made Galileo write the letter in the fashion that he did. Galileo actually perceived the world in the way that he described it in the letter as relating to observation of the cosmos and the power of the Holy Spirit to deliver one to the cosmos."

I continued, "One man saw the door way to the Cosmos in the Holy Spirit in Jesus and the other did not see any way to travel to the stars. One saw the way to be 'born-again' and the other did not." My friend replied, "Are we not born-again in our death? Were not both men born-again?" I answered, "No! No one is born-again in death. It's too late to be born again after death of our bodies. Either you obtain eternal life now or you never do. Jesus is the door we enter now in this present state."

He said, "I don't think you can be born-again until after death. How can you be in your mother's womb again." I couldn't believe he said that. My friend is an Episcopalian and totally familiar with the Bible and the story of Nicodemus, which I quickly reviewed with him (John 3:1-21). I said, "He that is not born again shall not see the Kingdom of Heaven. He that is born of the flesh is flesh and he that is born of spirit is spirit or space." He said that he was not born again. I said, "the death, resurrection and ascension of Christ Jesus is the alien birth canal that all men have access to the stars through. I am dead, resurrected and ascended with him now. **The hope of nations is here!**"

PART V - THE HOPE OF NATIONS HAS COME

CHAPTER 20 - SPACE TRAVEL

The way we will travel to the galaxies is not by the use of wave or particle behavior knowledge but by our conscious relationship to all space and time. We are the **Sons of Space** and we will be able to manifest and demanifest ourselves anywhere at any time instantaneously. We will be able to do this in any environment no matter how hostile.

What will space travel be like for the alienated? How big is the cosmos and the alien Kingdom of Heaven? Hyperspace Christian Aliens can ask the same questions modern scientists ask. Christians can actually arrive at the correct answers that scientists cannot perceive in their ignorance of their human relationship to space and time.

1.   What will aliens look like?
2.   How fast will aliens travel?
3.   Is history cyclical or linear?
4.   What kinds of environments will be accessible to us?
5.   What forms of manifestation will Christians have?

1.   What will our alienated bodies look like?

Our alienated glorified bodies will look like the one we presently have except they will be perfect and imperishable. However, we will be able to manifest them in any stage that they have ever been in on Earth and or could have been in. Just how imperishable will our bodies be and will they be similar to those we have now? Jesus says in St. Luke 12: 6-9:

> "Are not five sparrows sold for two farthings, and not one of them is forgotten before God?

> "But even the very hairs of your head are all numbered. Fear not therefore: ye are of more value than many sparrows.

> "Also I say unto you, Whosoever shall confess me before men, him shall the Son of man also confess before the angels of God:

> "But he that denieth me before men shall be denied before the angels of God."

We see that each hair of our head is numbered but does that mean we will retain them? Jesus makes it clear that not one hair of our head will perish (St. Luke 21: 17-19):

> "And ye shall be hated of all men for my name's sake.

> "But there shall not an hair of your head perish.

"In your patience possess ye your souls."

Wow! Jesus says that his disciples are going to see trouble for their allegiance to him, but they are going to retain every last hair of their heads, and that they possess their own souls which are the same as they will have while traveling in deep space.

2. How fast shall the alienated travel in deep space?

The speed at which the alienees will travel is the speed of "the twinkling of an eye" or the speed of thought and desire. Christ can now manifest or focus his physical body anywhere in the entire cosmos in the twinkling of an eye. The resurrected Christ Jesus has already exercised this power on Earth. You will recall earlier in this book that we discussed how Jesus entered into the upper room after the disciples had collected and closed the doors.

My Episcopalian friend, that I have mentioned before on two other occasions, said, "If Jesus could travel at the speed of light and if he came back to earth today he would only be about 32 years old." I said, "I don't understand why the speed of light in the case of Jesus is relevant at all. Why do we limit him who is the eternal Lord, creator, and sustainer of the cosmos with the speed limit of light?" He that fills and contains all of eternal space can manifest himself anywhere within that space at anytime he so determines. "And furthermore," I replied, "it follows, that if we likewise become like unto him, why do we limit ourselves with the speed of light?" This is precisely why we are not subject to particle physics, as St. Paul clearly speaks of the natural and the spiritual or the material and the spatial (1 Corinthians 15: 39-50:)

> "All flesh is not the same flesh: but there is one kind of flesh of men, another flesh of beasts, another kind of fishes, and another of birds.

> "There are also celestial bodies, and bodies terrestrial: but the glory of the celestial is one, and the glory of the terrestrial is another.

> "There is one glory of the sun, and another glory of the moon, and another glory of the stars: for one star differth from another star in glory.

> "So also is the resurrection of the dead. It is sown in corruption; it is raised in incorruption:

> "It is sown in dishonour; it is raised in glory: it is sown in weakness; it is raised in power:

> "It is sown a natural body; it is raised a spiritual body. There is a natural body, and there is a spiritual body.

> "And so it is written, The first man Adam was made a living soul; the last Adam was made a quickening spirit.

"Howbeit that was not first which is spiritual, but that which is natural; and afterward that which is spiritual.

"The first man is of the earth, earthy: the second man is the Lord from heaven.

"As is the earthy, such are they also that are earthy: and as is the heavenly, such are they also that are heavenly.

"And as we have borne the image of the earthy, we shall also bear the image of the heavenly.

"Now this I say, brethren, that flesh and blood cannot inherit the kingdom of God; neither doth corruption inherit incorruption."

Now Paul above is not speaking of the idea that a living man as opposed to a dead man going to the stars in heaven. Paul is referring to a man that has been transformed by the Lord into a spiritual or spatial man after the likeness of Christ on Earth. But he is also saying that even this changed terrestrial bound man will indeed obtain a fully spiritual body that will travel the galaxies and the stars of heaven. He that has been transformed is no longer corruptible as God is stronger than all, and no one has power to snatch him out of his hand, and nothing can take the joy from him that has been resurrected, and ascended with Christ. But there is one other step and that is the point at which the spiritual man receives a fully spiritual and eternal body. This spatial man in his indestructible body with every hair in place will manifest himself anywhere in the cosmos at the speed of desire, sufficient to take him across the vastness of space resident within himself.

3. History is Linear

We see here that God has also imposed a restriction on mankind more severe than the speed of light: and that is the law that corrupted man with a material body and mind will not inherit the kingdom of God or eternal space. Corruption will not inherit incorruption. Flesh and blood, without the transformation power of Christ, will not inherit the kingdom of God. This is to say that, at a point in the future when Christ Jesus operates upon the cosmos to close the door of salvation available at this present time, no man who is not born-again or translated will exist in heaven anywhere including planet Earth. These corrupted unrepentant men will live in the extreme contraction to nowhere. Each one will go there alone, and each one will know that the cosmos is the property of God, and that they have no bridge to get there forever. This is hell and eternal damnation. It is a place of extreme pain and insanity, which will last forever yet the cries from hence will not be heard by those in the kingdom of God.

The mere death of the individual is not the doorway into the Kingdom of God. One must be translated into the Kingdom of God, prior to the death of his earthy body, or he will never see life again. He will only know that it exists on the other side of the impassable gulf. Notice that this gulf can be likened to the one this same corrupted man has made for others trying to get to heaven. This man says that we can't know about heaven or hell or right and wrong until we die. This unregenerate man has built a wall between others and truth to prevent them from finding the truth, and being transformed by it into the kingdom of heaven or the cosmos about us. He has made a gulf that is stopping man from seeking God. The result is that this man will cut himself off from God in the end when he discovers that the entrance to heaven was in the earthy observable cosmos.

Paul assures mankind that he will not live in deep space or the kingdom of God along side the transformed. The unregenerate will not fly to distant stars in rocket ships or any other kind of craft along next to the glorified saints. There shall not exist any **state of being** other than that made by the death, resurrection and ascension of Christ. If you want to visit the galaxies and stars of heaven then you know where to enter into it. The door to the kingdom of God is Christ Jesus. Do not be deceived by the devices of man's thinking about particles and quantum physics and parallel world potentials becoming real with our selection. When Christ returns to shut the door to the kingdom of God all this probability will shrink to zero. There is one baptism, one body, one mind, one spirit, one space, one cosmos and one life. If you don't go through the alien birth canal of Christ's death, resurrection, and ascension, then you are cut off from all things for all time except your eternal knowledge of the same. This is hell beyond your wildest dreams. Don't go there!

4. Alienees will visit any environment

Alienees will be able to visit every kind of environment no matter how hostile to us presently. All environments will be beautiful and inhabitable (Daniel 3: 21-25):

> "Then these men were bound in their coats, their hosen, and their hats, and their other garments, and were cast into the midst of the burning fiery furnace.

> "Therefore because the king's commandment was urgent, and the furnace exceeding hot, the flame of the fire slew those men that took up Shaddrach, Meshach, and Abednego.

> "And these three men Shaddrach, Meshach, and Abednego, fell down bound into the midst of the burning fiery furnace.

> "Then Nebuchadnezzar the king was astonied, and rose up in haste, and spake, and said unto his counsellers, Did not we cast three men bound into the midst of the fire? They answered and said unto the king, True, O king.

> "He answered and said, Lo, I see four men loose, walking in the midst of the fire, and they have no hurt; and the form of the fourth is like the Son of God."

This is the type of body that the Son of God had 580 years before his appearance on Earth to walk as the Son of man (Christ Jesus). Notice how Jesus was able to protect not only himself but the others that had not his type of body but the body of humans. Now Shaddrach, Meshach, and Abednego came out of the fire without a singed hair nor even the smell of fire on their clothes while those that opened the door were burned to death (Daniel 3: 27):

> "And the princes, governors, and captains, and the king's councellers, being gathered together, saw these men, upon whose bodies the fire had no power, nor was an hair of their head singed, neither were their coats changed, nor the smell of fire had passed on them."

This miracle occurred on Earth to men of human form without their resurrected bodies because the Son of God joined them in the fire and protected them from it. This is not rich lore nor mystery, as the physicist Mr. Jones might call it in the preceding chapter, but the truth about what God and his children can do with glorified bodies through out all of the cosmos. Alienees will not only be able to manifest themselves anywhere but will be able to endure any environment without harm at all. The body or form of the fourth is the body that alienees will have after we obtain new glorified bodies upon Christ's return. Before that time alienees who die will be with Christ in the Kingdom, but without their glorified bodies as Christ has presently. The alienated will assume their own glorified bodies upon the "second coming" of Christ Jesus (1 Corinthians 15:51-54):

> "Behold, I shew you a mystery; We shall not all sleep, but we shall all be changed,

> "In a moment, in the twinkling of an eye, at the last trump: for the trumpet shall sound, and the dead shall be raised incorruptible, and we shall be changed.

> "For this corruptible must put on incorruption, and this mortal must put on immortality.

> "So when this corruptible shall have put on incorruption, and this mortal shall have put on immortality, then shall be brought to pass the saying that is written, Death is swallowed up in victory."

There seems to be a conflict or contradiction in the idea that one is born-again, possessing eternal life prior to the death of the body of man and that just said above. Was it not shown earlier that men must have new bodies on Earth to contain the new life that would be given them by Christ. Does this mean alienees do not get these new bodies until after the death of their earthly bodies. No! And does this mean that alienees sleep in the ground rather than live with Christ during the period between now and the Second Coming or the last trump? No! It means their bodies sleep in an imperfect state but their souls or spirit is with Christ where it is upon rebirth on Earth. St. Paul says in Philippians 1: 21-25 that he would like to depart and be with Christ rather than stay in the world:

> "For to me to live is Christ, and to die is gain.

> "But if I live in the flesh, this is the fruit of my labour: yet what I shall choose I wot not.

"For I am in a strait betwixt two, having a desire to depart, and to be with Christ; which is far better:

"Nevertheless to abide in the flesh is more needful for you.

"And having this confidence, I know that I shall abide and continue with you all for your furtherance and joy of faith;"

It seems clear that St. Paul was not looking forward to a sleeping in the ground but to being with Christ immediately. He knew this was the case because he was with him presently in the Holy Spirit. How could he lose the Holy Spirit in Christ in the death of his body? The possession of your soul in confidence and eternal life with Christ in the heavenly places is not lost for a period of time between the death of the alienees body and the second coming. This is again where the spatial model of alien physics plays a role. It has already been shown that the power of Jesus to save a man anytime is resident in Christ's power to implete and envelope the cosmos, and that his operation of death, resurrection and ascension was experienced by all things in the cosmos. Then the body of an alienee is all that is determined by Corinthians 15. The salvation or transformation of the alienee has already occurred in the operation of Christ. The operation of Christ upon his return at the sound of the trump will be to judge the world and to close the door to the kingdom of heaven at which time no man will be able to open it. Jesus speaks to John in Revelation 3:7:

"And to the angel of the church in Philadelphia write; These things saith he that is holy, he that is true, he that hath the key of David, he that openeth, and no man shutteth; and shutteth, and no man openeth;"

This is fact. Mere men had never entered into heaven by any manner until the appearance of Christ and his operation upon the cosmos (John 3:13). No man has been able to close the door but have done a good job of preventing others from seeing the door as we have discussed herein by occulting it with "science so-called." But when the trump sounds and Christ returns he will close the door and no man will open it again. The kingdom of heaven and the stars and galaxies will be cut off from all men that have not been alienated by the operation of the hyperspace alien Son of God, Christ Jesus.

5. Forms of Manifestation

Now we see that the manifestation of the body of Christ and our own bodies after the return of Christ will have any form consistent with the life we have and have had. There is evidence of several different manifestations of the same Christ Jesus after his resurrection prior to his ascension. It is recorded in chapter 20 of St. John that Christ manifested his physical body in the room where they were gathered on two separate occasions, eight days apart:

St. John 20: 19:

"Then the same day at evening, being the first day of the week, when the doors were shut where the disciples were assembled for fear of the Jews, came Jesus and stood in the midst, and saith unto them, Peace be unto you."

St. John 20: 26:

"And after eight days again his disciples were within, and Thomas with them: then came Jesus, the doors being shut, and stood in the midst, and said, Peace be unto you."

Notice that Jesus did not come in the room like the disciples but only after the doors were shut. His body was like that of his body prior to his resurrection and even had still the marks of crucifixion i.e., nail holes and a pierced side (John 20: 27-29):

"Then saith he to Thomas, Reach hither thy finger, and behold my hands; and reach hither thy hand, and thrust it into my side: and be not faithless, but believing.

"And Thomas answered and said unto him, My Lord and my God.

"Jesus saith unto him, Thomas, because thou hast seen me, thou hast believed: blessed are they that have not seen, and yet have believed."

That was no small experience for Thomas! That ended the doubt for Thomas. But what can we hope for who have not touched the resurrected and ascended Jesus? As we have seen earlier, we also obtain the same transformation that Thomas got. Yes, we have faith to believe, until we possess our souls in patience and confidence and all things in eternal space at one with God, in a state of perfection.

But on another occasion Christ Jesus appeared to his disciples in a different physical manifestation, even without immediate recognition or distinctive markings as he did in the room with the doors shut. Two disciples saw, talked and ate with him for a great period before realization of him, as recorded in Luke 24: 13-32. Christ vanished from their sight as recorded at St. Luke 24: 30-32:

"And it came to pass, as he sat at meat with them, he took bread, and blessed it, and brake, and gave to them.

"And their eyes were opened, and they knew him; and he vanished out of their sight.

"And they said one to another, Did not our heart burn within us, while he talked with us by the way, and while he opened to us the scriptures?"

The previous New Testament manifestations of Christ's body we have reviewed all occurred after his resurrection and prior to his ascension. Now we will look at the various manifestations of Christ's body after his ascension as recorded in the Scriptures. Christ Jesus revealed his glorified body to Stephen at his stoning, as recorded in Acts 7: 54-60:

"When they heard these things, they were cut to the heart, and they gnashed on him with their teeth.

"But he, being full of the Holy Ghost, looked up stedfastly into heaven, and saw the glory of God, and Jesus standing on the right hand of God,

"And said, Behold, I see the heavens opened, and the Son of man standing on the right hand of God.

"Then they cried out with a loud voice, and stopped their ears, and ran upon him with one accord,

"And cast him out of the city, and stoned him: and the witnesses laid down their clothes at a young man's feet, whose name was Saul.

"And they stoned Stephen, calling upon God, and saying, Lord Jesus, receive my spirit.

"And he kneeled down, and cried with a loud voice, Lord, lay not this sin to their charge. And when he had said this, he fell asleep."

Stephen sees Christ in heaven at the right hand of God. Stephen gave no description of how they looked under the stress of the moment. Where did he first look? It is recorded that he looked up into that same place that we look up to and see clouds and stars, etc. What did he see? He saw the heavens opened. Not one, but all three, with God in his glory and Christ at his right hand. Now had they been on a long light speed trip from beyond the stars? No! They manifested themselves in the twinkling of an eye, for the sake of Stephen while they remained in all three heavens, yet locally visible to Stephen. Space travel is simply no problem at all to those that contain all of heaven and fill all of heaven. Focused manifestation is in the twinkling of an eye anywhere, any time.

Notice that God and Christ protected Stephen very differently than they protected Shaddrach, Meshach and Abednego. Christ in this case protected him by revealing himself and his father from on high. Stephen was killed, but it is said that he fell asleep. Both in this case are true. Stephen is so moved by the sight that he is able to forgive and ask for the forgiveness of those who are at the very moment killing him. That's vision, truth and power indeed! This power is very different from the power of wave quantum physics, light speed, parallel universes and bent space. Notice that Christ received Stephen's Spirit and Stephen fell asleep rather than his death coming from the blow of a rock. This is vision is superior to the vision of horses and Chariots that Elisha's servant was shown. This means that the most powerful entity in the cosmos is Christ Jesus. This power exceeds that of nuclear power or any other power yet devised.

Now let's review the manifestation of Christ to Paul (Paul is Saul in the preceding verses) on the road to Damascus to persecute and arrest the Christians as recorded in Acts 9: 3-8:

"And as he journeyed, he came near Damascus: and suddenly there shined around about him a light from heaven:

"And he fell to the earth, and heard a voice saying unto him, Saul, Saul, why persecutest thou me?

"And he said, Who art thou, Lord? And the Lord said, I am Jesus whom thou persecutest: it is hard for thee to kick against the pricks."

Notice here that one cannot remove their guilt or shortcomings by punishing it in others. Saul was a sinner who was out to punish other sinners and Christ knew that it was painful to Saul's own mind.

"And he trembling and astonished said, Lord, what wilt thou have me to do? And the Lord said unto him, Arise and go into the city, and it shall be told thee what thou must do.

"And the men which journeyed with him stood speechless, hearing a voice, but seeing no man.

"And Saul arose from the earth; and when his eyes were opened, he saw no man: but they led him by the hand, and brought him into Damascus."

This manifestation of Christ did not reveal a body at all but a voice only and pure light that blinded Saul. The blindness was lifted when God sent a Christian to restore his sight in Damascus after three days. Is this account a valid description or body of Christ? Yes. If Christ wants to manifest his presence as light alone he certainly can do that just as well as he can manifest himself as a burning bush, a man, or a pillar of fire. You will be able to do the same for you will be like unto him.

Now we shall see how Christ manifested his gloried body to St. John after the ascension of Christ, as recorded in Revelation 1: 7-19:

"Behold he cometh with clouds; and every eye shall see him, and they also which pierced him: and all kindreds of the earth shall wail because of him. Even so, Amen.

"I am Alpha and Omega, the beginning and the ending, saith the Lord, which is, and which was, and which is to come, the Almighty.

"John, who also am your brother, and companion in tribulation, and in the kingdom and patience of Jesus Christ, was in the isle that is called Patmos, for the word of God, and for the testimony of Jesus Christ.

"I was in the Spirit on the Lord's day, and heard behind me a great voice, as of a trumpet,

"Saying, I am Alpha and Omega, the first and the last: and, What thou seest, write in a book, and send it unto the seven churches which are in Asia; unto Ephesus, and unto Smyrna, and unto Pergamos, and unto Thyatira, and unto Sardis, and unto Philadelphia, and unto Laodicea.

"And I turned to see the voice that spake with me. And being turned, I saw seven golden candlesticks;

"And in the midst of the seven candlesticks one like unto the Son of man, clothed with a garment down to the foot, and girt about the paps with a golden girdle.

"His head and his hairs were white like wool, as white as snow; and his eyes were as a flame of fire;

"And his feet like unto fine brass, as if they burned in a furnace; and his voice as the sound of many waters.

"And he had in his right hand seven stars: and out of his mouth went a sharp twoedged sword: and his countenance was as the sun shineth in his strength.

"And when I saw him, I fell at his feet as dead. And he laid his right hand upon me, saying unto me, Fear not; I am the first and the last:

"I am he that liveth, and was dead; and, behold, I am alive for evermore, Amen; and have the keys of hell and of death.

"Write the things which thou hast seen, and the things which are, and the things which shall be hereafter;"

Christ Jesus manifested himself to St. John with a glorified body, without the markings of the crucifixion, but instead those of the highest of priests. The following conversation was held by myself and a friend concerning all that is covered in this book.

I said, "The purpose of all history is redemption. When redemption is done then so will be the end of history as we know it. But a new eternal existence will begin."

Mark said, "I believe in God."

I replied, "But do you believe in Jesus?"

"Well the Bible was written by so many and interpreted."

I asked Mark this question, "If it works, who cares how many wrote and interpreted the work? I've been transformed, translated, and regenerated. Can you see why I don't care who, how many, how drunk, or how sane the authors were who wrote it?" I added, "Do you see why it should also appear as irrelevant to you if what you are hearing me say is true? I just want to tell you what happened to me. I have been altered and operated upon by the Son of God who is at one with all space and time. I have become like him by this operation and now I am at one with Christ, God and all of space and time. I also am now eternal. I also notified NASA SETI (Search For Extraterrestrial Intelligence) stating that I have become more alien then anything they have yet dreamed of or imagined and that I could prove it and describe how they too could become a hyperspace alienee."

Mark asked me, "What do you think happened at Roswell?"

"Nothing, and I can prove that as well, and again I am more alien than anything at Roswell alludes to. Let's start with how Christ operated upon me. Do you know the two capacities of Christ Jesus?"

Mark replied with a questioning answer, "He was killed and resurrected again?"

"No, that was part of his operation he performed but not his capacity."

Mark answered again, "He walked on water?"

"No, that was a miracle of many he performed by having these capacities. Jesus had two unique capacities that no other human had prior to him that permitted everything he did to have effect on everything else. They were complimentary capacities because it was not possible for him to have one without the other."

"OK, I understand the term complimentary."

"Jesus had the capacity to fill all space and then as a result contain all of space. And by those two complimentary capacities he contained all time as well. This is described in the Bible as the Baptism of Jesus by John the Baptist." I recited to him the baptism account at Matthew 3:16-17:

"And Jesus, when he was baptized, went up straightway out of the water: and, lo, the heavens were opened unto him, and he saw the Spirit of God descending like a dove, and lighting upon him:

"And lo a voice from heaven, saying, This is my beloved Son, in whom I am well pleased."

I said, "Now let me ask you what went up?"

"His soul?" he answered.

"Yes his soul or spirit. How far did his soul or spirit go up?"

"To God?"

"OK but how far is that?"

"To heaven?"

"Well right but what is heaven and how big is that?"

"I don't believe heaven is a place like Saturn or a planet but I believe its a place," he said.

"Well, I hope you don't believe it's in another dimension, because many Christians do in error."

"No I don't believe heaven is in another dimension."

I said, "Well, you are correct, heaven is not in another dimension, and you are also correct in that it is not in a restricted or isolated place in the cosmos, but it is the entire eternal cosmos or space."

Mark then astounded me with his perception of asking me, "Then where is hell?"

"Wow, that's a good question, I'm glad you asked that. There is a hell and we now know where it is and how it exists."

"Where is it?"

I answered, "It is the flip side of heaven or eternal space."

He quickly answered with, "But that's nothing!"

Mark looked astonished when I quickly replied, "You are so right and so correct." He could not believe that he answered that correctly. I went on, "That is precisely where hell is. Our definition of heaven defines also where hell is and how small it is by comparison. Hell is nowhere. Hell is non existence. Hell is the ultimate contraction totally outside of everything and all space and time."

Mark asked, "Do people burn there?"

"Oh yes! They will burn there because they will have knowledge that they are in nowhere and noplace without a way to get to or into life or all space and time."

"I see, the burning is the awareness of their entrapment outside of everything with no way to get back."

"Yes, and they will go there alone, there is no company in hell, all go there alone. If you want to be a loner, this is the place, the ultimate for aloneness and sensory deprivation, but with total knowledge of all that could have been. You see all the popular illusions of hell are a bit inaccurate."

"Then the popular pictures of heaven are also inaccurate as well."

"Yes, you are so correct again."

"No floating around on clouds?"

"Well, yeah."

I said, "Let's go back and define God. Jesus said in the Scriptures that God is a spirit and looks for those who will worship him in spirit and truth. Now let's draw a picture of heaven and God. We will start at earth. The rabbis had a convenient way of organizing heaven which is accurate and useful and is described or alluded to on several occasions in the Bible. They broke heaven down into three layers. The first layer was the clouds around the earth containing the waters above the earth. The second layer contains all the stars and celestial bodies and the third is the infinite space or endless Kingdom of God that contains all things which may or may not contain other matter and systems of matter." Now I asked again, "Now given that definition of God and heaven at one, how big is heaven?"

"Infinite!" he replied with confidence.

"Right!" I replied. "God and this infinite space are one are they not?"

"Yes," he replied again with confidence.

I continued, "So what happened to Jesus upon recognition of his going straightway up to fill all of heaven?"

Mark replied, "God came to him?"

As I drew a picture of a human figure representing Christ with waves of water under his feet, I said, "The Spirit of God or all space and time came down and rested in the physical body of Christ Jesus."

Mark said, "Well, I believe that Jesus could have stopped by some star or planet on his way back."

"First of all, he did not go physically or take his body into space or heaven at his baptism, only his spirit or soul filled all the heavens. Don't you see that it was not necessary for him to stop at one or two or all zillion stars because they all came to rest inside his physical body anyway. As Jesus stood in the Jordan River he then, and from then on, contained all the heavens, stars, galaxies, and all there is, to infinity. This state of being is called oneness with God."

I asked, "Now do you see how Jesus could walk on water?"

Mark answered again with a question, "He was the water?"

"No, he didn't become the water or the water become him. The water had its ultimate foundation in the body of Jesus."

He replied, "Jesus contained the water."

"Yes, absolutely correct."

"Now that we have established the capacities of Jesus, let's look at what he did or his operation he performed on the cosmos. When he was crucified, were not all things crucified with him?"

"Yes."

"When he was resurrected, what happened to all things?"

"They were resurrected."

"Yes sir, you are absolutely correct."

"And upon his ascension, were not all things taken back to fill all of heaven."

Mark replied with a simple, "Yes."

I said, "Now do you see why I can call myself a hyperspace alien without being a madman? Was Jesus from far away? You bet he was—he was from infinity. Does not his birth and baptism illustrate this?"

Mark listened as I continued, "Now back to your question about Roswell, and how I know nothing took place in Roswell, concerning visitors from other planets etc. coming to earth. I can do this by asking the question, What race through out all space and time is the most superior? Who has performed a more miraculous operation upon all of space and time then Christ Jesus?"

"No one," Mark answered with confidence.

As I drew a circle in red on the napkin, I said, "Now let's assume that there is a race on a red planet out in space and they have the power and intellect to come to earth. Does this mean they are more superior than us?"

"No," Mark replied with confidence.

"You are Correct, and why? Because a man, Jesus Christ, that looks like us and has shown us all that he knew of God and what power he had and can be ours, has operated upon the entire cosmos redeeming all space creatures as well as us. Jesus performed this redemption by his death, resurrection and ascension. All that is required to be transformed is the perception of the operation and the humility to accept it and surrender your body and mind to it."

I continued, "Would I not be compelled by the knowledge of Christ to tell all in the cosmos the good news of salvation for all things and baptize them in the name of the Father, Son and Holy Ghost?"

"Yes you would," Mark replied.

Finally, I asked, "Why would we presume that another race or being in space would be superior to us in space travel yet so grossly lost and decadent as a result of no knowledge of the salvation of all things? Why would we presume such a lost civilization could even last long enough to produce such technology? Our own history is replete with accounts of **civilization failure** because of gross ignorance of salvation. Even the Bible has many accounts of human kingdoms rising and falling as a result of moral decadence without knowledge of the operation of salvation wrought in Christ Jesus, the Son of God. As you can see Christ Jesus is the most profound and powerful event to take place in history and through out all space. Jesus is at one with God and is supreme over all creatures, races and civilizations. And we are like him and created in his image and now translated by his operation whereby we enter the Kingdom of Heaven and possess the same space and fill the same space at one with Jesus, his Father and the Holy Ghost."

"Well, Mark, it's 2:30 in the morning, why don't we head for the house?"

"That's a good idea," he replied, "But I believe we had a great discussion tonight."

"I agree Mark, I love nothing more than what we discussed tonight. Thank you very much."

PART V - THE HOPE OF NATIONS HAS COME!

CHAPTER 21 - SUMMARY

CHRISTIANS ARE HYPERSPACE ALIENEES

This chapter is a summary of all the concepts and theological categories that have been developed in this book. This chapter will ask the reader to answer the questions in the first chapter again. The purpose of this chapter is to consolidate all the theological discoveries discussed in this book into a whole that will demonstrate why it is completely accurate for Christians to call themselves, "hyperspace aliens."

Modern industrial society encourages us to believe in UFOs. Society will even entertain the idea that we have seen and been abducted by space aliens. Society will further consider the claims of some individuals that they have been implanted with some device by an alien. But modern industrial society will not tolerate the idea that you are a hyperspace alien. The reason is that opinion makers armed with media are designing a culture where certain "scientists, so-called," will become the priesthood in the quest for answers, supposedly to be found, in extraterrestrial intelligence.

Christians will also balk at the idea that you are a hyperspace alien because the theologians have modified the gospel to accommodate the ideas of *modern particle physics* e.g., lightspeed, curved space and blackholes may contain the hope for space travel for all of mankind. Theologians have also moved the kingdom of heaven into the "other world, or spirit world" beyond the impenetrable curtain of death. This is why they can acknowledge and participate in the death and resurrection of Jesus but not his ascension. They cannot perceive that they have entered into the kingdom of God, and sit in the heavenly places with Christ Jesus, because they perceive heaven as a place rather than the entire cosmos in which we live and breath at present.

Therefore, many Christians have adopted the idea that there could be aliens in space with more advanced technology than ourselves, and that no one knows about God or the kingdom of heaven until they die. They cannot perceive that the power of Christ to save all men is directly tied to the fact that he has operated upon the entire cosmos and everything therein. A perception of this fact does not permit a greater being than Christ Jesus, nor a form of life greater than ourselves, with the characteristics and familiar shape of Jesus and mankind. We are created in the image of God. We can take that to the bank and bet our lives upon it. This is proved beyond the shadow of doubt on Earth itself. Millions of life forms are observed around us and mankind is the only one that talks about God or claims to become the children of God. Jesus, and now all of mankind, is the only shape of eternal space that exists.

NASA SETI, SETI Institute, The National Science Foundation, Life Magazine, The Planetary Society, Texas Lutheran University professors, and many other so-called professors of science, will reject the idea that you are from eternal space. Yet after you have been transformed by your perception of the operation of Christ upon you, you are born of eternal space. You were created in the image of God with the **Two Complementary Image Capacities** to **implete** all of space and to **envelop** all of space. These capacities were activated and empowered by the perception of that same power in Christ Jesus that allowed him to operate upon the entire eternal space by his death, resurrection and ascension. All things on Earth and throughout all space have been operated upon and reconciled back to God. All things consist in Christ Jesus and all things have been brought together, both on earth and in heaven, in one body, the body of Christ. Amen.

The Christian is by necessity a product of hyperspace and a subject of the operation that Christ performed upon space. Therefore Christians were created by eternal space and operated upon by eternal space in Christ. You have been **predestined**, not by name, but by the comprehensive operation of Christ upon the entire cosmos. And you were predestined to be subject of that operation from the beginning of time. This is why you can't be smug about it. This is why it is God's will that all be saved because his method of salvation is the comprehensive operation upon the entire cosmos by Christ Jesus. It is the job of every Christian to make this operation known to every man and woman. We cannot discount people as not being predestined. **They are all predestined by the comprehensive spatial operation of Christ**. They either perceive the operation or they don't.

Modern astronomers and physicists are looking for extraterrestrial intelligence to learn about life and how to travel to the galaxies. And, all Christians have the answer. Christians are not only extraterrestrial but hyperspatial and will travel to the galaxies in the twinkling of an eye. All real Christians possess all things including the stars and galaxies and can one day go to them at will. A true **Christian cannot deny** this fact any more than they could deny their belief in God. Christians inherit this property and ability by the very operation by which they are saved. One cannot be born again without obtaining these benefits. If the Jehovah's Witnesses want to hang around on earth to farm it for eternity, they certainly can. But, if they want to travel the stars they can do that as well, if they are real transformed Christians.

Astronomers really have not properly identified what they are looking for. They say they are looking for extraterrestrial (ET) intelligence but they really mean otherterrestrial (OT). Christians are extraterrestrial. Christians are born of space itself, they are not merely from another planet or terrestrial globe. Scientists are looking for something from another planet far away. But we now know that the location of another terrestrial will not be much help. Without the operation of eternal space they will have nothing to contribute to what we know now. Such OT globes would become just more missionary fields in which to spread the gospel.

Not only are Christians hyperspatial born of eternal space but they are aliens. A more precise word would be alienees. However, an alienee is still an alien, but one made by the first (or alpha) hyperspace alien, Christ Jesus. We saw that the real root word of alien has to do with a state of being from far away or a foreign place as well as having possession of property and the power to transfer it to another and to change a person.

Part I: Sociological Equilibrium:

Chapters 1 through **4** demonstrated that our present equilibrium between the two most powerful fields of thought today is false. It is false because Christianity and science have made adjustments to their own fields in order to accommodate each other. The result is the occultation of the power of Christ in main stream Christianity. Science also has been altered from a mere mental discipline or method of approach, into a religious quest for the origin and destination of mankind while rejecting the truth of Christianity which explains that.

Part II: Alien Physics / Cosmic Operation:

Chapters 5 through **11** revealed the theological categories of the occulted reality of Christianity. Chapter 5 showed that Christianity has abandoned the mind, soul and strength of man to love God with only the "heart." In order to correct this false equilibrium, Christians must return to all four of the **quaternion** components of man to love God and his neighbor.

Chapter 6 developed the **Domain Triad** revealing God's location in this world in which we live, breath and have our being. God is not in another dimension that we cannot see nor perceive nor penetrate with our minds. This Domain Triad is expressed in the short paraphrase; "I am, One, of the Living." This phrase expresses the following three ideas:

1. The eternal nature of God without beginning nor end;
2. The oneness without separation of essence into one or more dimensions or domains;
3. And God's essence and life is found in the world that we inhabit and observe everyday. God lives only in the world of the living.

Therefore God and His Son are not to be found in a nonexistent world of the dead. Additionally, the human mind can be used with confidence to discover the reality of God in this observable reality we live in. This is the same mind that produced the scientific method of observation and proof and is the same mind that proves God and His power over the cosmos by experience and rationality.

Chapter 7 developed the theological category of the **Singular Essence of God**. Much has been said for centuries about the multiple characteristics of God, i.e., His beauty, power, justice, mercy. But most fail at identifying His actual essence, or worse, have denied that God has such an essence or entity. The power or mere ability to perceive and define God does not give one the power to become God. One becomes the child of God first and then is able to define God at one with Him.

God not only wants to be found, perceived and defined, but wants us to be at one with Him. Therefore we are incorrect in fearing to define Him or His Singular Essence. To do less is to quit and abandon the mind. One cannot diminish God's power or sovereignty by defining Him or defining His Singular Essence. Those that should fear God are those that attempt to rob Him or occult His reality and power over the cosmos.

To define God is to glorify Him, not to rob or occult Him. The old practice of **leaving letters out** of the name of God has returned, illustrating this fear of robbing

God by defining Him or even pronouncing His full name or spelling it out fully. Can we really fool God with such cheap tricks? Do we really become humble, obedient, righteous, and reverent by referring to God as G *d or Ya* way? If we become the Sons of God by the operation of Christ Jesus, and no act of our own, then why should we fear to write out God's name any more than to write out our own name? Furthermore, why should we fear defining God for our neighbor any more than we would define ourselves to our neighbor? Lastly, can we fully define ourselves to our neighbor if we cannot define God? In fact, Christians have adopted a false doctrine that says God is not, and never will be, definable. God has worked and grieved and gave His only begotten Son to reveal Himself to us and we have responded with the doctrine of eternal ignorance! God forbid!

Let it be proclaimed that we now know God and His Singular Essence through the revelation of His Son Jesus Christ. God's Singular Essence is Eternal Space without beginning and without end. This Essence has been occulted in main stream Christianity in fear of modern philosophy and physics (Decartes and Einstein). But this doctrine is error. Space does exist without field or objects and is the very most Essential Singular Essence of the reality of God.

Chapter 8 reviewed the **Trinity of Personality** that traced the development of the theological category of the Trinity. The doctrine of the Trinity took some 300 years to develop fully. Yet this doctrine has lost its power altogether and now is avoided intellectually as something merely to be accepted in "faith." Again, theologians today fail to define the Trinity just as they fail to define God. The result is the doctrine of "the Mystery of the Trinity." This "mystery" provides no power and no way for Christians to explain their salvation.

The Trinity is not a mystery and cannot be a mystery if we are to explain our transformation by the power of Christ into new creatures. The Trinity is the **spatial union** of the Father God who created all things, and His Son, who created all things with God, in eternal unity, and the Holy Spirit which was given by Christ Jesus to His disciples to dwell with us. They are one in spatial unity, and yet they are different in personality in God the Father, God the Son and God the Holy Spirit in the disciples.

Chapter 9 explained the **Two Complementary Image Capacities** that Christ possessed and transferred to us. These capacities are the power to **implete** (or fill completely) the cosmos and as a result the power to **envelop** (or contain completely) the cosmos and all therein. Christ Jesus exhibited these two complementary capacities in the description of his baptism. It is this power of Christ to contain all space and therefore all time that permitted anything he experienced to occur to the cosmos and all therein. When Christ experienced the death, resurrection and ascension, all things on earth and in heaven experienced the same to the ends of the galaxies. All things are therefore reconciled unto God, both things that are on earth and things that are in heaven.

Chapter 10 presented the evidence that with the **occultation of the real power** of Christ over the cosmos and all things therein that Christians are just as vulnerable to the notions of superior alien life forms in space as the secular atheist and agnostics. Evidence is also shown in this chapter for the correctness of the proposition that Christians have accepted the erroneous idea that God, Christ and angels live in another dimension that is imperceptible and impenetrable by the human mind or "spiritual mind" for that matter.

Chapter 11 demonstrates that Christ Jesus conforms to and exceeds the definition of an extraterrestrial alien developed by modern society. The definition of the word alien and all its meanings reinforces the idea that **Christ Jesus is more alien** than any scientist has ever imagined. The root word alien refers to the possession of property and the power to transfer that property to another and to come from a foreign place and to transform another person. Christ meets and exceeds all those definitions.

Part III: Clarification of Theological Terms:

Chapter 12 shows how the new categories of theology developed in this book and others can be have a **heuristic value** to check and correct modern science. This heuristic value extends to the checking of other theological notions held by Christians and those claiming to be Christians. Several conversations with those of other denominations and those outside Christianity are used to demonstrate the power of Alien Physics based upon the power of Christ to transform the cosmos from death into eternal life.

Chapter 13 uses the results of the physical operation of Christ over the cosmos to show how it defines the **essential difference between faith and grace**. Faith and grace are used interchangeably by modern theologians without perception of the essential difference that must be in effect to acknowledge that Jesus Christ has done anything in the real world we live in. Faith is seeking and Grace is the possession of that which we sought in Faith. Faith is the attraction we feel for the truth that God grants us as an unmerited free gift. Grace is the operation of Christ upon the cosmos in his death, resurrection and ascension. Grace is also the unmerited gift of salvation to us. Once we possess grace, we live in a state of perfection in the kingdom of heaven in the observable cosmos, prior to the death of our bodies.

In **chapter 14** other theological terms are defined in conformance with the power of Christ to transform the cosmos. Terms such as **Justification, Sanctification, Reconciliation, Regeneration, and Redemption** are all shown to be merely different qualities and conditions of the Christian after they have been transformed by the operation of Christ. None of these terms are defined by our works or growth in Scripture but are all provided by the operation of Christ Jesus. Our work or the work of those to become Christians is to believe in Christ and the one who sent him and to know that the will of God is that all men be saved. Christianity is not a continually growing walk where in we never really know God or perfection as is suggested by many theologians. Therefore we should be suspicious of terms like "enrichment, growing, and deeper," etc. This is not to say that our perception of Christ does not unfold, but after the transformation of "old man" into a "new creature," it is not "growth" that matters. Christ is really good news for all men because they indeed will know God fully, be transformed into his children to be at one with him forever, to travel throughout all of heaven or infinite space above us in every direction.

The Spatial Model of Christian Theology is more completely stated in **chapter 15** to show the real world power of Christ to transform the cosmos and all things within it. The Spatial model is used to demonstrate why modern theologians are void of the power of the apostles and cannot explain what the apostles meant accurately. The great questions asked by the men of the Old Testament concerning the magnitude of God are examined to show that it is Christ Jesus who did all these works with God. Can we really comprehend the unsearchable riches of God? The answer is "yes" in that Christ did those things and we now have oneness with him and God. Who has measured the waters, meted out heaven, comprehended the dust, weighed the mountains and hills, counseled and instructed with the Lord? All these Old Testament questions are answered in the New Testament gift of Christ Jesus. Jesus did all those things and more with his Father.

We examine why modern theologians do not have the perception of their oneness with God. We show that it is because they do not possess a real world spatial model to describe the salvation of mankind or themselves. They have shirked from the task in fear of modern science. But science is merely a mental discipline to be used by men to find answers to questions.

I would not exaggerate one bit to compare the infamous mental model used by Einstein to present his idea of simultaneity and its resulting theory of relativity with the mental models Christ's relationship with space to establish God's power to physically operate upon the cosmos. Einstein presented his thought with the example of a train car traveling in one direction on a track and lightning striking the track at both ends at the same time. Einstein then asks, "Did the two bolts of lightning appear to strike at the same time to the passengers?" The mere speech of Christ himself, as recorded in the Bible presents us with a mental example, or model, of what he was. Scripture reveals that Christ contained all space and time, it follows therefore, that any thing he would then experience would be experienced by all things in the cosmos. It could be said then that "science" is the discipline of clear and logical thinking in any field of thought. New visions of truth springs from correct thinking.

We show in chapter 15, that modern theologians still present the Trinity as a mystery, and tell men they are finite and cannot comprehend the infinite. We show that this cannot be true if we can claim we are born again. Not only must we comprehend that the operation of Christ **makes us infinite**, but we must allow this truth to operate on us. We are not saved if we are yet finite. The finite cannot by definition contain eternal life. The possession of eternal life requires us to be infinite. That is to say the finite cannot contain the infinite.

Christians are amazed when it is said that Jesus is the shape of eternal space and contains it. Yet these same Christians will tell you they believe Jesus is the Son of God. However, **they cannot tell you** what God is, how Christ is his Son, or how Christ can save all men for all time. All they can tell you is that they just have faith. But faith is clearly insufficient, because the men of the Old Testament had faith and it was not enough.

In modern industrial society the notion of Christ and the Son of God, and any power that might accompany such a being, is eclipsed (or occulted) by the notion of aliens and outer space potential and higher civilizations. And, in fact, these ideas coexist in the minds of many "Christians." This state of mind is shown to result from ignorance of the power of Christ to operate on anyone at anytime. The result of this operation on a person 2000 years after the crucifixion, resurrection and ascension of Christ implies directly that there is no being, in all of the cosmos, that is superior to Christ Jesus. Jesus and now, those that he has operated upon, are the crown of creation. The notion, that superior life forms exist in deep space, is therefore, abolished in our salvation by Christ Jesus. There is no sane hope in meeting an alien superior to Christ for even that creature has been operated upon by Christ and a ripe candidate for the good news of salvation.

Would not the Son of God have some unique quality? Yet many Christians will look at you with suspicion when you attempt to explain this quality. Faith for them is the **substitute for thinking** and analysis of what Jesus did and how.

The notion of **heaven as a restricted area** in the cosmos is challenged and shown to be **inconsistent with the power of Christ** Jesus to save all human flesh. It is inconsistent with the full operation of Christ in his death, resurrection and ascension into heaven. The reason for this misconception that heaven is a restricted finite place is because there is a lack of a real world spatial model to describe salvation. The Bible contains much on the subject, but it has never been developed into theological concepts and categories.

It is further shown in chapter 15 that many modern theologians cannot discern between the infinite spatial world and the unseen "spiritual world." Most Christians will laugh at the notion of "parallel worlds" presented by wave physicists yet they have accepted the false idea of a separate and unseen spiritual world. Most Christians have made a more serious error believing that this separate parallel spiritual world is heaven and that they will go there in death. They have then concluded in error that the kingdom of heaven, or this "other world," is not penetrable by the human mind and is therefore unknowable until death. All of this is error of the worst kind and unsupportable by scripture.

These **theological errors** render the power of Christ to save all men powerless. The power of Christ to save is not explainable under these notions. Again all that "Christians" can say who hold these erroneous views is that, "all must be accepted on faith." But again this is the **abandonment of the mind**, one of the four main components we are to use in loving God. The good news of Christ is that we can penetrate the Kingdom of God and Heaven with our minds and we can know the secrets of the cosmos and we can become one with God the creator of all things. This is salvation, the finish of our faith and the possession of our own souls in confidence in a perfect state of grace. Amen.

Heaven is not a place in space as a **glass bubble** that only good people can enter or good "spirits" etc. It is the totality of all space. Only those who have experienced the operation of Christ upon all space will live with Christ there. There will be no unrighteousness anywhere in all of space. Hell is the flip side of all space and time. Hell is a contradiction to life and space and to go there is to burn with the knowledge of your separation from all space, things and beings. Hell is an intolerable perception that one has no alternative but to be continually eaten by the worm of knowledge that eternal space is not accessible to you. Heaven cannot be a planet or a bubble and be consistent with the power of Christ to reconcile all things unto God.

Even the mainstream "fundamental" churches in America have accepted these errors and developed a theology, which could be termed the **theology of the indescribable God**. This theology is no better than the one the Athenians made a monument to—"To the Unknown God" This theology suggests that one is a heretic if one makes an attempt to describe God and his relationship to us. The result is that God only exists, for them, in their desire, rather than in a describable reality, mental or otherwise. God, therefore, cannot exist in their perception of reality but **exists only in their forced assertion** that he exists somewhere and somehow. But if God existed in their perception they would not be able to deny his definition. Is it not true that Christ spent his entire earthly ministry trying to define himself and his Father and our relationship to them? Why then do we hesitate to take on the job of clarifying this in our minds and then showing it to others? Christ came to reveal, and modern theology is busy concealing. If not, why then do modern theologians insist on "mystery and faith?" They choose to be ignorant to avoid the challenges they perceive they would receive from modern science. Yet modern science cannot challenge the truth revealed in Scripture. It is rather the truth of revealed Scripture that can challenge modern science.

Part IV "Contact" Collision - Alien Answers Message

Chapter 16 begins the effect of the perception and knowledge of Christ and how he has operated upon the entire cosmos. This perception causes a clash with modern industrialized culture or the point of "contact" between two cultures. This contact is more accurately termed a collision of the truth of Christ with the made up pop culture of today. This is where as some say, "the rubber hits the road." This is where the reality of the physical operation of Christ Jesus upon the cosmos collides with the false equilibrium between occulted mainstream Christianity and science falsely "so-called."

Chapter 16 also records the real challenge of modern so-called science by an actual hyperspace alien (the author). Chapter 16 proves that the challenge presented publicly to NASA SETI and SETI INSTITUTE cannot be intellectually or scientifically dismissed based upon the only reasoning conceived by SETI, which follows:

1. The message did not come from a radio telescope.
2. The contents of the message were hard to believe.
3. The evidence of the message was insufficient to prove experience.
4. The source of the transmission experience was available on earth.
5. The alien does not look different.
6. The message in the contact was offensive.
7. The contact never got to NASA SETI via Life Magazine.

Under number 4 (above) it is shown why it is essential to know the difference between **faith** and **grace** so that we don't stop seeking until we possess what we sought in faith. Faith is not the end, it is the attraction to the end. The end is the perfect state of grace or salvation to sit down with Christ in the heavenly places right now before we die on this earth.

Under number 4 (above) it is also shown what the scioreligionists have been doing with their science "so-called." They have been building a ladder to "climbeth up some other way" via Einstein and Rosen Bridges. Rather than enter the "door" to the kingdom of God via the **death, resurrection and ascension** of Christ Jesus, they have attempted to get in another way and to persuade others to attempt the same.

Under the same number 4 (above) it is also shown why it is important to know where heaven is and where God is via the **Domain Triad** expressed in the short phrase "**I Am, One, Living**."

Rejection theory number 6 (above) is shown to be the most likely motive for NASA SETI and SETI INSTITUTE to dismiss the challenge by a real hyperspace alien. This was also predicted in Carl Sagan's book, *Contact*.

The real question becomes "Who has had a real physical transformation, the alienee Avery or Carl Sagan and his friends in their dreams of Einstein Rosen Bridges and deep mathematics?" The fact is that not one of them has confessed to a transformation from one type of creature to another as the alien Avery has with his perception of the operation of Christ Jesus upon the cosmos.

In **chapter 17** it is shown that the failure to distinguish between grace and faith has led to the stagnation and slowing of the spread of Christianity. Two processes are revealed at work in modern society to pervert and slow Christianity. The first process is to call Christianity a mere "faith" equal to all other "faiths." The second process is to elevate the practice of the scientific method to a search for truth concerning ultimate questions of nature, origin and destiny of mankind.

Scientists have banished Christianity to the "other world" along with all the other "faiths." Thus scientists become the only priests of the "real world" the scioreligionists define for us. This false notion produces a mental "split-world view," and it is exposed in Sagan's book, *Contact*. In his book, Sagan describes his perception of a **finite heaven** and an **infinite world of the living** with an "**impenetrable curtain**" between the two—until death. **This is false—there is only one world and that is the world of the living**. This is shown in the written words of Jesus Christ himself.

The new theological category of the Domain Triad locates God and His Son by the short paraphrase, "I Am, One, of the Living," in our present world that we observe everyday. This is the world that we presently move and live and have our being in as stated by St. Paul.

Carl Sagan's book is used to illustrate how these sociological processes are in operation. Science becomes the superior "faith" compared to all the others. Sagan compares a telescopic view of the Galaxy, Andromeda, to the resurrection and suggests that this mere view from afar is superior. Sagan asks the question who's more religious would you say, the people who follow the bureaucratic religions or the people who teach themselves science?

Sagan ascribes more authority to an encyclopedia's discussion of the "mysterium tremendum" than to Biblical scripture. He finds from reading it that all religions, including Christianity, will become extinct in favor of the "mysterium tremendum." Chapter 17 shows that Christianity has become occulted by applying the "mysterium tremendum" to the Holy Trinity and other doctrines to blend with science and other religions. But in Christ we have the revelation of all mysteries, including the mysterium tremendum (God) and the Trinity. If the Trinity remains a mystery in the mind, so is salvation a mystery in that mind. One cannot be saved by mystery, but only by knowledge and clear perception.

Also chapter 17 shows that any experience is "religious" under the "mysterium tremendum" doctrine of the New World order. Once a person knows the truth, and perceives the reality of the operation of Christ Jesus, they will be in violation of the "mysterium tremendum" and pose a threat. Sagan makes it clear in his book that radically different religious views are coming to your local church. He's right on that point! Most congregations have accepted many of them already and have been doing so over the last 50 years. The only Christianity that will be socially acceptable in the future will be one that does not claim that Jesus did anything but give good speeches on doing good. Those that claim power and transformation and speak out against society and its evil practices will be deemed intolerant of other equal faiths groping for truth in futility with their "spiritual minds."

Chapter 18 presents the two types of Christians that will be acknowledged in the 21st Century, and discusses the two-fold attack on Christianity. The movement underway is making Christianity into a mere faith, as shown before, and faith is equal in all religions for the term "faith" is defined as the hope in something not seen. What group does not hope in something not seen? Therefore all are equal. But you will recall, in real Christianity, that Christ is the finisher of faith and the establisher of the perfect state of grace, enabling his followers to become the children of God.

Then the lost world's logic follows that Christianity and the other equal religions are in conflict and this conflict has caused all the evil and bloodshed since the dawn of man. This leaves the "faith" of modern science as the only possible chance for mankind. However, it was Darwinism and modern philosophy and "empty field theory" which were in full swing during World War I and II.

Only two kinds of Christians will be perceived by the New World Order. First will be the quiet, sophisticated, and impotent Christian. The second type will be the hateful, lunatic, sociopathic preacher types that become terrorists to stop the pursuit of truth which is obviously only perceivable by modern scientists. Even Carl Sagan considers himself to be a "type one" Christian. But "type one" does not believe in the deity of Christ nor the operation that he performed to give eternal life to all flesh in the cosmos.

A paradoxical aspect of the attack on Christianity is revealed in chapter 18. It is the difficult position of distracting the world with the hope of aliens in space to help us while simultaneously discrediting the idea that the alien (or the superior idea of Godhood) has already come in the person of Jesus Christ. After all what would a God Man be like? Would he not have power superior to a mere space neighbor living in a nearby galaxy? The occulting of many Christian realities is required to perform this paradoxical task. A list of occulted realities appears in this chapter. The main concept of space versus heaven is discussed as well as the resultant "other spiritual world." The term spiritual in the Bible means spatial. The term spirit in theology today, many times, means "other worldly" or "other dimensionally." There is a big dangerous difference!

Part V - The Hope of Nations Has Come! - The Hope of Nations

Chapter 19 presents the good news that the life, death, resurrection and ascension of Jesus is the fulfillment of the "Hope of Nations," and all faiths, all science, and all men. The hope of nations is the transformation from death into eternal life. This operation has already occurred in Christ Jesus 2000 years ago. This operation is referred to in Haggai 2:5-9 as a "shaking" of heaven and earth and all nations. This shaking is also referred to as the creation of the present heavenly Jerusalem and Mount Zion in Hebrews 12. Shaking is God's term for a harvest or separation, certainly a big event.

Also chapter 19 compares the New Jerusalem to what the scio-religionists are creating for us via science "so-called." Several major men are reviewed who are offering what they think is hope for the future. Fred Allen Wolf fails to deliver the hope of nations via his Quantum Psychodynamics. He says all things exist in other dimensions and that they become real when we select them to happen. He also says that all motion and time have the effect of evolving matter into consciousness. He later says all suffering is the result of man not letting go of his apeness he evolved from. This holding on to the past prevents the ape from evolving into man. In other words all evolution has stopped because man has not let go of being an ape.

Einstein fails to deliver the hope of nations via his theory of Relativity. He admits that his theories do not effect the Newtonian model of the gravitational motion of bodies. Therefore, for all practical purposes, mankind is still living in the Newtonian world, according to Einstein himself.

However, chapter 19 shows that the great contribution of Einstein is in his success at convincing mankind in the last 50 years that the eternal space we live in does not exist outside of objects that define it. When physicists got rid of the idea that space alone exists without anything in it to define it, they got rid of God. Then Einstein speaks of a finite, yet unlimited, universe in which it is either spherical or elliptical and we exist on its surface. In other words, Einstein projects his experience of the earth upon the entire cosmos. The earth is limited in that there is a fixed number of spaces able to be marked on its surface by longitudinal and latitudinal rods or chains. The earth is unlimited or infinite, in that one could walk in one direction infinitely, given that they begin to walk a well-trod path upon it, a point he ignores.

Obviously this is bunk, but we don't want to argue with genius. There is only one shape of eternal existing living space and that is the shape of Christ Jesus. And now each one who humbly seeks after him and perceives of the operation Christ performed upon the entire cosmos will also form the shape of eternal space.

Chapter 20 presents a biblical description of the way we will travel in the kingdom of heaven or to the galaxies and beyond. It is shown that all the **powers of redeemed mankind** over the material world was demonstrated by Christ Jesus and witnessed by his disciples and many others. Manifestation and demanifestation are discussed and illustrated according to the Holy Scriptures.

The speed limit for the regenerated in deep space will be shown not to be the "speed of light" but the "twinkling of an eye." One could very well say that going to the stars by rocket and machines is as ridiculous as going to God by the effects of the pyramids. Therefore the "estimated time of arrival" for the redeemed to the galaxy Andromeda will be one twinkle. That which has the capacity to fill all space and contain all space has the capacity to manifest itself in it anywhere at the power of desire and thought. This is how Jesus moved after his resurrection, and prior to his ascension. And this is how Jesus moves at this present time in space. The only thing preventing his immediate reappearance on earth is that it is God's will that the present period of the dispensation continue. When God wills it to be over, it will be **over in a heart beat** and the door to the kingdom of heaven will be closed forever.

This then brings us to the notion of linear history. Things were different before the fall. Things were different before the great flood. Things were different before the Advent of Jesus Christ. And, things will most definitely be different after the return of Christ. This means that the dream of unregenerate man to travel to the stars in a continual quest will come to a rapid and disastrous awakening. Only those who have been transformed by the operation of Christ Jesus will travel eternally in the stars. Those who refuse the redemption in Christ shall not visit the stars or remain on earth on in any other dimension or location. These evil persons shall be cast into eternal darkness away from all things for all time. This is a necessary reality when the mechanics of salvation are understood. The spatial power of Christ to save all mankind also demonstrates on the flip side that hell is, by necessity, that which is outside the **operational dimensions of Christ**.

If the operational perimeter of Christ be all space and time that leaves, by necessity, that hell is that which is outside Christ's domain which is all things. Therefore hell is the only "other world" or no-where or no-place. This is the ultimate **contraction to nothingness** with the knowledge that you are there with no way to get back. This is eternal damnation where the worm does not cease and where all that is heard is your own wailing and gnashing of teeth. **All go to hell alone**. The transformed go to heaven with Christ and all the other redeemed. The day is coming very soon in which **only those translated** by Christ will exist anywhere in the heavens.

Chapter 20 also shows, through the harmony of scripture, that no environment will be too hostile for the enjoyment of the redeemed hyperspace alienees in deep space. We will be able to live in the ocean floors or the midst of fire or the chemical clouds. The power of space over all matter will be ours to possess in Christ Jesus.

The forms of our own manifestation will be those similar to those recorded of Christ Jesus. The different forms of manifestation revealed to the disciples of Jesus after his resurrection will be available to us. It is clear from Holy Scripture that we will not lose one hair of our head that we presently have or had. Our glorified heavenly bodies will be manifestable in several forms, but all with the likeness of human beings.

Ronald F. Avery

Appendix

Exhibit A

HYPERSPACE ALIEN ANSWERS NASA SETI VIA LIFE MAGAZINE 1992

Ronald F. Avery
1955 Mt. Vernon
Seguin, Texas 78155
(512) 372-5534

CERTIFIED MAIL
P 859 324 106
RETURN RECEIPT
REQUESTED

Oct. 28, 1992
Ms. Jill Tarter, Project Scientist
NASA SETI
C/O

Mr. James R. Gaines
Managing Editor
LIFE Magazine
Time and Life Building
Rockefeller Center
New York, N.Y. 10020-1393

Dear Ms. Tarter,

I learned of your message beamed into deep space from a Sept. 92 issue of LIFE Magazine and considered it in terms and knowledge I have obtained. I can answer all of NASA's questions concerning travel and survival in deep space. I also want to thank the NASA SETI program for establishing this format for search and discussion with an alien. I have long desired a forum with Sagan and his Colleagues and fellow believers. They are right in their attempt to contact extraterrestrials and they are right in their concern for the survival of their kind and the planet earth. This letter should represent the "one signal that makes sense" rather than "random, irregular and crazy signals." I will number the answers to your "signals" so that readers can correspond easier. I will divide the answers into two parts. The first part is the "break throughs" possible for all, and the second part is risks of rejection of this letter and its contents

PART I
1.1
My Origin has received all your questions documented and written about in LIFE magazine, not just those sent into space via Arecibo Radio Telescope. You understand your perimeters well and your concern for your future is appropriate.
1.2
You are not meant to be bound to a dying planet. You are correct in your implied hypothesis that: your only hope of survival is through space.
1.3
You shall travel in outer space and to distant stars. The speed of light barrier has been broken and materialization and manifestation is in your grasp and you have capacity for it.
1.4
There is a metamorphosis for all to experience in order to escape the dying earth and dwell in deep Space.
1.5
You cannot continue to travel or live in "deep" or shallow space as you exist at present.
1.6
There is a physical means accessible to you at this moment in time to prepare you for continuous and distant life. This will not always be true.
1.7
The human creature is capable of much more sophistication than you ever supposed and it is capable of existence beyond your wildest imagination. In fact some of your kind have already evolved into aliens and inhabit earth and space at this moment.
1.8
You are as much a slave to your own self imposed culture as you are to the confines of nature and space which you perceive accurately.
1.9
Without the evolutionary process which the writer is prepared to describe in detail to you, you and your kind will die chained to a dying planet.
1.10
I am an extraterrestrial and my Origin is beyond your universe. My Origin is not beyond eternal space but beyond what you define as the universe. I did not arrive here by any mechanical means you are familiar with or imagine. I was born on earth, just as I assume you were, but I have had to learn three dialects and pass through a alien physical process in order to reveal any cosmic secrets to you.

1.11

I have been translated into the parallel universe over a period of 20 years through a physical evolutionary process. When this process first began I did not know what it was, or where it was going, or how to talk about it. But I am now ready to describe the process and purpose of it in detail.

1.12

I assure you that the message described in LIFE Magazine is received by my Origin. My Origin has also prepared me to speak to you at length and make known to you all that you want to know concerning human survival in deep space.

1.13

Dava Sobel is correct in saying; "It is hard to imagine a more exciting astronomical discovery or one that would have greater impact on human perceptions than the detection of extraterrestrial intelligence." But consider the possibility of contacting such intelligence living next door to you who had all the answers to man's deepest questions of time, space and survival and upon his visit you slam the door in his face? If I did not respond to your message I would be in defiance of the desire of my Origin.

1.14

I agree with Dava Sobel's statement that "this could be the best bargain in history." I hope that you will be happy to read that you are wrong and have vastly underestimated the potentials of space and time when you were quoted as saying "Jill Tarter, now 48, would be the first to tell you that extraterrestrials have never visited earth and probably never will."

1.15

I do hope that this message can be "detected" by the NASA SETI system. I also hope.. "such a message would be sensed by Culler's software, causing a telephone to ring." I also hope that you will tell the world as you have said "Once we are sure we're right, we have to make that information public right away, any signals that arrive are rightly the property of humankind. They were sent to the planet earth, not to NASA. After millennia of wondering, all humans should know - we are not alone." So be it! I invite you and Frank Drake, Carl Sagan, Dava Sobel, Authur Clarke and all other human beings to test and retest the authenticity of this message. Maybe LIFE Magazine would like to publish our forum in a series to be permanently recorded for all to read and consider.

1.16

I recognize the truth of Clarke's notion that there are two aspects of the search for extraterrestrial intelligence - the technological and the philosophical. The SETI project at present, has error in both aspects but the potentially fatal errors are in the assumptions in the technological aspects. I will respond to the second aspect first. I totally agree with his statement that "The second (philosophical) should be the concern of every living person, because it deals with one of the most fundamental questions that can be asked: What is the status of that recent arrival on the scene, Homo sapiens, in the cosmic pecking order?" The status report is; if Homo sapien does not evolve by alien physical means established by my Origin he will not survive to dwell in any place, much less deep space. I possess the principal and have undergone the process and I am given the awesome responsibility to rescue as many as possible with it. Those I fail to rescue will be without rescue.

1.17

Mr. Clarke is absolutely correct when he states "the detection of intelligent life beyond the earth would change forever our outlook on the universe. It would prove that intelligence does have some survival value, despite what we see on the evening news." Contact with intelligence beyond the earth may begin evolutionary change resulting in a physical transformation of humans into beings that are capable of continual life in deep space.

1.18

In answer to Mr. Clarke's first question he would ask of an ET "What does it look like?" They are totally indiscernible from yourself except in their audio waves. However, I am completely amazed that anyone would suggest that I "would look far more, well alien, than a gorilla. They would certainly be stranger in appearance than an octopus, or a mantis or a dinosaur."

1.19

I will assure you that such "mantis" creatures do not possess the capacity for enduring life or travel in deep space. This capacity is reserved for your likeness alone, unique through out all of eternal space.

1.20

Mr. Clarke is correct in his hope that higher civilizations are out in the milky way and he is also correct in his hopes that "perhaps they are continually broadcasting an easily decoded "encyclopedia Galactica" for the benefit of their less advanced neighbors." He is also absolutely correct in his hope that "It may contain answers to almost all the questions our philosophers and scientist have been asking for centuries, and solutions to many of the practical problems that beset mankind." I assure you that all he hopes is, in fact, true and I know the contents of the "Galactic encyclopedia" and I am prepared to discuss the contents of it at length in a suitable format.

1.21

I am also in complete agreement with Clarke that "Even the most well-intentioned contacts between cultures at different levels of development can have disastrous results." Mr. Clarke is also most astute in his fear over the great question and doubt in his mind about his and his kind's ability to "absorb such a flood of knowledge, and would its very existence not give us a - perhaps terminal - inferiority complex?"

1.22

I assure Mr. Clarke and all thinking men everywhere that I have not "stolen his dreams" but I have merely taken hold of them to possess them for myself and to demonstrate how he and his fellows can also obtain them.

1.23

I, like Mr. Clarke "believe the promise of SETI is far greater than its perils. It represents the highest possible form of exploration, and when we cease to explore, we will cease to be human". It is in that belief that I seek to make contact and reveal myself to you and attempt in all sincerity to discuss your many questions in great detail and show you the gateway to the stars that you seek.

1.24

Now we must turn our attention to the more serious error in the "technological" aspect of the SETI project. Mr. Clarke has defined this aspect as "the concern of engineers and scientists: Where and how do we search, and with what equipment?" He goes on to say that "The spectrum of conceivable answers is enormous..." However, one very simple scenario is completely overlooked. This is the prospect of contacting a local extraterrestrial in Texas as a result of a magazine article. And just as Clarke has said "A spaceship landing on the White House lawn is considerably more exciting than a lot of staticlike hisses collected by a radio telescope - though hearing, rather than seeing (telescope), is the much more likely scenario." And to carry this thought further; staticlike hisses heard by a mile wide radio telescope is a lot more exciting than getting a letter in the mail. Or is it! Herein lies the danger and the doubt that Clarke is concerned about.

1.25

The answer coming in does not conform to our method of data retrieval and analysis. It does not fit because we are READING our answer instead of "hearing" it or "seeing" it. It does not fit in terms of the location expected for alien habitation or the "WHERE TO SEARCH." It does not fit in terms of "HOW WE SEARCH" It does not fit in terms of "WHAT EQUIPMENT DO WE USE." It does not fit in terms of how our beamed message was retrieved. It does not fit in terms of how the message or answer was sent back. Therefore you must ask "does the answer we are receiving by letter have validity? Have we really contacted an alien? What is an alien? Is our hypothesis so flawed that we may never contact an alien or get help with anything?"

1.26

But be assured you have contacted a true alien and the first part of your mission is completed with success. It is now the time to move on to the other purposes of the NASA SETI mission which your Philosophic aspect addresses, namely does the alien have any power to share? He does and he is ready to meet you and discuss it and this fact should be more exciting than any spaceship on the White House lawn. This alien has been equipped to translate you to a safe and secure parallel universe that will neither contract or expand for your particular and general habitation to enjoy eternally.

1.27

I will, however, measure your response to this communication the same way Mr. Clarke has measured the motives of those who are against the search for extraterrestrial intelligence: "Perhaps they sense it is ticking like a time bomb at the foundations of our pride - and of many of our religions." If you do not contact me and treat me with mutual respect as I have contacted you in order that we may continue our dialog, or if you attempt to discredit this contact as a farce in any way, you will be guilty of the very charge you have lowered upon the religions. I will know, LIFE will know, my Origin will know. Therefore starts part two, the risks of rejecting this letter.

PART II
2.1
Not only will you be measured by the comments of Mr. Clarke about the opponents to the search for extraterrestrial intelligence but Science itself will measure you by its own definitions. All scientist recognize that precepts lead to formulation of hypotheses. But the experiment, no matter how well devised and controlled, can lead to new discovery of a totally new concept or a more encompassing explanatory truth. Therefore, it must be true that even if an elaborate and expensive experiment is established upon the wrong hypothesis or partially wrong hypothesis that certainly a different and most unexpected truth will result. This event will require a modification or abandonment of the old precept when its falsehood is demonstrated.

2.2
Does this mean the hypothesis is wrong? Not necessarily. It might only mean that the experiment set up was not sufficient or adequate to test the hypothesis correctly. In fact in this hypothesis the equipment for the experiment is actually a hindrance not an aid in terms of actual message transmission. The equipment in this case might be allowed to screen out and misdirect the information available and may lead to exclusion of the actual truth concerning the questions the hypothesis asks.

2.3
The questions asked by the NASA SETI hypothesis are in fact the most important questions concerning mankind. The experiment was to find extraterrestrials. And if located, it was further hoped that the alien would have special knowledge to share with man. This knowledge, it is hoped again, will help mankind survive in the face of facts scientist have discovered concerning decay and death both on earth and in the universe.

2.4
The error may occur if the data, received by nonconforming means, is rejected and the old flawed assumption that should test the hypothesis is retained as the only legitimate source of data. SETI scientist overlooked the real potential of having such knowledge immediately available to them.

2.5
The experiment could have included a search for a local alien at "home" on Earth by sending out an appeal, possibly in LIFE Magazine, on the questions and subjects desired. Each answer could have been reviewed and considered for truth and power. If no good explanation was received then the search could have included the milky way and beyond as appropriate. Lucky for us however, NASA SETI did not do that. Your giant expensive devices may not act merely as a veil to prevent communication but it may act as a purifier or true filter. The result is that a true

extraterrestrial will have less competition for an audience with NASA SETI. Few will attempt to challenge the authority of science and giant government contracts except on the grounds of "little green men" (humiliating the notions) or other "academic scientific argument". I answer on the ground that I have become the missing link, the answer to the yearnings of your imagination to live and travel deep space forever. I have done so through a process not my own nor is it mine to withhold but I must share it with all. I am merely answering your transmission and advertisement to locate an extraterrestrial alien. I have answered on my own transformation I have discovered and experienced which addresses all the questions you have asked. I understand science and I can communicate with you. I am an alien superior to that which you have defined and seek.

2.6

The oversight of the potential that human beings have evolved to an alien state of being right here on earth is only a mistake in experiment design. It does not render the primary purpose or hypothesis of this project a hoax or trivial. But the potential is there for failure to modify the original notions and definitions of aliens and means of their detection and communication. It certainly does not dismiss the need to know what an alien from deep space knows about mans survival and travel in deep space. This experiment may result in either catastrophic error for a civilization or complete joy and surprise at a wonderful new world opened to all men upon acceptance of an alternate source of data retrieval.

2.7

However, If NASA SETI says, "this is just another "cracked pot" similar to all those recorded in tabloids at the grocery counter!" they make a devastating error. My Origin is space itself not a planet any where not even earth. Your beamed advertisement into deep space seeking an alien who must be from just another terrestrial planet who must look odd reveals complete misunderstanding of the scheme of space, matter, time and physics. Your hypotheses overlooks the notion that a real alien may have SPACE itself as an ORIGIN rather than matter of any kind located anywhere.

2.8

If NASA SETI says, "this message is not from a parallel universe or deep space for it was just mailed to us by the post office!" each one of you personally risk permanent existence alone in a contracted universe unable to contact aliens, friends or anything even though you will try desperately to do so, always.

2.9

If NASA SETI says, "this message is in a crude language and we received it by a crude means!" they are contradictory to all space and its design and they will surely destroy the ecology and utterly fail in this mission as well as all other missions to preserve the planet earth or yourselves.

2.10

If NASA SETI says, "This letter is ridiculous and reveals the desire of a nut who wants media exposure after reading a magazine article" do not blame the writer, he did not create the language, he only has translated the truth and his experience of it into your own imposed culture and language. The writer has taken you and the culture at face value sincerely believing you mean what you say. And he wants to help you, just as you have hoped.

2.11

If NASA SETI says, "this message cannot be to us because it does not relate to our coded message or did it arrive over our "fifth of a mile wide" receiver nor was it decoded from another language by high tech computers!" I will have to respond that your message was most crude, worse than a child's drawing, and your receiver is most crude, incapable of receiving the ideas or processes necessary for your survival.

2.12

Frank Drake has imagined correctly that "messages from alien civilizations in space are passing through our offices and homes right now, like a whisper we can't quite hear". I have received them and have already decoded them for you.

2.13

It is not the intention of the writer to make light of the NASA SETI program or those involved. Quite the contrary, it is the writers intent to assent to SETI's importance and he respects the leaders of the SETI program as the best minds on earth. Further, it is his intent to have meaningful and productive dialog with the project directors and movement leaders and mankind and any individual concerning all the questions raised by NASA SETI. The writer has longed for a forum with you and welcomes your message and reply to his letter. He will sincerely answer all your questions in your dialect concerning the future of man in space and his mode of escape from the universal contraction to come. It is the intent of the writers Origin that no human being be left in the contracting universe and the Origin has provided a physical means of escape for all.

2.14

However, If you decide to disregard, laugh off, or humiliate the writer - you will remain locked in the dead and decaying universe.

2.15

The writer has told you nothing of the methods by which you can evolve or translate yourselves. But he is ready to do so, depending, only, on your response to him.

2.16

The question is: Are the NASA SETI scientists able to prove to the world that they are in fact as OBJECTIVE and FLEXIBLE in their notions upon the introduction of evidence which disproves their original hypotheses? Or will they fall into the bigotry and blind practice of pseudo science which has plagued the earth for centuries sharing the blame of deceit and corruption equally with dead religion?

This concludes my message in answer to your transmission. All true scientists are on the edge of the adventure of their dreams. All SPACE and aliens through out eternal space await to celebrate the response of scientists who establish an open format for the complete divulgence of the process of human evolution and space travel. If you want to undergo physical evolution which we have taught children to believe in for decades (without imparting to them any knowledge of its Origin or purpose or process) then contact me at will. The NASA SETI project has just started and if modified to accept alternate transmissions of data it will indeed be the most productive and meaningful bargain in history. There is much to be discussed and implemented in terms of revision of the way humans are instructed and educated in this world. The NASA SETI budget should be used to explore, document and disseminate all the concepts it addresses in its hypotheses.

Sincerely Yours,
Ronald F. Avery

Ronald F. Avery

Glossary / Index

M

N

O

P

Ronald F. Avery

About the Author

Mr. Avery is a licensed architect and interior designer in the corporate State of TEXAS. He has operated the Silver Eagle Taphouse in McQueeney Texas for the last five years where he has the opportunity to discuss many ideas with ordinary people. He has tested the ideas in this book in reality to prove his thesis. You may visit his house of conviviality at www.SilverEagleTaphouse.com.

Mr. Avery wrote a letter in response to a September 1992 Life magazine article about the NASA SETI project, to be forwarded to NASA SETI, wherein he proclaimed to be an extraterrestrial hyperspace alien with the answers to their questions. He has never heard from any of them. He sent the SETI INSTITUTE emails asking if Jill Tarter, Project Scientist, ever got his letter. No one has ever replied to him about his claim. *Alien Physics* explains why he can make such a claim. You may read his emails to the SETI Institute and others on his website at www.AlienPhysics.com.

Mr. Avery has been a translated Christian for 26 years and is a laymen theologian. He worked with an ordained Methodist Minister for two years on *Alien Physics*. He is also a student of the principles and laws of civil liberty discovered and established by Christian philosophers and thinkers. His next book will analyze the impact of Christ Jesus on civil government and the stand of Christian Patriots in the Global Order at hand.

www.ingramcontent.com/pod-product-compliance
Lightning Source LLC
Chambersburg PA
CBHW030254290526
45785CB00001B/85